ACCOUNTING FOR BUSINESS OR(

ACCOUNTING FOR BUSINESS ORGANISATIONS

A Practical Approach

Graham Taylor and Chris Hawkins

M
MACMILLAN

© Graham Taylor and Chris Hawkins 1984, 1988

All rights reserved. No reproduction, copy or transmission of this publication may be made without written permission.

No paragraph of this publication may be reproduced, copied or transmitted save with written permission or in accordance with the provisions of the Copyright, Designs and Patents Act 1988, or under the terms of any licence permitting limited copying issued by the Copyright Licensing Agency, 90 Tottenham Court Road, London W1P 9HE.

Any person who does any unauthorised act in relation to this publication may be liable to criminal prosecution and civil claims for damages.

First published 1984 by
MACMILLAN EDUCATION LTD
Houndmills, Basingstoke, Hampshire RG21 2XS
and London
Companies and representatives
throughout the world

ISBN 0–333–37406–1

A catalogue record for this book is available from the British Library.

Printed in Hong Kong

Revised reprint 1988
10   9   8   7   6   5   4   3
00 99 98 97 96 95 94 93 92 91

Contents

1	**ORGANISATIONAL OBJECTIVES**	**1**
	1.1 The nature of objectives	1
	1.2 The nature and complexity of business decision making	4
	1.3 The need for and nature of information	4
	1.4 Desirable properties of an information system	6
	1.5 The stages of the information system	9
	1.6 The need for accounting	11
	1.7 Who wants the information?	13
	1.8 Managers and decision making	15
	1.9 Levels of decision making	17
	1.10 Financial and management accounting	19
	Summary	21
	Assignments	21
2	**PRODUCING ACCOUNTING INFORMATION**	**23**
	2.1 The extent of understanding required	23
	2.2 The accounting system	24
	2.3 The double-entry system	25
	2.4 The key financial documents	32
	2.5 Accounting guidelines	34
	Summary	39
	Assignments	40
3	**COMPUTERS AND ACCOUNTING**	**44**
	3.1 The data processing cycle	44
	3.2 What is a computer?	47
	3.3 Costs	51
	3.4 Advantages of computerisation	52
	3.5 Problems with computers	55
	3.6 Steps in the creation of a working computer system	58
	Summary	60
	Assignments	60
4	**THE VALUATION OF ASSETS**	**63**
	4.1 Introduction	63
	4.2 Stock	64
	4.3 Stock valuation	65
	4.4 Cost bases	66

	4.5 Choosing the final figure	70
	Summary	71
	4.6 Depreciation of fixed assets	72
	4.7 Methods of provision for depreciation	75
	Summary	80
	Assignments	80
5	FINAL ACCOUNTS OF PARTNERSHIPS	**85**
	5.1 Introduction	85
	5.2 The partnership agreement	86
	5.3 The personal accounts of partners	87
	5.4 The Profit and Loss Account	87
	5.5 The Balance Sheet	91
	Summary	94
	Assignments	94
6	THE FINAL ACCOUNTS OF LIMITED COMPANIES	**100**
	6.1 Introduction	100
	6.2 Sources of company capital	100
	6.3 The Profit and Loss Account	103
	6.4 The Balance Sheet	106
	6.5 Published Accounts	107
	Summary	108
	Assignments	108
7	FUNDS FLOW STATEMENTS	**115**
	7.1 Introduction	115
	7.2 Measuring working capital	116
	7.3 The Sources and Applications of Funds Statement	117
	7.4 The Cash Flow Statement	121
	Summary	122
	Assignments	123
8	THE ANALYSIS OF FINANCIAL STATEMENTS	**129**
	8.1 Introduction	129
	8.2 Analysis of accounts	131
	8.3 Profit ratios	133
	8.4 Liquidity ratios	135
	8.5 Funds flow analysis	137
	8.6 Investment ratios	137
	8.7 Employees	140
	8.8 Inter-firm comparisons	140
	8.9 Problems with the use of ratios	142
	Summary	143
	Assignments	143
9	CURRENT COST ACCOUNTING	**149**
	9.1 Introduction	149
	9.2 The main features of current cost accounting	150

	9.3	The current cost Profit and Loss Account	150
	9.4	The current cost Balance Sheet	156
		Summary	162
		Assignments	162
10	**PREPARING ACCOUNTS FROM INCOMPLETE RECORDS**		**166**
	10.1	Introduction	166
	10.2	The reasons for incomplete records	167
	10.3	Final Accounts from incomplete records	167
	10.4	Budgeted Final Accounts	172
		Summary	175
		Assignments	176
11	**MANUFACTURING STATEMENTS**		**181**
	11.1	Introduction	181
	11.2	Classifying costs	181
	11.3	The Manufacturing Statement	185
		Summary	191
		Assignments	192
12	**COSTING SYSTEMS**		**198**
	12.1	Introduction	198
	12.2	Costing procedures and documents	199
	12.3	Job costing systems	202
	12.4	Process costing systems	206
		Summary	208
		Assignments	209
13	**BREAK-EVEN ANALYSIS: THE ANALYSIS OF COST/VOLUME/PROFIT/RELATIONSHIPS**		**214**
	13.1	Introduction	214
	13.2	The break-even model	214
	13.3	The break-even point	216
	13.4	The margin of safety	216
	13.5	Contribution/sales ratio	217
	13.6	Calculation of estimated profit	217
	13.7	The break-even chart	218
	13.8	Changes in the variables	221
		Summary	223
14	**COSTING TECHNIQUES**		**225**
	14.1	Absorption and marginal costing: differences	225
	14.2	The nature of a marginal cost	225
	14.3	Basis of marginal costing	226
	14.4	Analysis of contribution	227
	14.5	Stock valuation	229
	14.6	Marginal costing and pricing policy	230
	14.7	Advantages and disadvantages of marginal costing	234
		Summary	235

Assignments · 235

15 BUDGETING — **243**
15.1 Introduction · 243
15.2 Planning by means of budgets · 243
15.3 Preparing a set of budgets · 245
15.4 Control and review · 251
Summary · 253
Assignments · 253

16 STANDARD COSTING — **258**
16.1 Introduction · 258
16.2 Labour variances · 260
16.3 Materials variances · 261
16.4 Variable overhead variances · 262
16.5 Fixed overhead variances · 263
16.6 The variance report · 265
Summary · 266
Assignments · 266

CASE STUDIES — **269**
1 The Dog and Firkin · 269
2 Soccer finances · 272
3 Taylor's Toys Ltd · 274
4 Northborough Motors Ltd · 278

ANSWERS · 282
INDEX · 335

A booklet containing answers to the assignments is available to lecturers. Contact the Further Education Department, Macmillan Education on 0256–29242 for details.

To Gladys, Naomi, Doug, and Sharon

1 Organisational Objectives

When you have read this chapter you should be able to:
- appreciate the main objectives of business organisations
- know the desirable properties, stages and levels of information
- know the types of users of accounting information
- distinguish between financial and management accounting

1.1 The nature of objectives

Most organisations have broad aims which they are trying to achieve even if these are not stated explicitly. For small businesses these aims are often of a fairly general nature but larger concerns, which are accountable to various interest groups and may be using other people's money, need more specific aims. It seems sensible, therefore, to set down their aims and philosophy in some kind of statement of intent such as the Memorandum and Articles of Association. Subsequently these aims have to be converted into much more precise quantifiable objectives (e.g. return on capital employed, market share), and in turn these strategic objectives must be translated into much more detailed tactical objectives, budgets and action plans at the operational level (see Figure 1.3).

These objectives are important because they give the organisation, or rather the people within it, a sense of direction and purpose. If they are imaginatively and realistically set they may even act as a motivating force and everyone will do their best to achieve them. This will usually entail careful co-operation and participation with employees to gain their acceptance. Clearly defined objectives should help throughout the organisation to provide better control over existing operations and sounder planning for the future if only because the whole process of setting objectives provides useful experience for the next time around. Clear objectives are a pre-condition for successful decision making although there are many problems involved with setting and implementing them.

Different organisations place different emphases on what areas it is best to set objectives in, and obviously objectives will vary according to the legal or financial status of the organisation. This can be wide-ranging, particularly in the private sector where there are sole traders, partnerships, public and private limited companies, and owner managed and managerial businesses.

Some of the commoner objectives for businesses such as these might be (in no particular order):

- profitability
- sales growth
- market share increase
- risk spreading (diversification)
- innovation

These are not necessarily compatible, and in any case they may be tempered by aims relating to social or public responsibility.

Public corporations (nationalised Government-controlled companies), on the other hand, have social and political objectives as well as economic objectives and are not always run to make a profit. However, most operate under government guidelines and have a government-fixed rate of return on investment, although specific sections of the business may be subsidised for various reasons, for example:

Organisation	*Service or product*	*Reason*
British Rail	Country branch lines	Social service
British Coal	Old coal mines	Jobs

Certain services and charities measure their success by the quality of service offered rather than profits made or markets won. Thus education and health, by their very nature, are rarely run on a profitable basis, at least in this country, nor are charities, e.g. the Royal National Life Boat Institute. But all organisations are seeking to maximise the use of scarce resources. Even charities strive to be efficient in attracting resources, e.g. people, machines, materials and money, and in using them well.

Not only will objectives differ between the various types of organisation but also between the groups, such as management, workers, shareholders and customers, involved with a particular business. The various 'pressure groups' and their objectives can be seen in two ways. Either the belief is that the organisation is a coalition of groups each with a common goal (the unitary view) or that conflict will inevitably result (the pluralist view). But whatever your beliefs, managers have the unenviable task of balancing the wishes of the various interest groups and if one (or more) of these groups is alienated then problems of conflict arise. Further still, the goals of individuals within these groups may be different. This is particularly important for owners and management, who have the authority to direct, and must interpret the objectives set. Different factors in the organisational structure, e.g. top management, middle management etc., may have moral or cultural beliefs which affect their decisions or they may be concerned with self-interest and empire-building in varying degrees.

This self-assertion by executives, coupled with company tradition and the public image of the organisation, may make it appear that the business has its own unique set of objectives and personality.

Problems and constraints

Objectives provide the goals towards which the organisation is moving. Any decisions made to achieve these goals depend largely on the constraints which exist and on the information available. If goals are ambiguous and inconsistent, and the choices not always clear cut, then there may be mixed consequences. This generally leads to a search for *satisfying or satisfactory* alternatives.

The problems have to be clearly defined and their cause(s) correctly pinpointed; only then can ways of overcoming them be worked out.

There are usually *constraints* in arriving at any business solution. Generally there will be limited resources in terms of time and money, but there may be other key factors which restrict the possible choice of options. These other constraints can be either internal or external to the organisation:

Internal constraints include scarce resources (e.g. skilled personnel, finance, materials) which may have alternative uses (i.e. opportunity costs).

External constraints include economic factors (e.g. markets, competitors, government policy), legal factors (e.g. trades description and consumer credit acts) and technological factors (e.g. computerisation), all of which can force changes on an organisation's operations.

It is important to identify and quantify the key constraints in any problem so that research can be directed towards finding: (a) the optimum solution within these limits, or (b) the best way of overcoming them.

In reality information in business is seldom adequate, particularly forecasting data. So in a situation of incomplete information, the selection of objectives requires the application of judgement, opinion, belief and subjective estimates plus whatever objective (hard factual) information is available.

1.2 The nature and complexity of business decision making

Running a business successfully is not easy. Doing so requires that managers try to use the resources (people, machines, materials and money) at their disposal to achieve the best results, i.e. the best return consistent with the objectives of the organisation. This, in turn, obliges them to give constant attention to operational problems. They will have to deal with hindrances to the desired performance level due to such internal factors as staff sickness, plant breakdown or malfunction, and friction in employee/management relations. The details, order and timing of productive operations will have to be defined and re-defined to ensure that objectives are met on time. Progress must be constantly monitored, so that what actually happens matches what should happen.

In addition to obtaining and responding to this *internal information*, managers should also keep an eye on the outside world and any *external factors* which might affect their operations. Organisations do not exist in isolation, and they should be constantly aware of outside influences such as the behaviour of competitors, and the impact of government planning measures. Such factors are often outside the control of any one business but they should, nevertheless, be taken into account. The difficulty and complexity of the manager's task is made greater by the fact that both the *internal* and *external* factors influencing the organisation are constantly changing – often in an unpredictable way. An information system should handle all these factors and serve as a basis for business decision making, and helping managers to plan, control and review their operations to the best effect.

Additionally, information will have to be provided to meet the legal obligations of various interest groups who have a stake in the business. Such an information base will inevitably include the main internal source of data – the accounting system – as well as other subsystems such as market intelligence.

1.3 The need for and nature of information

Complexity can only be eased by information, defined here as relevant and accurate data. This might be thought an obvious enough statement, but many businessmen still base their decisions either on intuition, unfounded hope or the blind acceptance of figures supplied by 'experts'. Consequently they often face crises which they could have avoided had they kept proper *records* of what they were doing and made use of data available to them. It is true, of course, that some of these businessmen will survive, particularly in small-scale operations, but that will probably be because they are subconsciously using information which is at their fingertips.

It is also true that decisions are often made on *incomplete evidence*. This may be quite justifiable if the cost of obtaining the extra information is prohibitive, or if there is not enough time to collect it.

Managers have to deal with both *qualitative* (non-numerical) and *quantitative* (numerical) data. They are concerned mainly with the *future* and, because this is uncertain, much of the quantitative data on which they have to rely is only approximate (accounting is historic data after all). Forecasting is a good example of *approximation*, and an 'innumerate' manager who does not understand this may treat forecasts as if they were matters of fact, and be suitably derogatory when they seem to be 'wrong' compared with actual performance.

Despite the approximation involved, accounting information, just because it is expressed in figures, may convey an impression of being more 'real' or accurate than qualitative information, which is based on data not readily lending itself to statistical or accounting treatment. It may be possible, for example, to use such material to gain a complete picture of the human and industrial relations of an organisation, but these factors can have a profound effect on performance. Even here, however, there may be *indirect measures* for something that at first sight appears unquantifiable. The state of employee morale, for example, may be indicated by such things as absenteeism, lateness and productivity per worker.

The apparent greater firmness and accuracy of accounting data leads to a common mistake: that of *simplifying* a complex problem by excluding from consideration those features which do not lend themselves to accounting analysis, and cannot easily be expressed in monetary terms. The problem in its simplified form is then solved, and this solution is taken, quite falsely, to be the solution of the original (whole) problem. Businessmen must guard against this danger, and not allow themselves to be bemused by accounting 'solutions'.

Accounting information

An organisation must devise 'information systems' to provide the correct data in an appropriate form as quickly and as efficiently as possible. A major part of this system is accounting, which involves long-established concepts, doctrines and conventions concerned with the collection and processing of financial data.

This book deals separately with accounting information because the financial consequences of an organisation's performance are so vital that they warrant separate attention.

The early chapters are largely concerned with mechanical procedures and techniques which can aid the production of relevant, accurate and up-to-date accounting information. Later chapters concentrate more on the use and interpretation of these pieces of information and show how they can be drawn together and applied to business forecasting and evaluation, and to the planning, controlling and reviewing of an organisation's activities.

Accounting is part of the overall information system which should include data on:

- the economy
- markets
- products
- personnel
- competitors etc.

Less reliable *external* data must be balanced with *internal* data, including accounting.

The value of accounting information is that it is hard, quantifiable information which indicates what *has* happened and what *is* happening to the business, and therefore should provide an objective basis for rational decision making and the assessment of risk. Judgement as to the likelihood of different risks and the relative importance of the various influences working on the business is equally important, and both *qualitative and quantitative information must be weighed up before a decision is reached.*

On balance, decisions which might otherwise have been based on intuition alone should be improved. The whole decision making process benefits from the combined use of quantitative and qualitative information and it is important that the decision maker has the right background knowledge to handle the 'accounts side' with confidence.

1.4 Desirable properties of an information system

Information is essential if an organization is to operate effectively, but is it always worth having? It may be difficult or costly to obtain and even then there may be an in-built margin of error in the historic information which devalues any forecasts based on it.

Organisations usually measure the worth of information according to certain criteria. To be of value any information should be:

- cost effective
- relevant

- accurate
- up-to-date

The 'right information should get to the right person at the right time'.

Cost-effective information

Information should not cost too much to produce. Clearly, the more accurate and up-to-date information has to be, the more expensive it will be to generate. The costs of collecting, processing and analysing the data must be balanced against the possible benefits gained from the work. The problem is, therefore, one of 'cost-benefit analysis' although it is often extremely difficult to estimate the future benefits of information gathering.

Relevant information

Information should be provided according to *need* rather than on what data is available. Information should be sufficient to meet the needs of the user and no more. Concise relevant summaries are more likely to convey the essential message; massive output defeats the purpose.

If a problem is precisely defined and there are clearly defined objectives to guide the choice of data, then there is less chance of wasting time and money generating irrelevant or redundant information – a problem all too common in many organisations.

For example, it would be wrong for an organisation to ask an accountant to carry out an investigation into 'labour' and 'wages'. What does the term 'labour' imply? Must the figures concern all employees or should they include 'manual services' only? Again, what does the term 'wages' mean exactly? Is it the actual amount of money earned including overtime or is it the 'wage rate' only? Should lost time and bonus payments be allowed for? How about receipts in kind? The information required must be described in unambiguous and consistent terms aimed at meeting a specific purpose. Any reputable piece of research should normally explain what it has done and what its definitions are, stating clearly its terms of reference and research procedure.

Accurate information

Information should be as accurate as it needs to be to suit the purposes of the user. Where health, safety or large sums of money are involved, accuracy becomes that much more important than in other instances where a rough guideline may be quite adequate. For example, it would be spurious to predict sales to such levels of accuracy.

Accuracy will depend on the stages of collection, processing and presentation of information, and the care taken at each step. In particular accuracy will depend on:

- *The definition of the problem*
  This relates to what exactly is being measured.

- *The method of investigation*
  It is rarely practical to undertake a total investigation and so methods have been developed which can produce information with the required levels of confidence and accuracy from relatively small samples. The key point is that the degree of likely error should always be stated.
- *The method of collection*
  Poorly supervised or inadequately checked input data can result in misleading output.
- *The method of processing and presenting*
  Similarly careful checking and control of the findings must be undertaken and information should be interpreted and presented in an honest way. Elimination of many of these inaccuracies may largely be a matter of cost as there is often a close link between the cost of a survey and its validity.
- *The need for up-to-date results*
  Information, no matter how good, is of little use if it arrives too late. Therefore, it is often necessary to trade accuracy or depth of analysis for quick results. Generally, the faster information is required, the more expensive it is going to be to retain high levels of quality and presentation.

Decision making may take place within three contexts which depend on the amount of information available and the time which is at the disposal of the decision maker:

1. Decisions must be made instantly, with no time to obtain relevant information. In this case, managers must rely on snap judgements based on intuition and experience.
2. More time may be available, but there may be no formal system within the organisation either to provide the required information or to adapt the existing data.
3. The organisation has a formal system which can provide information where necessary, e.g. access to current stock levels via a computer terminal.

Managers will be faced with a mix of all three types of decisions, and the appropriate facilities and aids should be available to help. Nowadays there is no real excuse for avoiding objective analysis because of lengthy and complicated calculations since facilities are usually available even for non-routine problems. This *data processing* now offers the opportunity to perform analyses cheaply and quickly. In addition to standard computer programs for routine commercial and financial procedures (e.g. payroll) there are now packages available in the area of management decision making, e.g. quality control, sales forecasting, planned maintenance. Now that desk-top facilities are economically viable for even the small organisation, management can access relevant information more quickly than ever before.

Well-presented information

Information should be presented in an easy-to-read 'user-friendly' manner. Pictures and graphs, which highlight any significant trends, are more likely to be acted upon than pages of figures whose implications may be ignored or misread because they are not fully understood.

Similarly, concise, relevant summaries are more likely to convey the essential message than massive output which defeats the purpose.

Accountants seem to like tables of figures, which are not easily understood by the beginner, although supplementary pictures and graphs have crept into their communications.

Good presentation and explanation will minimise the risk of misinterpretation and help the non-specialist to understand and use accounting information.

So the value of any information depends upon answers to the following basic questions:

- What information is required? (relevant)
- Who wants it? (relevant and well presented)
- How much time is available to collect it? (up-to-date)
- How much money is there to spend on it (cost-effective)
- How accurate must the information be? (accurate)

If these objectives are clear, and care and attention are given at each stage of the information system, then useful information will result.

1.5 The stages of the information system

To be of value, raw, internal or external data must be processed into information, defined here as relevant, accurate and up-to-date data.

This process can be broken down into several stages (Figure 1.1).

- *Define and identify the problem.* There is a need for clearly defined objectives to guide the choice of data for the other stages of the decisionmaking process. This should help to avoid the production of irrelevant or redundant information – a problem all too common in many organisations.

- *Establish source and type of information required.* Information can come from historic data; the feedback from previous decisions or from research into new problem areas. The source(s) of information, internal or external, has to be agreed upon together with the question of whether it can be obtained at the right time for the right price with the required level of accuracy.

- *Decide on method and collect information.* This will be a choice between primary and/or secondary sources and the collection method will be chosen in the light of the constraints of time, money and accuracy. The collection stage will provide the basic raw data for analysis.

Data relating to items of activity, e.g. goods received, is recorded in some way and classified or sorted into some kind of prearranged sequence in which it is required for subsequent operations. It is processed and selected, and from this, summarised information is produced. This involves careful analysis in order to decide which key factors to highlight. Care and accuracy are particularly important at this stage and the computer can be of great assistance, especially with routine work.

Selected data is subjected to the arithmetic operations of addition, subtraction etc. Fundamental to any information system is the need to update *by* addition, deletion, amendment and combination.

Store/retrieve/copy If necessary, data is filed away for future use. Among the main organisation files are sales, purchases, stock records and payroll. Files are updated whenever relevant data is posted to them at the calculating stage.

A good filing system is a good information retrieval system, i.e. information can be easily accessed in a form which is useful and copies are available for the right people in the right place at the right time. Ways of extracting relevant information have been much enhanced by modern technology.

Interpret and present information Good presentation and explanation will minimise the risk of misinterpretation and help the non-specialist to understand and use numerical information. Output should be simple, concise, easy to read (or listen to) and thereby easy to understand and act upon.

Control It is essential to emphasise the importance of control at all stages of the system, i.e. the need for constant monitoring and checking of the data to ensure its accuracy and reliability for its end use.

Figure 1.1
Stages of the
information system

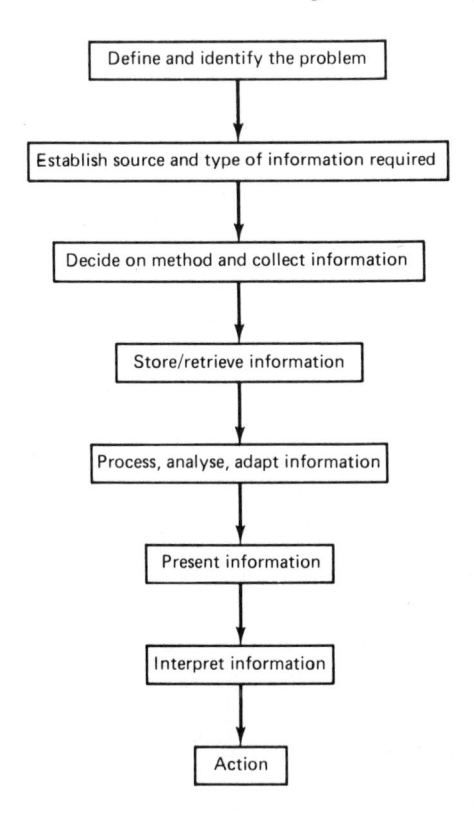

```
Define and identify the problem
            ↓
Establish source and type of information required
            ↓
Decide on method and collect information
            ↓
Store/retrieve information
            ↓
Process, analyse, adapt information
            ↓
Present information
            ↓
Interpret information
            ↓
Action
```

1.6 The need for accounting

Organisations need efficient information systems if they are to be managed effectively and achieve their objectives. Most decisions have financial consequences; a major throughput of data in any business concerns its financial position. This information is provided through the accounting system which is usually the main formal internal source. It is essential to keep records of performance and of all relevant transactions, e.g. expenses, revenues, assets and liabilities. The needs for accounting are therefore:

- to provide managers with information needed for decision making (management accounting)
- to meet the legal obligations of various interest groups (financial accounting)

Accounting has developed to meet these two needs, and is the process of collecting, recording, processing, analysing, summarising, presenting and interpreting business transactions in monetary terms.

Records should act as an aid to management in planning and controlling the organisation. Businessmen who wish to survive and prosper must know their financial position on a weekly (or even on a daily) basis. This means that they must produce information that shows:

- the amount of cash they have to spend
- the true profit or loss they are making

It is important to realise the difference between these two. Making a profit does not necessarily mean having any cash to spare, any more than having a large sum of money in the bank means that a large profit has been made.

Recent surveys into the causes of bankruptcy among small organisations have shown that the main reason for failure has been a general absence of reliable records. Lack of information means that management is unable to plan to meet known expenditure, assess demands such as taxation, or to meet any sudden expenditure which arises but cannot be anticipated with accuracy. It is essential, therefore, to maintain records which can provide relevant, up-to-date and accurate information for management decision making.

People outside the organisation will also be interested in its performance. These include:

- shareholders, who need to assess their investment stake
- creditors, who will want to gauge the degree of risk involved in lending to the organisation
- trade union representatives, who may base pay claims on business results
- the Government, which will require information for macro-economic planning and tax assessment

Accounts must be kept for legal purposes and must be audited so that they give a 'true and fair view' of the organisation's position. This ensures that the interests of outside parties (e.g. shareholders) are properly protected. Companies are required by law to publish certain information and many are becoming increasingly aware of their social and commercial obligations, so that they present accounts in an easy to understand manner which conveys their essential message to such interest groups as employees and customers.

Let us consider the needs and objectives of organisations and of the various interest groups in more detail.

1.7 Who wants the information?

A consideration of information requirements would be incomplete without an understanding of its users. There will be a variety of interest groups concerned with an organisation but their needs will differ widely. Some information will have to be prepared by a business for internal control purposes, as a public or industrial relations exercise, or as a result of legal requirements. Table 1.1 shows the main groups, their possible interests and their access to information.

Table 1.1 *Interest groups and their access to information*

Interest group	Main interest(s)	Access to information in addition to published accounts
Managers	Decision making	All information
Employees	Security of job and income	House magazines and bulletins
Shareholders	Present and expected earnings, security	
Creditors/banks	Future orders, security of payments	Credit report, auditors' certificate
Customers (public)	Price, product/service quality and reliability	
Government (central and local)	Economic and social planning, tax calculation	In theory all information but not usually asked for; treated in confidence
Competitors	Comparative performance measures	Limited exchange of information via Trade Association

Shareholders — Shareholders are primarily interested in the security and growth of their earnings and will be particularly interested in profits and the proportion distributed as dividends. Share prices reflect the performance of the organisation which can be assessed by referring to the annual Reports and Accounts which companies are required to publish by law. These results will be compared with similar-risk investments in the market.

Creditors/banks — Banks and trade suppliers will be concerned with the recovery of money advanced and will therefore be looking for adequacy of income rather than large profits, preferring security to speculation by the organisation. A bank manager may need to agree on cash flow forecasts before granting an overdraft. In turn, potential trade suppliers may call for credit-ratings from the bank.

General public, including customers

Most organisations are becoming more conscious of their social and environmental responsibilities and try to project a good corporate image by emphasising their value to society, the number of workers employed and their support of good causes. The general public are, after all, potential customers. More specifically, organisations are keen to gain customers and keep their existing customers satisfied by promoting price, product/service quality and support (e.g. after-sales services and guarantees). This is to gain consumer loyalty and so strengthen market position. Increasingly company reports and media publicity are being slanted towards these 'consumer groups'.

In addition, organisations are increasingly stressing their contribution to the econmy as a whole. ICI, for example, has advertised the importance of its exports to the balance of payments.

Government

The central Government requires businesses to provide sufficiently detailed information about their operations to enable liability for *income* or *corporation tax* and *value added tax* to be calculated.

An organisation may also be called upon to provide quantitative information to enable a Government department to carry out regional or national surveys for economic planning.

Competitors

In most circumstances no statistics will be prepared specifically for this group for obvious reasons. There are, however, occasions when the exchange of information may be mutually beneficial, for instance, in research to solve common problems or, anonymously through a trade association, in setting performance standards based on inter-firm comparisons.

Limited companies must, of course, publish a great deal of information about themselves, and this is available to any competitor ready to take the trouble to seek it out.

Employees

It is being increasingly accepted that all employees of an organisation, managers and others alike, have the right to know what is happening and what plans exist for the future. A number of companies now provide supplementary reports for their employees, who are naturally concerned about the level and security of their incomes (and pensions) and about prospects for promotion. These factors are closely allied to the success (or otherwise) of the organisation, and they will therefore need to know how well the organisation is doing. Various performance measures, such as profitability, market share, the achievement of planned targets, as well as proposed future developments will thus be of direct interest to them.

For example, the 'worth' of each worker can be indicated by calculating sale or profit per employee, to give an idea of the average contribution each person is making to the organisation's results.

For comparative purposes, employees will want to see wage statistics at all levels inside the organisation, by section, department, etc., as well as average wage rates for the industry and for the country.

1.8 Managers and decision making

Managers are employees, so the previous section applies to them too. In addition, managers need information in their role as decision makers. It should also be remembered that they are responsible, either by law or voluntarily, for providing information to the other interest groups.

In outline, management tasks may be described as a process involving the following elements:

- establishing and evaluating objectives
- developing long-term forecasts and short-term plans and devising operational targets in line with objectives
- choosing between alternative plans
- implementing plans, initiating action, organising resources, co-ordinating and controlling activity
- measuring actual performance against the planning and assessing achievement
- reviewing operations at regular intervals

If an organisation is to operate successfully some logical approach to decision making is necessary. In this respect a structural framework should help to identify the key features which are common to most decisions so that risks are minimised and optimum decisions are made. The framework shown in Figure 1.2 places an information system in the context of the management decision-making process. It can be seen that the system is interlocking.

Objectives

Objectives have already been outlined in general terms. From a management viewpoint, however, objectives will have to be expressed in more precise and quantitative terms stating clearly

16 Accounting: A Practical Approach

**Figure 1.2
Information for
management
decision making**

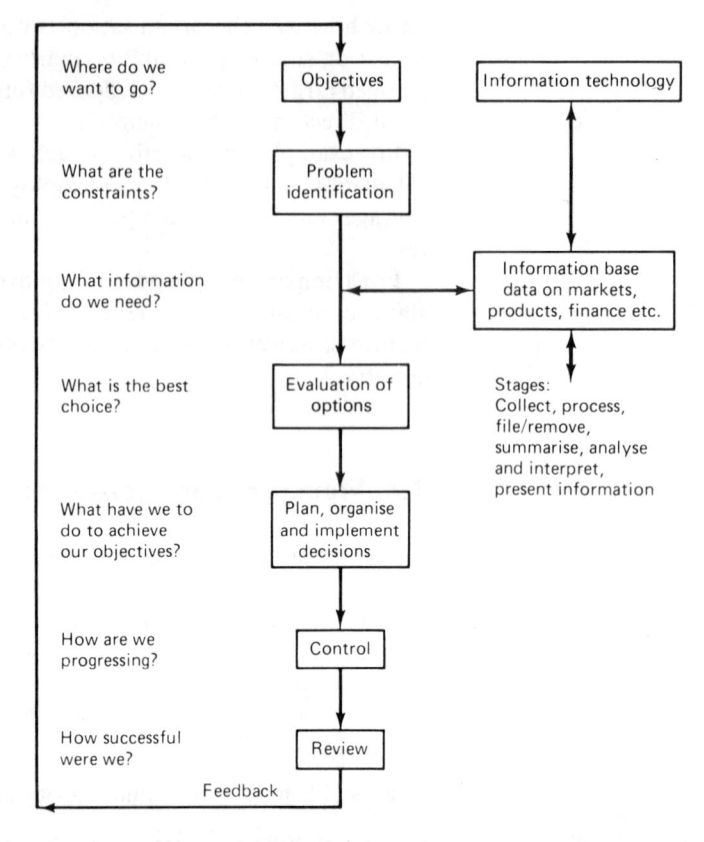

Question	Process	
Where do we want to go?	Objectives	Information technology
What are the constraints?	Problem identification	
What information do we need?		Information base data on markets, products, finance etc.
What is the best choice?	Evaluation of options	Stages: Collect, process, file/remove, summarise, analyse and interpret, present information
What have we to do to achieve our objectives?	Plan, organise and implement decisions	
How are we progressing?	Control	
How successful were we?	Review	

Feedback

which areas of the organisation they cover and the time period over which they should be achieved. With this in mind, consideration should be given to the different levels of decision making.

A hierarchy of objectives is shown in Figure 1.3. This links with

**Figure 1.3
Levels of information**

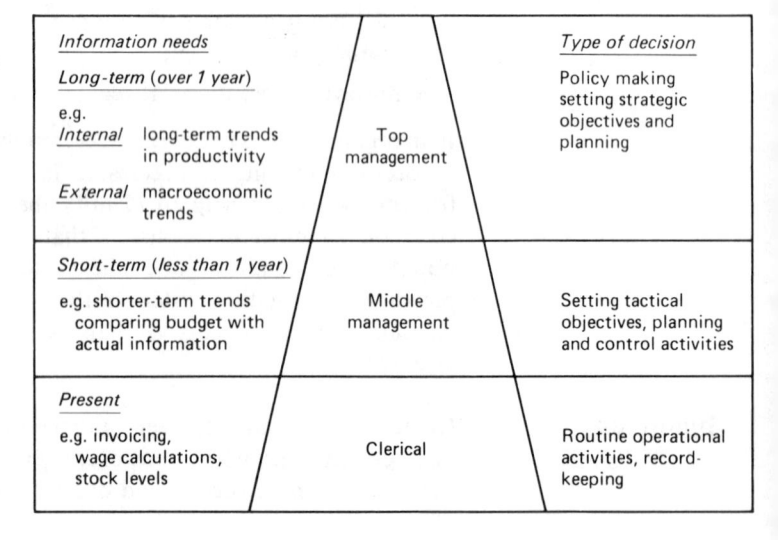

Information needs		Type of decision
Long-term (over 1 year) e.g. *Internal* long-term trends in productivity *External* macroeconomic trends	Top management	Policy making setting strategic objectives and planning
Short-term (less than 1 year) e.g. shorter-term trends comparing budget with actual information	Middle management	Setting tactical objectives, planning and control activities
Present e.g. invoicing, wage calculations, stock levels	Clerical	Routine operational activities, record-keeping

1.9 Levels of decision making

At the *strategic* level, broad objectives are set by top management for the company as a whole to aim for. These might include return on capital employed, market share etc., and will have implications for strategic decisions on such things as new products, diversification and new technology. Strategic decisions and objectives tend to affect the whole business and usually have a long-term influence.

There is a need, at this level, to balance internal information with less reliable external information on market trends etc. Similarly, hard quantitative information such as that obtained from accounting must be assessed in the light of qualitative information before decisions are reached.

Strategies must be translated into *tactical objectives* which are much more detailed and therefore need information on action plans and budgets. They usually specify the target to be aimed for, when it is to be achieved, and who is responsible for seeing that it is. These tactical objectives are set jointly by middle and senior managers and must dovetail with the corporate strategic objectives. Their implementation is usually at the departmental level and they tend to have a shorter-term effect on the organisation.

Finally, there are the low-level routine or operational decisions which have little uncertainty and require detailed, accurate information on day-to-day operations.

Figure 1.4 shows that the information requirements at each level differ mainly in terms of: time-span, scope and detail, sources and frequency.

Figure 1.4

	Straegic	*Tactical*	*Operational*
1. Time-span	Long (one year or greater)	Shorter (up to one year)	Short (even daily)
2. Detail/scope	Broad	Detailed	Detailed
3. Sources	Mainly external	External/internal	Internal
4. Frequency	Irregular	Mixed	Routine

Information

So, just as the information *need* must be clarified in precise terms, so must the *level* for which the need exists.

With both of these established, a suitable information system for gathering, processing and presenting information may be evolved. Figure 1.2 indicates that different information is needed at different stages in the decision-making process. The provision of this information allows problems to be clarified and risk areas to be identified and should improve the organisation's performance by aiding the planning, controlling and reviewing of resources as well as providing information for external purposes.

Accounting is clearly a vital part of this information system.*

Forecasting

A prerequisite of planning is to try and make forecasts of likely outcomes. If relationships between key variables (i.e. variables which significantly affect the organisation's future) can be quantified and current conditions accounted for, then figures can be projected into the future which form the basis for planning resource. This is where statistical, market research, and intelligence and economic data can add to the internal and historic accounting data.

The forecasting process should at least screen out unrealistic proposals so that only feasible ideas go forward to be evaluated at the next stage. There are long-term forecasting techniques which can help organisations to determine likely outcomes and feasible projects. Clearly qualitative judgements are important at this stage.

Evaluation of options

Before an actual decision can be made, there are usually a number of projects or courses of action to be considered and these must be assessed as (usually) only one can be chosen. There is a need to devise a method of assessing these feasible options and acceptance criteria have to be devised. Chapters 13 and 14 examine techniques which can help the organisation make this choice, and plan and direct their operations accordingly.

Planning and implementation

Once the decision is made, it has to be planned for and put into action. Planning in this sense means setting operational targets, say by department, and making sure that people are made responsible for carrying out the plan. Clearly the plans made must be budgeted for and the details, order and timing of events will have to be defined. The separate targets then have to be co-ordinated to ensure that they fit in with the original objectives of the organisation. A budgetary control system will be outlined in Chapter 15 along with some of the problems of target setting.

Control

Once the plan is put into action its progress will have to be monitored to see if what is actually happening matches what should be happening. Control techniques such as variance analysis (see Chapter 16), stock and quality control methods should help to

* See sections on properties and stages of an information system

(a) measure planned against actual performance, and (b) set standards for future measurement. Where possible interim corrections can be made on any significant variations found. This means that the organisation should keep on course towards meeting its objectives.

Review

Periodically, usually once a year, decisions are reviewed to give an overall picture of the progress made. The findings of the review can then be incorporated into subsequent decisions which, in theory, should be better because of the knowledge and experience gained. Review should help to provide feedback information to frame new objectives, problems and key variables for the next round of decisions. Chapters 7 and 8 on Funds Flow Statements and ratios examine the ways in which an organisation might evaluate its overall performance.

1.10 Financial and management accounting

Because there are both internal and external demands for accounting information many organisations regard accounting as consisting of two quite distinct parts – *financial* and *management* – to the extent that in large businesses there may be two separate departments, albeit run by one senior manager. This split shows up in the training of the two types of accountant, so each may be relatively unfamiliar with the other's role, although there are often cases where the roles are combined or there is a need to work together or with the auditor (the outside financial accountant).

Perhaps the best way of describing the differences is to show the job descriptions, requirements, qualifications and personal attributes needed by a typical large company. Each branch of the profession places a different emphasis on various aspects of the work but it should be remembered that although the management and financial accountants may have different objectives they are dealing with the same records, rules and methods.

The main aim of an accounting system should be to provide management with sufficient information to run the business. This will involve maintaining a well-designed record-keeping system, and the documents in the system should contain sufficient detail on products, customers, outlets, sales regions etc. to help in decision making. Information to satisfy external needs (financial accounting) will then be a natural by-product of such a system.

Financial accountant

Job description A financial accountant is responsible for supervising and controlling record-keeping by examining closely all financial aspects of the day-to-day running of the organisation. This might involve making regular payments for bills, wages and other transactions as well as managing and controlling stock movements.

In addition the financial accountant must arrange and present a summarised version of these activities – the Final Accounts – in accordance with the companies acts and the auditors' requirements.

Job requirements   The job demands:

- a knowledge of accounting techniques, company and tax law and auditing needs
- a liking for figures and an honest regard for accuracy and precision
- an ability to work to tight deadlines
- an ability to motivate office staff of all ages, male or female, and to deal with people at all levels

With few exceptions a formal qualification is now required. This involves passing a series of examinations as well as gaining practical experience by working as an articled clerk with a firm of auditors. There is talk of making accountancy an 'all-graduate' profession – a degree will be followed up by 2 or 3 years of theoretical and practical training in an accounting practice. To date there is still little emphasis on management training, however.

The management accountant

Job description   A management accountant is responsible for supplying management with information to help improve business efficiency and decision making. This involves generating up-to-date, accurate and cost-effective information in a form which is easy to understand and therefore to act upon.

Job requirements   The job demands:

- a knowledge of financial accounting concepts and methods
- a broad understanding of management techniques and decision-making methods

This entails a thorough understanding of how the organisation works, how the management accountant fits in and, nowadays, it is vital to be familiar with data processing methods and equipment. A good management accountant should have an imaginative and enquiring mind and be able to win the co-operation of all employees, including management, by conveying the usefulness of any accounting information produced so that it can be understood and acted upon.

Today's successful applicants usually possess a formal accounting qualification, a general management qualification (e.g. BTEC) and/or considerable general management experience.

Summary of job differences

The practical differences between financial and management accounting can be understood if it is appreciated that management information should be much more:

- detailed
- frequent
- up-to-date
- understandable

than the production of the annual set of financial accounts where format is standardised, and structure and content are dictated by the various companies acts.

Summary

This chapter has examined the nature of business objectives and how information, and in particular accounting information, can help in the achievement of such objectives. The desirable properties, stages and levels of information have been explained and it has been shown how financial and management accountants meet the needs of the various interest groups who use accounts.

Assignments

1.1 Naomi Hooper, a successful business lady, is talking to John Muir, her accountant, who has just completed the organisation's annual accounts. 'Thank goodness that's out of the way again, I can get back to running my business now. What a waste of time it all is!'

John Muir gave a wry smile; he was used to this sort of reaction from many of his small business clients. 'You're not suggesting that my job is useless, are you?'

'Well, put it like this,' said Naomi, 'if it wasn't for the wretched taxman I wouldn't bother with accounts.'

'Surely you don't really mean that,' replied John. 'Your bank manager always wants a copy of the accounts, particularly this time, because you're asking for a large advance to open a second shop in town.'

'Yes, you've got a point there; and come to think of it, the Building Society insisted on seeing the signed business accounts when we bought our house.'

'Moving on a bit,' said John, 'I know that you've been thinking of going into partnership with Dave's Shops. Surely you wouldn't decide until you had seen Dave's up-to-date accounts?'

'OK, point taken, but I've got better things to do than spend my time dealing with accounts; I'm in business to sell things, I look after my employees and my customers, get the best terms from my suppliers and earn enough for myself as well as helping with the family budget. All this takes up time, as you'll appreciate, John.'

'Of course, I do, but don't you think that accounts can help you make decisions to help you achieve these things?'

'Well, maybe that's true for a large, limited company but not for little old me!'

'But can't you see that accounts can be useful to everyone we have mentioned, including you? Using accounts can help you to achieve your objectives.'

(a) In groups discuss the interests of each of the various people mentioned. What do you think the objectives are of the:
taxman
bank manager
building society
potential partner?

(b) How can the business accounts help them to achieve their objectives?

(c) Are Naomi's objectives different to the objectives above? If so, why? If not, why not?

(d) List how Accounts can help the business owner/manager to achieve objectives.

(e) Consider how accounts can be of use to:
suppliers
customers
employees

(f) List the objectives which businessmen, or others, have which accounts *do not* help them achieve. Do these goals make it unnecessary to consider accounts?

1.2 Give examples of strategic, tactical and operational information for the following organisations:
British Rail
supermarket
college/school

1.3 Write to a public limited company (preferably choose one which you like and is newsworthy) and get a copy of their Annual Accounts prepared for shareholders. Design and present a brief version of them for employees. Comment on the different goals of the various people for whom they are designed. (These accounts can also be used for ratio analysis; see Chapter 8.)

1.4 Search newspapers and periodicals for recruitment advertisements for financial and management accountants and other accounting jobs (bought-ledger or sales-ledger clerks etc.). What qualifications or experience are necessary? What other personal characteristics are organisations looking for? What pay scales are offered?

2 Producing Accounting Information

When you have read this chapter you should be able to:
- identify the sources of financial information
- explain how it is classified and recorded for the purposes of analysis and control
- explain the value of the key accounting statements – the Balance Sheet, the Profit and Loss Account and the Funds Flow Statement
- understand some of the concepts and guidelines which underlie accounting procedure

2.1 The extent of understanding required

Accounting is vital to most aspects of business decision making as there are few business situations where money is not involved. This is not to say that you should be an expert accountant, but that you need an understanding of basic accounting procedures and techniques, and their applications. With a basic understanding of accounting it is more likely that these techniques will be used and acted upon properly. This understanding depends on:

- an appreciation of where to find source data
- a grasp of the principles of data collection and processing with particular reference to the accuracy and validity of the data
- a working knowledge of the concepts, conventions and procedures concerned with the accounting process
- a thorough grasp of the meaning of the various statements prepared by the accountant and an ability to interpret and present the information contained therein

2.2 The accounting system

The previous chapter showed the stages of an information system of which accounting is a part. The problem is to produce a statement of profit or loss for a given period together with the financial position at the end of that period. These two statements are described as the Profit and Loss Account and Balance Sheet respectively. The system of input of data, processing and output is illustrated in Figure 2.1.

Records can be kept in several ways, in books, invoices or in a computer; and it should be emphasised that the method of recording of accounting data should suit the needs of the particular organisation. More often than not a small business, particularly a sole trader, will not keep accounts so carefully and comprehensively.

In larger firms, however, accounting systems may be partly or wholly computerised, speeding up the process of sorting and summarising the data. Accounting usually involves a series of routine steps which readily lend themselves to computer processing, and output can be tailored to specific needs. In the not too distant future many businesses will have fully integrated accounts systems with direct computer links to suppliers, customers etc.

The accounting system is the essential core of all financial information within an organisation: this information is the main

Figure 2.1
The accounting system: the major information system of the organisation

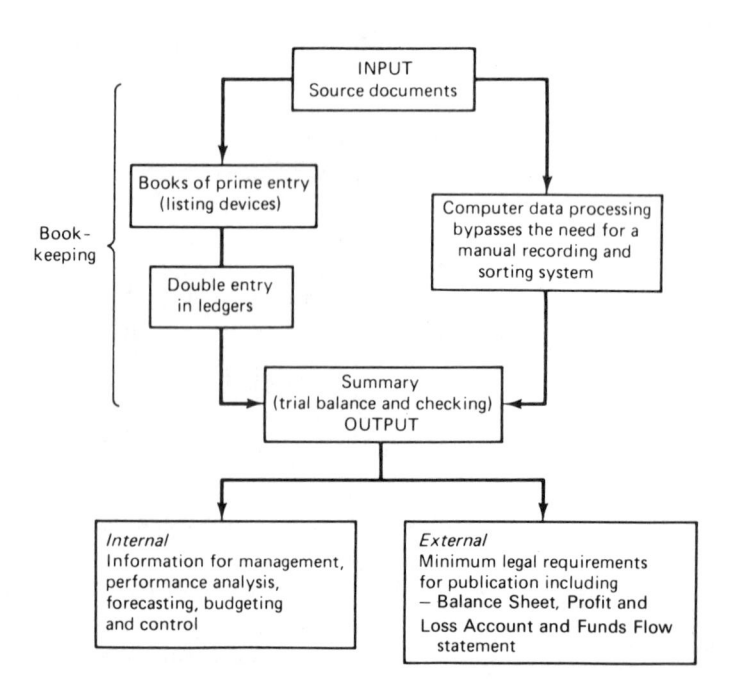

```
                        INPUT
                    Source documents
        ┌───────────┘          └───────────┐
        ▼                                   ▼
  Books of prime entry
  (listing devices)              Computer data processing
Book- {                          bypasses the need for a
keeping                          manual recording and
                                 sorting system
  Double entry
  in ledgers
        │                                   │
        └──────────┐          ┌─────────────┘
                   ▼          ▼
                     Summary
                (trial balance and checking)
                      OUTPUT
              ┌──────────┴──────────┐
              ▼                     ▼
      Internal                External
      Information for         Minimum legal requirements
      management,             for publication including
      performance analysis,   – Balance Sheet, Profit and
      forecasting, budgeting  Loss Account and Funds Flow
      and control             statement
```

clue to the organisation's success or failure, and the main measure of its value and standing. The statements, will accordingly, be liable to scrutiny and, perhaps, challenge. The shareholders of the Limited Company will be protected by audit, and accounts rendered can be questioned by Government officials for purposes of tax assessment. For this reason every transaction should be supported by a document of origin, known as a *voucher*, and such vouchers should be retained for inspection.

It is not necessary to detail every form of voucher, but the kinds of documents commonly in use include:

- Cash transactions: cash receipts, cash register tally rolls, bank paying-in slips, cheque stubs, bank statements, petty cash vouchers
- Purchase and sales transactions: invoices, credit notes, coupled with evidence of cash transactions

In addition a business will handle a host of correspondence, rates demands, energy bills, contract agreements etc., all of which will support the validity and amount of single transactions.

Using the prime data provided by this multitude of vouchers, it is normal for each transaction to be entered in the financial records, known as *books of account*.

2.3 The double-entry system

Books of account are created by means of a system of *double-entry* bookkeeping. This system is based on the simple fact that when a piece of business is arranged there are always two parties involved: a giver and a receiver. Thus each business transaction has a dual effect on the financial position of the organisation. For example, when the organisation makes a sale the increase in cash is matched by the reduced value of stock. If both these effects are recorded, then the following equation must hold:

$$\text{Assets} = \text{Capital} + \text{Liabilities}$$

This is called the *accounting equation* or Balance Sheet equation and is made up of:

- **Assets:** these are resources such as premises, stock, equipment and cash which are acquired by the organisation and put to use with a view to making a profit
- **Capital:** This is the owner's financial interest in the organisation and initially will be represented by the assets introduced to start up the organisation
- **Liabilities:** these are the amounts of money that the organis-

26 Accounting: A Practical Approach

ation owes to others in return for the goods or services they have provided

Thus, if the assets of the organisation increase, this must be accompanied by an increase in capital or liabilities or both. The converse is also true. Sometimes, however, an increase in one asset will be accompanied by a decrease in another and therefore the equation is not affected.

Example To illustrate the validity of the equation, consider the following example of eight typical business transactions, A to H.

A R. Stornaway forms a company and puts £40,000 into a business bank account
B Buys property £20,000 (cheque)
C Buys stock on credit £20,000
D Sells stock which cost him £5,000 for £8,000 on credit
E Pays wages and expenses £1,000
F Raises a bank overdraft to pay off creditors
G Collects debts
H Pays off overdraft

If after each of them, assets are marshalled together under capital and liabilities, then the result is a series of consecutive balance sheets showing that the equation is maintained.

Consecutive Balance Sheets, R. Stornaway (£000)

	A	B	C	D	E	F	G	H
Capital								
Capital	40	40	40	40	40	40	40	40
Profit				3	2	2	2	2
Liabilities								
Creditors			20	20	20	—	—	—
Bank overdraft						20	20	—
	40	40	60	63	62	62	62	42
Assets								
Property		20	20	20	20	20	20	20
Stock			20	15	15	15	15	15
Debtors				8	8	8	—	—
Cash/bank	40	20	20	20	19	19	27	7
	40	40	60	63	62	62	62	42

The changes resulting from each of these transactions can be explained as follows:

A Both capital and cash have increased, thus giving the first balance at £40,000. Note that the capital is the owner's interest, his contribution to the business

B Some of the initial cash is used to acquire property; one asset has increased while another has decreased with the balance of the equation unaffected

C The organisation acquires stock valued at £20,000 and therefore its assets have increased; but at the same time, it has also incurred the liability to pay for them; the suppliers of the stock are now the organisation's creditors

D The cost of the goods sold is £5,000 and the company makes a profit of £3,000 by selling them on credit for £8,000. So the company now has debtors owing £8,000 but no longer has the stock of £5,000. The assets have therefore increased by £3,000 and this is accompanied by the same increase in the owner's capital, shown in the above table as profit

E Cash is reduced by £1,000 and profit is reduced by the same amount

F One liability (creditors) is removed, to be replaced by another (the bank overdraft). Notice that the equation is not affected by this transaction

G Cash is collected from debtors and therefore one asset increases while the other decreases by the same amount – the equation is unaffected

H The asset of cash is reduced and at the same time the liability to the bank is removed

Keeping books of account

The above example illustrates the principle of double-entry bookkeeping but it would obviously be impractical for a new balance sheet to be drawn-up after each transaction that an organisation enters into. Therefore, in practice, transactions are recorded in books of account, the chief one of these being the *ledger*. Every page in the ledger is called an *account*, the format of which appears below:

Figure 2.1b

DEBIT				CREDIT			
Date	Details	Folio	Amount (£)	Date	Details	Folio	Amount (£)

Each account records the transactions relating to the person or thing named at the top of the account.

Basically, accounts fall into three types:

- *Nominal:* e.g. sales and expenses
- *Real:* e.g. assets such as stock, fixtures and fittings, and motor vehicles
- *Personal:* e.g. individual debtors and creditors.

Notice that the account has two sides which are identical, the left-hand side referred to as the *debit* side and the right-hand side referred to as the *credit* side. The general double-entry principle for recording transactions can be summarised as follows:

1. Each transaction always affects two accounts, one of which will have an entry *posted* (written) on the debit side and the other which will have an entry posted to the credit side.
2. With asset or expense accounts, an increase is shown by a posting to the debit side; a decrease, by a posting to the credit side.

   With liability, revenue or capital accounts, the reverse is the case. An increase is shown by a posting to the credit side; a decrease by a posting to the debit side.

Figure 2.1c

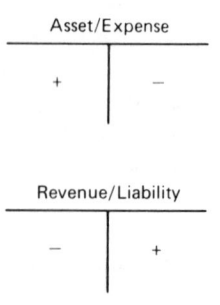

```
         Asset/Expense
        ───────────────
           +  │  −
              │
```

```
        Revenue/Liability
        ───────────────
           −  │  +
              │
```

3. Periodically, the values on each side are totalled and the difference between them found. The difference is called a *balance*; either a *debit balance* or a *credit balance*, depending on which total is larger.

Example The simple example which follows illustrates the double-entry principle, starting with the source information and finishing with the completed ledger accounts.

Source information

		£	Transaction
Jan 1	Mr AB commences business with the introduction of cash	100	1
2	He purchases shop fittings for his premises, paying cash	30	2
3	He pays rent for the premises in cash	10	3
3	He buys goods for resale on credit from CR Co	50	4
6	He pays wages of his helper in cash	5	5
6	He sells the goods on credit to Mr DR	90	6
6	He borrows cash from Mr XY for use in the business	10	7
10	Mr DR pays cash to business (Note that this is a cash payment in part settlement of debt.)	85	8
10	CR Co is paid cash (Note that this is a cash payment in part settlement of debt.)	40	9

Note: The persons involved in the credit dealings have been identified, and it is now necessary to maintain a control on the extent of indebtedness.

Double-entry involved

Transaction	Debit account	Credit account
1	Cash	Capital
2	Shop fittings	Cash
3	Rent	Cash
4	Purchases	CR Co
5	Wages	Cash
6	Mr DR	Sales
7	Cash	Loan
8	Cash	Mr DR
9	CR Co	Cash

Transactions 4 and 6 refer to opposite movements of the same volume of stock which have different values. The accounts are separated into purchases and sales. Figure 2.2 on page 30 shows how these transactions may be recorded in the accounts.

Sectionalisation of accounts

To free ledgers from excessive detail and to save time and expense double entering every single transaction, groups of transactions are often brought together and supported by listing systems known as *subsidiary books*.

The four main groups to which this method is applied are Sales and Sales Returns, Purchases and Purchase Returns. In each case, the subsidiary book is referred to as a *day book* or *journal*. Transactions are listed in these subsidiary books and the totals are transferred periodically to the relevant accounts (via the double-entry system) in the ledger.

Figure 2.2
Sample transactions recorded in the accounts

Cash account No. 1

Date	Debit	Ref	Amount	Date	Credit	Ref	Amount
Jan 1	Capital account	2	100 00	Jan 2	Shop fittings account	3	30 00
6	Loan from XY account	6	10 00	3	Rent account	7	10 00
10	Mr DR account	10	85 00	6	Wages account	8	5 00
				10	CR Co account	9	40 00
				10	Balance c/d*		110 00
			195 00				195 00
10	Balance b/d*		110 00				

Capital account No. 2

				Jan 1	Cash account	1	100 00

Shop fittings account No. 3

Jan 2	Cash account	1	30 00				

Sales account No. 4

				Jan 6	Mr DR account	10	90 00

Purchases account No. 5

Jan 3	CR Co account	9	50 00				

Loan from XY account No. 6

				Jan 6	Cash account	1	10 00

Rent account No. 7

Jan 2	Cash account	1	10 00				

Wages account No. 8

Jan 6	Cash account	1	5 00				

CR Co account No. 9

Jan 10	Cash account	1	40 00	Jan 3	Purchases account	5	50 00
10	Balance c/d		10 00				
			50 00				50 00
				10	Balance b/d		10 00

Mr DR account No. 10

Jan 6	Sales account	4	90 00	Jan 10	Cash account	1	85 00
				10	Balance c/d		5 00
			90 00				90 00
10	Balance b/d		5 00				

*b/d = brought down   c/d = carried down

In this way the double entry has been completed but streamlined. In addition to this grouping, the Cash account, which tends to have the vast majority of entries, will be housed in a separate *Cash Book*.

Thus most large-scale accounting systems, whether manual, semi-automated or fully computerised, will be broken down into working units:

- *Sales Ledger:* all credit customers' accounts
- *Purchases Ledger:* all suppliers' accounts
- *Cash Book:* for all cash and bank transactions

Example
Sales Day Book

Date	Account number	Customer	Invoice number	Amount £
Nov. 17	10600	Smith	7/135	45
	51000	Hunt	7/136	15
	13124	Peters	7/137	80
	34256	Wales	7/138	30
	22578	Stead	7/139	50
			Batch total	220

The individual invoices will be debited to the customers' accounts in the sales ledger and the batch total will be credited to the sales account in the nominal ledger.

Summaries of these are fed into the

- *General Ledger:* for all other accounts, subdivided between:
- *Nominal Ledger:* all expenses are posted from the cash books and purchases ledgers to the left-hand side of the nominal ledger. Revenue from sales, rent received, dividends etc. are posted to the right. It is important to keep expenses on the left and income on the right if the books are to balance
- *Capital Ledger:* any land, buildings, machinery, furniture and vehicles owned will be entered on the left of this ledger showing the cost of such items at the time of purchase

A comparison of expenses with sales will show the profit for the period. The cash book totals will show the cash in hand. The total sales and purchases ledgers balances will show how much the organisation is owed by customers and how much it owes to suppliers.

For management purposes, frequent summaries of the accounts can be accessed for investigation. For example, the credit control manager would take charge of the sales ledger to monitor debtor pay-back.

The trial balance At any time, and certainly at the end of any accounting period, the data, now sorted into its various categories, can be listed in two columns and the columns totalled to produce a summary as shown here.

Trial Balance of Mr AB as at January 10

Account	Debit £	Credit £
Cash	110	
Capital		100
Shop fittings	30	
Sales		90
Purchases	50	
Loan from Mr XY		10
Rent	10	
Wages	5	
CR Co		10
Mr DR	5	
	£210	£210

If the double-entry recording has been done accurately, the two columns will agree – producing the *trial balance*. The trial balance tests the accuracy of the recording up to this stage, although it would not detect some bookkeeping mistakes, for example:

- complete omission of transactions
- entries posted to the wrong accounts
- correct double-entry but with the wrong amount
- double-entry maintained, but to the wrong side of each account

However, the trial balance is also useful as a convenient list from which the final stage of presentation can be completed, and, if re-ordered, it can be used as the basis of key financial documents – the Profit and Loss Account and the Balance Sheet.

2.4 The key financial documents

The financial statements which together comprise a set of final annual accounts are:

- the Balance Sheet
- the Profit and Loss Account
- the Funds Flow Statement

The main aim of any accounting system will be to produce these summary documents.

The Balance Sheet   The Balance Sheet is a statement of the financial position of an organisation showing what the organisation owes and what it owns at a point in time. It is convenient to think of an organisation as a resource-converting machine or an input–output mechanism. It collects funds (inputs) and uses them (outputs) as shown below; because these two must be equal, the Balance Sheet will, by definition, always balance, since the document represents two aspects of the same situation.

A stylised Balance Sheet

Where does the money come from? (Input)	Where does it go? (Output)
1 Share capital – owner's equity	Fixed assets (i.e. items to be used and kept in the business)
2 Reserves—retained profits once the organisation has started trading	Current assets (i.e. items for sale)
3 Loan capital – outsiders' loans	Outside investments (i.e. shares in other companies)

For example, re-ordering the figures in the trial balance gives the following:

Balance Sheet of Mr AB as at January 10

Capital		£	Assets	£
Capital	100		Shop fittings	30
Profit	25		Debtors (Mr DR)	5
		125	Cash	110
Liabilities				
Loan from Mr XY		10		
Creditors (CR Co)		10		
		145		145

The rest of the items from the trial balance have been used to calculate the profit figure of £25 as the following section explains.

The Profit and Loss Account

This statement shows the extent to which management has succeeded in increasing funds or capital during a given time span. This mainly results from making profits while carrying on the normal operations of the organisation. Profit is the excess of revenue (income) over costs (expenditure). If expenditure is greater than income, then a loss is incurred and funds will shrink.

Revenue is the value of an organisation's sales plus any non-trading income (e.g. rent received from sub-letting).

Costs are expenses incurred in making those sales and will

include the cost of buying or of manufacturing the goods sold (or of providing the services rendered) as well as the other day-to-day running expenses of an organisation.

A sample Profit and Loss Account is shown below.

Profit and Loss Account for the period ended January 10
(from trial balance)

	£	£
Sales		90
Purchases	50	
Rent	10	
Wages	5	
Total expenses		65
Profit		25

If a profit is made, the owner can withdraw it for personal use, known as drawings, or retain it within the business for expansion.

Funds Flow Statement

The summarised data has been arranged into two key statements and there are already links between the two – profit being the most obvious. In fact, another statement, called the *Funds Flow Statement*, can be produced which looks at the Balance Sheet from a different angle. It is concerned with the changes in the availability and use of funds since the previous statement, and it is used to show either the cash or the 'liquid' position of the organisation and its ability to pay off short-term debts. The preparation of this statement is explained in Chapter 7.

Shareholders and creditors examine the historic sources of funds and the uses to which they are put in order to highlight trends and potential liquidity problems. In addition, certain types of creditor will demand a cash flow forecast which attempts to predict the flow of funds into and out of the bank account. This forecast is based on expected output and sales, and is vital if the organisation is to be sure that it will have enough money to pay its bills at all times.

Accounting guidelines

Accounting is not the straightforward, mechanical set of procedures that it at first appears. Accounting involves matters of opinion and judgement, and this could lead to two accountants reporting different results from the same set of figures.

This has led to the development of a number of generally agreed guidelines and laws which act as the framework for preparing accounts so that a reasonably 'true and fair view' of the organisation is given.

Role of accounting standards

The various accounting bodies have tried to devise, agree on and implement accounting standards for such things as the valuation of stock and the treatment of inflation. These are precisely the areas where there is a lot of scope for argument and judgement as to which accounting method is most appropriate. Accordingly, in these areas, managers sometimes aim to show the most favourable view instead of the truest and fairest one. The establishment of broadly uniform practices should make inter-firm comparisons more useful as well as minimising the risk of misleading and fraudulent statements.

Since 1970, the Accounting Standards Committee, which includes members from the principal accounting bodies, e.g. CACA, CIMA, has issued a series of *Statements of Standard Accounting Practice* (SSAPs) aimed at narrowing differences of accounting treatment by restricting the range of choice in accounting practice.

To issue an SSAP the committee first publishes an Exposure Draft (ED) which serves as a discussion paper for comment by the profession (cf. a Government Green Paper). At the end of the exposure period, the SSAP is issued in its final form. Although not legally binding, SSAPs have the force of house rules and are obeyed by all qualified accountants.

There are several important SSAPs which will be outlined in this book; the others cover areas beyond its scope.

SSAP 2 is called the *Disclosure of Accounting Policies* and sets out the main assumptions (usually referred to as *fundamental concepts*) which provide the general framework for the preparation of financial statements. SSAP 2 requires that the accounting policies adopted and any fundamental differences from the fundamental concepts must be disclosed in the Final Accounts.

Fundamental concepts

There are four assumptions which accounting is based on:

The going-concern concept It is generally assumed that the organisation will carry on trading 'for the foreseeable future'. It follows that financial statements should reflect this by valuing (for example) assets accordingly, not as if they were going to be sold.

The matching (or accruals) concept Another problem of measurement is to try to ensure that costs and revenues 'belong' to the correct accounting period. In practice profit should be determined by including revenue and costs as they are earned or incurred and not as cash is received or paid.

A transaction is recorded in the books when goods enter or leave the premises or when a service is provided. So revenue arises on the date of sale when goods are sent out to customers either for cash or some legally enforceable debt. Similarly, purchases are recorded when the goods arrive and not necessarily when they are paid for. Likewise, payments in advance (say rent for next year) are excluded from this year's profit calculations. For example, if a business pays for the next 12 months rent and the payment is made half-way through the financial year, then obviously only half of this amount can be related to the current year as an expense. The remaining half is a current asset at the end of this financial year to be carried over to next year when the benefits will be gained and it becomes an expense of that year. Conversely, unpaid (accrued) expenses (say an electricity bill) must be included because they 'belong' to the present period. A quarter 4 electricity bill (October–December) may not be paid until the final demand in late January but the amount owing is really a part of the previous year and should be charged as such. The outstanding amount appears on the Balance Sheet under current liabilities.

A further problem exists where expenditure provides benefit over several accounting periods. This *Capital Expenditure* includes spending on such items as fixed assets which should have several years of useful life. The cost should be spread over the active life of the asset and 'matched' against the revenues (benefits) it is estimated to make – a process known as *depreciation*. Clearly the matching principle is quite complex and reference will be made to various aspects of it throughout the book. SSAP 12 deals specifically with Accounting for Depreciation and this is covered in Chapter 4.

The consistency concept It is important that accounts are prepared on a consistent basis from year to year so that like can be compared with like and meaningful conclusions drawn. To prevent manipulation of the figures and the possibility of misleading or defrauding outsiders, any change in the accounting methods or policies affecting the valuation of assets and the profit figure, such as depreciation or stock valuation, must be noted in the accounts. Similarly, any departure from the four fundamental concepts must be explained (disclosed).

The prudence concept This concept boils down to 'when in doubt, assume the worst' and is the reason why accountants are often seen to be cautious or pessimistic.

It is customary to hold back from showing profits until they are more or less certain. For example, on long-term contracts such as building an office block, an organisation will often delay the reporting of the bulk of the profits until the job is completed. If, however, losses are anticipated, these will be taken into account at once by means of a provision, even if such a loss does not subsequently come about.

Another example of the prudence concept is stock valuation. Stock is always valued at 'the lower of cost and net realisable value' (see Chapter 4 for SSAP 9 Stocks and Work-in-Progress).

The rationale behind the accountant's prudent approach seems to be that fewer problems are caused by understating rather than overstating profits.

Other key assumptions

Apart from the four fundamental concepts referred to in SSAP 2, financial statements are usually based on the following:

Money In order to preserve a certain amount of objectivity only data which can be reduced to a common standard of measurement, i.e. money, can be recorded. Therefore, qualitative data is not easily handled in accounting as it cannot easily be expressed in money terms. As a result, factors such as competitive changes, new product development or key managerial moves, which can all have a major effect on business performance, are not dealt with directly although their impact should reflect indirectly in future financial statements.

Historic cost The need to report accurately and honestly also requires basing records, statements and estimates on historic costs. The money values assigned to assets are original purchase costs and these are used as the basis for future valuation. Historic costs are facts, not opinions, and can therefore be said to be objective. However, there are important exceptions to this principle which allow for the fact that certain assets depreciate (see SSAP 12 and Chapter 4), whereas other assets (e.g. property) appreciate. There are further difficulties concerning out-of-date or damaged stock (see SSAP 9 and Chapter 4) and the much greater problem of recording historic values in times of inflation. This final point led to the development and adoption of a system of Current Cost Accounting as explained in SSAP 16 (see Chapter 9). However, because of the fierce controversy it caused and the resulting uncertainty, most companies have stopped producing Current Cost Accounts.

Separate entity For accounting purposes the organisation is regarded as a separate entity quite distinct from the proprietors or owners of the business, so records are kept from the standpoint of the organisation rather than its owner(s). For example, if a sole trader introduces money into his own business the convention is to treat the transaction at 'arms length', i.e. the books will show that the organisation has received money from him. Only the extent of the owner's financial interest will be recorded, not his private possessions or wealth. The distinction is more easily seen in the case of a limited company because a company is technically and actually separated from management. Managers look after the business for their shareholders, who own the company, and, as we have already seen, provide information such as annual reports to meet these outside obligations. This notion of stewardship resulted in the development of financial accounting.

Double-entry The concept of separate entity requires an organisation to record each transaction in two separate accounts, one showing a loss in value and the other a gain. These two sides of any business transaction – the giver and the receiver – are noted in the system of bookkeeping called double-entry (as discussed in Section 2.4). This system can be manual, or partly or wholly computerised.

The Accounting Standards, were built on traditions and conventions and have led to greater uniformity of practice in terms of principles adhered to, presentation and disclosure which should add realism to accounting figures.

Laws Additionally organisations have certain statutory (legal) obligations to keep certain interest groups, like shareholders and the Inland Revenue, properly informed. The majority of these statutory regulations can be found in the Companies Act of 1985, but there are other Acts of Parliament which deal with special parts of the organisation. The Finance Acts, for example, detail how a company should fill in its tax returns and how VAT records should be kept. For companies quoted on the Stock Exchange, there are further rules. Although these are not strictly laws, the quotation is discontinued if the rules are broken.

Most of the laws strengthen many of the principles and practices already outlined by limiting the accountant's discretionary powers; other laws introduce additional rules which organisations must keep to.

Disclosure The law requires limited companies to keep records, and an annual summary – the Company Report – is drawn up for shareholders and the Government. There is a minimum amount of information which must appear in these published accounts but many organisations volunteer extra information. Any change in accounting method or policy must be displayed (see the Consistency Concept). This is again backed up by the law so that changes which can significantly alter profit are brought to the attention of the investor or creditor. Any organisation is required to maintain sufficiently accurate records for tax assessment and to meet its obligations for the collection and payment of income tax for its employees and VAT from its customers. Government departments are authorised to inspect these records and can do so at short notice.

The annual audit For limited companies, the law requires an annual audit which aims to ensure that the information shown is a 'true and fair view' of the organisation's affairs. The auditor must satisfy himself that the fundamental concepts and the law have been followed and severe penalties can be imposed where published accounts deliberately mislead or show signs of negligence or carelessness.

Future developments

There is a growing acknowledgement by organisations of all types that accounting information should be honestly, correctly and clearly presented to the various interest groups. Already some companies are adapting this information to meet the particular needs of employees and customers alongside the existing, and more formal, approaches to shareholders and Government.

There appears to be a general trend towards better presentation and a greater disclosure of results.

Summary

This chapter has taken a broad view of the need for and the problems of preparing financial accounting information.

Three key documents – the Profit and Loss Account, the Balance Sheet and the Funds Flow Statement have been identified. Each of these documents will be examined in detail in later chapters.

The chapter also introduced a number of assumptions which provide a framework for the accounting system. These include 4 fundamental concepts:

- going-concern
- matching
- consistency
- prudence

and 4 key assumptions:

- money
- historic cost
- separate entity
- double entry

A familiarity with these will be essential when the actual processes are examined.

Assignments

2.1 (a) Try and get hold of examples of a:
Sales invoice
Supplier invoice
Wage analysis printout
Bank statement
Credit note

(b) Explain what each document is and how its contents would be entered up into an organisation's books.

2.2 Draw an outline diagram (a sample of which is shown in Figure 2.3) to illustrate the double-entry bookkeeping system which you might expect a small retailer to use. Indicate on your chart the prime entry documents which start the recording of the main business transactions. Ignore day books.

Figure 2.3

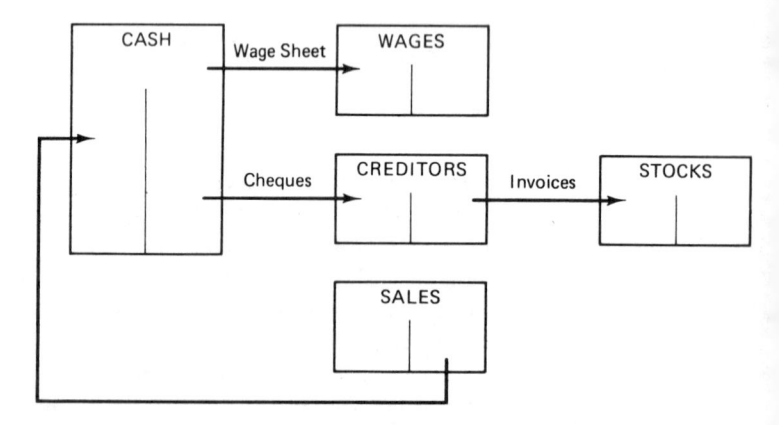

```
┌─────────┐  Wage Sheet  ┌─────────┐
│  CASH   │─────────────▶│  WAGES  │
│         │              │         │
│         │              └─────────┘
│         │
│         │  Cheques  ┌───────────┐  Invoices  ┌─────────┐
│         │──────────▶│ CREDITORS │───────────▶│ STOCKS  │
│         │           │           │            │         │
│         │           └───────────┘            └─────────┘
│         │
│         │           ┌─────────┐
│         │           │  SALES  │
│         │           │         │
│         │           └─────────┘
└─────────┘
```

2.3 Your local village general store and newsagent, Rupert Digger, knowing you are studying BTEC 'Business Studies', asks for your help. He wants to know how the company stands at the year end and what sort of year it had. He provides you with the following information about his company. All the figures refer either to the year ended 31 March or to that date itself.

	£
Wages paid to sales assistant (part-time)	4,000
Value of delivery van at 31st March	1,800
Cost of goods sold to customers	25,320
Salary paid to self	10,000
Sales of goods to customers	45,147
Value of shop building and land as at 31st March	90,000
Cash in the till and in the bank	1,350
Sundry expenses paid (e.g. rates, telephone, petrol etc.)	2,750
Amounts owing to suppliers at 31st March	1,600

During the year property values in the area have risen but because the general state of repair of the shop has deteriorated its value has, on balance, stayed the same as a year ago. The van, on the other hand, was worth £2,000 a year ago but has now been valued at a lower figure because it is older.

Be sure to explain why he needs to keep a:
Profit and Loss Account
Balance Sheet
Cash Book
and point out what each statement is designed to show.

2.4 (a) Find out and explain what it means when an auditor 'qualifies' the accounts.

(b) Try and find recent examples of accounting 'fraud' (sometimes known as 'creative accounting'!).

(c) What guidelines exist to minimise the chances of accounting malpractices happening?

(d) Give examples of the following concepts:
going-concern
matching
consistency
prudence

Why do you think these concepts are so important?

2.5 According to the assumptions in accounting, how would the following events be treated? Give reasons for your answers.
(a) A competitor announces the launch of a new rival product.
(b) Motor vehicles are depreciated by half the rate of last year.
(c) A new sales manager is appointed.
(d) The office is fitted with a central heating system.
(e) The premises are painted and decorated.
(f) Goods sold towards the end of the accounting year are not paid for until the following year.
(g) The owner takes cash out of the business for private use.

2.6 Draw up the accounts and prepare a trial balance from the following information.

	Debit	Credit
(a) A. Wainwright (owner) pays £10,000 into business bank account	Cash	A. Wainwright (capital)

(b) Take out a £5,000 bank loan
(c) Purchase a machine for £3,000 in cash
(d) Purchase goods for £1,500 from A. Toplis on credit
(e) Pay wages of £1,000 in cash
(f) Pay general expenses of £1,000 in cash
(g) Sell goods (cost price £500) for £750 cash
(h) Part payment to A. Toplis of £500

Why is accounting information recorded in this form?

2.7 Demonstrate by means of successive balance sheets the effects of the following transactions:
(a) Start business with £60,000 cash
(b) Buy shop for £15,000 cash
(c) Buy stock on credit for £10,000
(d) Pay business expenses in cash £2,000
(e) Sell stock which cost £7,000 for £12,000 on credit
(f) Pay creditors amount owing
(g) Collect cash (£9,000) on account from credit customers

2.8 1st January 19–8, A. Toplis starts a business with £6,000 in a bank account. He purchases furniture and fittings for £1,200 paying by cheque.

During the first month he buys stock on credit:

		£
Jan 8	G. Fogg	450
Jan 13	E. Brush	250
Jan 20	P. Bancroft	150

His sales of stock on credit are:

Jan 9	J. Todd	650
Jan 21	B. Williams	800
Jan 29	J. Todd	350

Cash sales during the month totalled £800 and are paid into the bank.

Other purchases and payments made by cheque are:

Jan 7	Rent	70
Jan 18	Electricity	125
	Motor van	1,200
Jan 20	Packaging	100

On 30th January, J. Todd settles his account in full by cheque and Fogg, Brush and Bancroft are paid off. Toplis buys additional fittings on credit from Office Furnishing Ltd for £400 and cashes a £300 cheque for his own spending. Set out all the accounts, including a bank account, in A. Toplis ledger and extract a trial balance.

2.9 From the following trial balance draw up the Profit and Loss Account and Balance Sheet.

Trial Balance of K. D. Hull, year ending 31st December, 19-8

	£	£
Sales		22,000
Opening stock	2,000	
Purchases	12,000	
Light and heat	250	
Rent and rates	200	
Insurance	100	
Discounts allowed	50	
Rent received (sublet)		100
Land & buildings	20,000	
Furniture & fittings	5,000	
Motor vehicle	2,000	
Debtors	500	
Creditors		1,500
Capital		18,000
Bank overdraft		500
	42,100	42,100

Additional notes
(a) Closing stock at 31st December, 19-8   £3,000
(b) Insurance prepaid   £20
(c) Light and heat owing   £50
(d) Depreciation   £700

3 Computers and Accounting

When you have read this chapter you should be able to:
- explain the main components of the data processing cycle
- understand what a computer system is and how it can help the accountant
- appreciate some of the relative costs involved in computing
- outline some of the advantages and disadvantages of computerisation
- outline the steps in the creation of a working computer system

3.1 The data processing cycle

An accounting data processing system can progress from simple hand-written bookkeeping, through various stages of computerisation, to a fully integrated computer-based system for financial and management information. Any system requires an ordered procedure by which data is first introduced (input), then stored, processed and finally extracted as information (output). This output may be used again (feedback) or become the input of another system. Figure 3.1 gives a flow diagram of such a system.

Figure 3.1

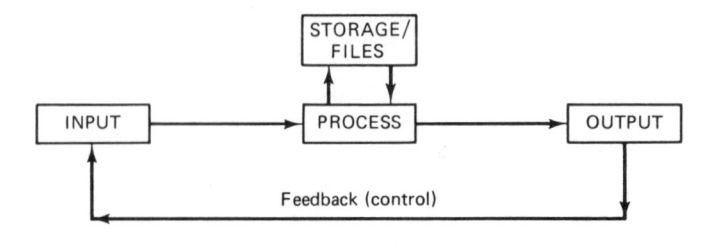

```
                    ┌──────────┐
                    │ STORAGE/ │
                    │  FILES   │
                    └──────────┘
                         ↕
┌───────┐        ┌─────────┐        ┌────────┐
│ INPUT │──────→ │ PROCESS │──────→ │ OUTPUT │
└───────┘        └─────────┘        └────────┘
    ↑                                    │
    └──────────── Feedback (control) ────┘
```

Input

The nature of the input depends on the system; for example, purchases recorded over a day on a pre-list (*journal*) form the basis of a purchases accounting routine and the individual purchases would be used in the creditors' accounts.

Care should be taken to check the accuracy of the incoming data. Some sort of validation or editing procedure, designed to sift out any errors, should be included at this stage.

Process Any accounting routine features arithmetic operations, data transfer and maybe comparisons. The process may be manual, such as writing up a ledger or totalling a column of figures, or it may be a computerised process for manipulating the same information.

Output Systems are designed to produce useful, up-to-date information and this can take the form of:

- business documents, e.g. invoices, statements, exception reports
- files, i.e. copies stored for later use

Data storage The storing of data is basic to any accounting information system. It is often useful to distinguish between data which will have long-term use (e.g. annual figures for a five years sales history) and data which is likely to be of value only in the short term (e.g. daily sales). The former is sometimes known as *archive* data and the latter as *current* data. There is little point in saving data which is no longer of use to the organisation and so regular purges of files to remove the redundant data should take place.

In addition, data is sometimes classified as:

Standing data This is data, often held on a master file, which is relatively constant. Examples could be a customer address or account number, which change infrequently, if at all. Changes to standing data can be of three types:

- additions, e.g. creating a new customer account
- amendments, e.g. changing a customer's address
- deletions, e.g. removing an old customer

The updates should be carefully checked as a mistake made here can be serious.

Transaction data Conversely this type of data changes, as the name implies, with each transaction, e.g. an account balance or date. Transaction data can be created during processing, e.g. by calculating interest on a customer's account, perhaps by reference to another file.

Types of files A *master file* is used to hold data similar to that held in a ledger in a manual system. This can include both standing and transaction data. A master file such as one containing the sales ledger balances may be the input to a process, which is itself a set of stored instructions (a program) and may be updated by that process to become output in the form of new balances. In general, the master files will contain the main records of the system.

A *transactions file* will contain details of movements (or transactions) that have taken place since the master file was last updated.

A *working file* is a temporary file created during processing and will not be retained.

Occasionally *reference* (or common data) *files* are held. These might contain prices for example.

File structure and method of access will help to determine the frequency and speed at which data can be retrieved.

Sorting and Accessing

Some tasks may require the sorting of data into a particular order so that it can be processed easily. For example, sales invoices received at random may have to be sorted to match a sales ledger held in customer account number order. Some data may even have to be sorted several times in different sequences, e.g. customers by area or outlet type. Where required, utility sort and search programs should be available to organise and retrieve files in the required manner.

System control

The various parts of the system should be related and held together by set procedures and controls.

In a computer, there will be a stored program known as an operating system which controls and co-ordinates activities. But whether they are manual or computerised, it is important to have controls and checks at all stages to ensure that the system is running properly. This involves decisions on how to detect, locate

Table 3.1

System	Manual	Computer
INPUT	Basic business documents	Data captured on magnetic disk/tape usually keyed in from basic documents. Also direct 'reading' devices, e.g. bar code readers
PROCESS	Clerk sorting & analysing data	Central Processing Unit (CPU) performs arithmetic and sort operations according to stored instructions
OUTPUT	Business documents accounts, ledgers	Preprinted business documents, disk/tape containing updated data
STORAGE/ FILES	Subsidiary books, ledgers, microfilm	Magnetic disk/tape (or other media)
CONTROL	Clerk following written/unwritten rules of procedure	Programs on 'Procedure' stored in the 'Memory' Computer checks and controls

Table 3.2
SYSTEM OUTLINE: Sales Ledger

INPUTS
Customers' orders
Payment information
Credit information
	PROCESSES
	Update sales ledger with:
	  order information
	  payments
	  credits
	Calculate new total owed
	Apply discounts, credits and VAT
	Prepare invoices
	Prepare summaries and totals

FILES Customer master file Stock master file Sales file Transaction file Print files (various)	OUTPUTS Invoices and copies Control totals Exception reports e.g. credit and bad debt status Summary reports

and correct errors to ensure accuracy, security and privacy, and it is useful to get the auditor's approval for such controls. As a rule of thumb it seems sensible to trap errors as early as possible and put them right so that complications do not arise at later stages.

Table 3.1 shows how the five elements of the data processing cycle might appear in a manual accounting system and in a computer system.

Another way of showing a system is given in Table 3.2. This format is known as a system outline, and this one depicts the various components of a sales ledger system in non-technical terms.

What is a computer?

In simple terms a computer is a machine which can accept and store data, process a list of instructions which act on this data (known as the program), and output the results in printed form or onto a screen. This data comprises numbers, letters and special symbols which can be read by humans but must be held in the computer in the form of an electronic code called the binary system. This is a system of numbering using only zeros and ones. In most small computers each character, number or symbol is represented by 8 or 16 binary digits or bits. This collection of 8 bits is known as a byte. The machine detects these zeros and ones by recognising different voltage levels.

The computer can perform arithmetic operations on the data or make comparisons between sets of data. This ability to make comparison tests and act accordingly gives the machine apparent 'intelligence'. The computer has to be given a set of rules (the program) in order to do this and these rules are stored in the memory as bytes. Whilst the program can be input in binary or some other form of machine code the usual method is to have a special program which translates English or near-English into machine code. Commonly, program instructions are typed in at a keyboard to be coded and stored into memory. To run such a program the computer uses a special program known as an interpreter which translates each pseudo-English instruction into machine code and then feeds it into the processor to be carried out. The nearer the programming language is to English, the easier and faster programming becomes. These so-called high-level languages, e.g. COBOL, PASCAL and BASIC, have opened up the world of computing to non-experts, children, teachers and businessmen alike. They are fairly easy to learn and simple to use.

Components of a computer

A computer consists of various main components (see Figure 3.2)

Hardware is the general term for the physical components of a computer system as opposed to *software* which means the programs needed to make the system work.

Figure 3.2

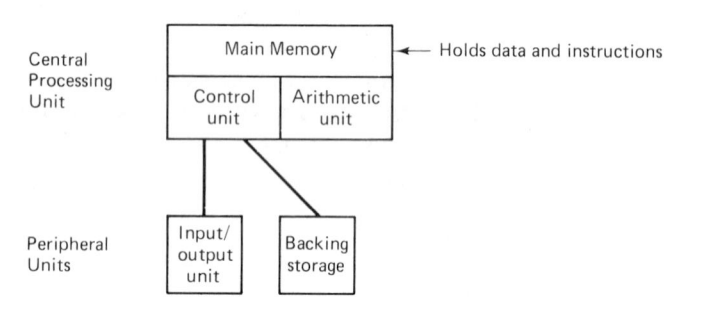

```
                         ┌──────────────────────────────┐
                         │        Main Memory           │◄── Holds data and instructions
    Central              ├──────────────┬───────────────┤
    Processing           │   Control    │  Arithmetic   │
    Unit                 │   unit       │  unit         │
                         └──────────────┴───────────────┘
                                │              
                                │              
                         ┌──────────────┐  ┌──────────────┐
    Peripheral           │   Input/     │  │   Backing    │
    Units                │   output     │  │   storage    │
                         │   unit       │  │              │
                         └──────────────┘  └──────────────┘
```

Central processing unit   At the heart of a computer system is the *central processing unit* (CPU) which consists of:

An *arithmetic and logic unit* (ALU) which, as its name suggests, performs calculations and logic operations.
A *control unit* which performs the fetch/execute cycle:
1. it fetches an instruction
2. decodes it
3. if necessary fetches any data from the memory
4. performs the actions specified by the instruction
5. if necessary stores the results in the memory
6. determines the location of the next instruction
7. repeats the cycle from 1 step.

This component, therefore, monitors and controls operations and acts as a link between the various parts of the system.

The *basic functions* of a computer are:

- arithmetic
- data transfer (from input units to the main memory and within the main memory)
- writing data to output devices
- assessing instructions for processing
- transferring instructions into and out of the main memory
- carrying out instructions

It is important to distinguish between *memory* (the computer's working capacity) and backing store. The CPU needs memory in which to keep data being processed and the programs for doing this. Microcomputers generally have two types of memory: RAM (Random Access Memory) and (ROM) (Read Only Memory). The CPU can read data stored in RAM and also put data into it. But RAM loses its contents when the power is switched off. On the other hand ROM retains its contents permanently so interpreters and the like are often stored there. The CPU can only read the ROM's contents and cannot alter them in any way although special programmable and erasable ROMs can be bought.

Peripheral units These are generally anything linked to the computer that is not part of the CPU. They include:

The *backing storage* which is usually necessary because of the size limitations of the main memory. Any data which will not fit into the main memory may be copied into backing store and read back later, so tapes and disks are used to save programs and data files for later use.

With small microcomputers, audio-type *tape* recorders are often used which convert data into a series of audio tones and record them; later the computer can reconvert these tones back into data. As with any tape recorder it can take a long time to record and it is difficult to locate one specific item among the mass of data held; therefore, to overcome these problems of serial access, *floppy* or *hard* disks are used which have direct (or random) access, cf. a record player.

A *floppy disk* is made of thin plastic, coated with a magnetic recording surface rather like that used on tape. The disk in its protective envelope, is placed in a *disk drive*, which rotates it and moves a read/write head across the disk's surface. The disk is divided into concentric rings called tracks (cf. music LP tracks), each of which is in turn subdivided into sectors. Using a program called a disk operating system, the computer keeps track of exactly where data is on disk and it can get to any item of data by moving the head to the appropriate track and then waiting for the right sector to come round. This can be done by recording special signals on the surface (known as *soft sectoring*) or by holes punched through the disk around the central hole, one per sector (known as *hard sectoring*).

Hard disks are commoner in large systems. They are still expensive but store more information, are more reliable in the long term, and transfer data much quicker. The advantage of direct access on disk lies in the speed with which any particular data item can be located.

The user must be able to communicate with the computer. *Input/output units* are electromechanical devices for getting data into and out of the computer. The bare essentials for this are usually a visual display unit (VDU), which looks like a TV screen with a typewriter-style *keyboard*, which may or may not be built into the system. For a written record (hard copy) of the computer's output, a printer is necessary.

In special circumstances optical character mark recognition (OMR/OCR) or magnetic ink character recognition (MICR) devices can be used to 'sense' each character. Bar codes in libraries and supermarkets are read by passing a light-processing pen over them and translating them into a numeric code for computer processing.

Communication–data transmission

The computer can send out and receive information in two forms: parallel and serial. Parallel input/output (I/O) requires a series of wires to connect the computer to another device such as a printer and it sends out data a byte at a time, with a separate wire carrying each bit. Serial I/O involves sending data one bit at a time along one piece of wire with extra bits added to tell the receiving device when a byte is about to start and finish. The speed that data is transmitted is referred to as the *baud rate*.

To ensure that both receiver and transmitter link up without any electrical problems, standards exist for interfacing the two. Finally a *modem* connects a computer, via a serial interface, to the telephone system allowing two computers with modems to exchange information. A modem must be wired into the telephone systems and this needs British Telecom's permission; instead you could use an *acoustic coupler* into which the hand set fits. This has no electrical connection with the phone system – so you do not need permission – but they are less reliable. Developments in communications have led to the growth of *networks* and *distributed computer systems* where computers are linked to each other and can share expensive peripheral devices such as disk drives and printers.

3.3 Costs

The rapid development of computer technology, advances in solid-state electronics, and in particular the advent of the microprocessor has caused major changes in the past few years. Microelectronic circuits printed on a tiny silicon chip can now provide the main units of a computer.

Computers are not only becoming much cheaper but much more powerful in terms of what they can do. Each new generation of computers delivers more power for the same price. One measure of this 'power' is memory size/capacity: the ability to store and process data. The relationship between costs and performance (as measured by memory size) is shown in Figure 3.3.

As memory costs tumble (about tenfold in 10 years) the price of software – the programs which drive the computer – is growing and can now be the most expensive part of any computer package (Figure 3.4). Organisations are buying 'problem-solving systems' not pieces of hardware; computers alone are valueless unless there is software available to make them run. This is why 'brain-power' – the expert programmers' time – is so expensive. Program development costs are increasing. It takes many hours of skilled programmers' time to write a workable program, and this is why tailor-made software can be so dear.

But once written, the high fixed development costs become sunk costs (accounting jargon for 'the money is spent and there's no going back') and the add-on costs are marginal, i.e. many copies of the program can be made and sold to many customers (cf. video). The only add-on costs are the costs of the media (tape or disk) which are a matter of a few pounds, and some marketing expenses to help push sales along. Therefore, development costs can be

Figure 3.3
Cost/Performance ratio

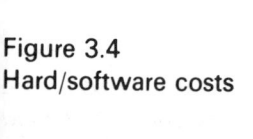

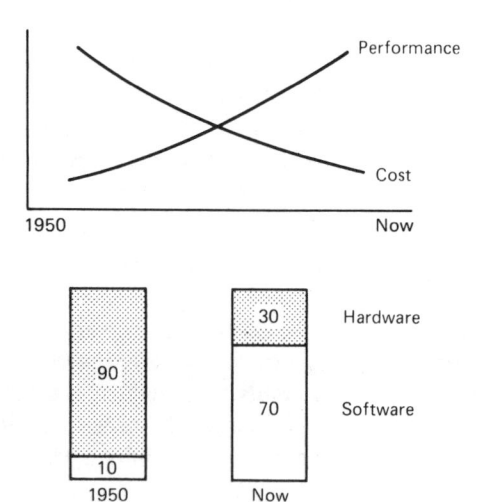

Figure 3.4
Hard/software costs

recouped and profits made if programs are marketed to many users. If sales are good, unit prices can fall drastically and so second-hand programs, (known as 'application packages') can be purchased quite cheaply. A major benefit of pre-written systems is that they are well-tested, simple, easy to use and can be managed by existing staff with minimal retraining; there is less need for computer expertise within the organisation.

It is now becoming economically feasible to computerise even the smallest business with relatively small data processing and accounting needs. Indeed falling prices and easy-to-use systems have opened up a whole new personal market for home and leisure activities.

Most business systems require a disk drive for keeping files, and a printer for hard copy. These 'peripherals' can be more expensive than the computer itself and are more susceptible to breakdown (they have moving parts). It is important, therefore, that these items are given careful consideration, as they are as much a part of the buying decision as the software and the computer itself.

Small business computer systems: a micro computer with a disk drive, a VDU, a printer and software packages for all the basic accounting routines can be bought for under £2,000 nowadays and this could become cheaper in the future. Available application packages might include:

- stock control
- purchases and sales ledgers
- nominal ledger and trial balance facility
- payroll and pay as you earn (PAYE)
- value added tax accounting

Software might come with the hardware as part of a package deal or be available at an extra cost.

There are now literally hundreds of integrated accounting packages for microcomputers. Best selling ones include SAGE and PEGASUS. Most are made up of *modules* so, for example, a business can start with the sales, purchases and nominal ledgers and add the stock control module later on when users are familiar and happy with the workings of the package.

3.4 Advantages of computerisation

The repetitive nature of the processing

Accounting by its very nature is a formally structured, rule-governed set of procedures which are repeated at frequent intervals. This lends itself readily to computer operation. The drudgery can be taken out of book keeping routines by using a computer. It does not get bored, drink tea or go to the lavatory (but you can!).

All advantages are only potential, because there are inevitable problems involving acceptance and implementation: things are easier said than done!

Think back to the information system outlined in Chapter 1. Recall that for management purposes it is desirable that information is timely (up-to-date), inexpensive (cost-effective), as accurate and reliable as need be, relevant and in the format required.

Timely There is a need for information to be produced quickly. Information, no matter how good, is of little use if it arrives too late. The computer can manipulate and process data at incredible speed, and with direct access to backing stores and desk terminals located around the organisation, information can be available at the right time in the right place. Computerisation means a vast improvement in readily accessible information. Obviously, files must be carefully designed so that search and locate procedures can operate well. Significant improvements should be available; statements could go out on the same day rather than suffer the delays inherent in a manual system, i.e. posting up-to-date, balancing-off, addressing statements. The trial balance should be available within hours rather than days of the end of the accounting period.

Cost-effective In most businesses there is a need to process much data. Clearly, the greater the volume of data to be processed the more economical computer processing becomes. Although initial capital costs for a computer-based system can be high there are major potential savings over manually based clerical systems. These savings may be direct in terms of measurable reductions in labour and overhead costs, or they may be indirect, the net benefits of having a faster and more accurate system which might indirectly improve future sales revenue because customers are getting a better service.

Data can be used for many purposes. For example, a person's weekly pay could affect job costs, departmental labour costs, total wage bill and profits etc., and each would need to be individually updated in a manual system. In an integrated computer system, however, accounting data may only need to be input and stored once to effect operations on the different files or applications. Hence unnecessary duplication of data can be reduced.

Accurate and reliable The computer is the most reliable and therefore the most accurate machine ever devised. Solid-state technology means no moving parts. Only rarely does computer equipment malfunction. Invariably if errors are produced it is because the wrong data has been input or because the program is wrong. Even then there are various control and validation checks and balances which can be built in to minimise the chance of error, although no system is perfect.

Relevant and in the format required

(a) More detailed and specific analyses can be made available on request.
(b) There can be a facility to interrogate the system by asking such questions as:

- How many debts are more than three months old?
- How much PAYE do we owe?
- Who has a birthday this week?

This flexibility means that managers can call up at any time information which is relevant to their specific needs and in the format they want. Such exception reports are more likely to be acted on. The three queries above might lead to: reminder letters to debtors; a cheque to the Inland Revenue; birthday cards to appropriate employees.

Spreadsheets and financial modelling

Sometimes there is a need to process data relating to complex systems and problems. Most accounting information systems are characterised by a mass of input data, a fairly simple set of calculations, and a mass of output data. There are specific problems of an operational research type where the arithmetic is quite complex. A computer is invaluable in finding solutions to such problems as financial planning (budgets and projections), the best level of stock to hold, the optimum method of distribution, and the best product mix.

To help the accountant forecast likely business performance there are spreadsheets and financial modelling programs available which permit the user to 'simulate' behaviour over several time periods. This is a powerful tool as it permits the decision maker to play the 'what-if' game (What if wages increase by 10%? What if prices drop by 5%?) and, given stated assumptions, to examine the likely consequences of any proposed change over several decision periods perhaps up to a year ahead.

Imagine how long it would take to produce such results manually. The benefits of such improvements in management information should increase the profitability and liquidity of the business.

Computers where you want them

The capability of computerised systems to analyse and summarise data, in whatever form required, increases the effectiveness of the accounting system. Furthermore, the linking of data *processing* with data *transmission* means that data can be sent instantly to, or received from, all over the world. Such information can be called up as required on VDUs without moving from your desk. Computers which are linked together in networks are particularly important where organisations are decentralised. Distributed data processing provides local desk-top computer facilities which are linked to the area/head office computer. Thus the organisation has the best of both worlds.

'The office of the future'

New technology provides the opportunity to co-ordinate a wide range of office procedures and tasks, which have previously been undertaken separately. Thus data and word processing, computerised filing/storage, retrieval, copying, mailing/transmission and general communication networks can all be planned from the same computer system, and the 'functional' divisions of the organisation, e.g. the accounts, marketing and production departments, can be linked together in an integrated system. This joining of operations is the basis of the new concept of *information technology* and of the so-called electronic office – the office of the future.

Systems of this complexity, however, need powerful computer backing and sophisticated software. This, in turn, means capital expenditure and a major upheaval of administrative systems and procedures with all the problems of staff retraining and development that go with this. Because of this many organisations are taking a step-by-step approach to change.

Management information systems and computers

So computers can improve information systems and therefore management efficiency because they are good at:

- processing large volumes of data
- analysing complex problems
- producing relevant information which is timely (up-to-date), inexpensive (or cost-effective), as accurate and reliable as need be, and in the format required

There are precisely the desirable properties of a good information system as outlined in Chapter 1. Therefore better decisions should be made.

3.5 Problems with computers

All the advantages outlined are, however, potential because several problems can hinder successful computerisation unless care is taken to overcome such obstacles. These include:

Choice of system

Nowadays there is a vast choice between systems. A useful checklist of questions might be:

- Is the software and hardware well developed and tested?
- Are there users similar to ourselves?
- Can we approach other users and see their systems in operation?
- What type of after-sales service and training is provided? (This is particularly important to the small, first-time buyer.)
- Is the system compatible with our existing systems (if any) and our suppliers'/customers' systems?

It is easy to be sold an expensive toy which lies idle in the corner. Rather it is wiser to buy a machine which does what you want it to do plus a little bit more for possible future growth in the business. Care should be taken not to misuse the speed of computers; more useless bits of paper can be produced very quickly.

Staff/management participation

One of the key ingredients in the successful introduction of computer systems is the full backing of management and employees. Even small business computers need careful planning and control both prior to and during the period of implementation and change-over. If the decision to proceed is made it is vital to have backing from the top, and proper management of the computer once it is fully operational. It is essential that all staff and union representatives are involved from the outset with any proposed computer system (either first-time or up-date). Participation and co-operation should lead to understanding and therefore change is more likely to be accepted if user departments are consulted early on. Careful planning might avoid redundancies, and retraining/-redeployment schemes can be agreed well in advance.

Security and control

Another problem is that of ensuring proper control over the use of the computer itself. An organisation must protect itself against:

1. the malicious abuse of equipment, fraud
2. errors and accidental mistakes (e.g. as disks are 'wiped clean' of key data because someone has pressed the wrong button)

The first type of danger, damage or fraud, demands physical controls, e.g. limited access to the computer room, and even restricted access to parts of the operating system. Hence a clerk might gain admission with a passkey, log in to the system with a specific password but still be prevented from discovering the boss's salary because that has been designated restricted or confidential information. The Americans call these levels of access 'rings of confidence'!

The second type of danger, the accidental error, can be minimised by making the system as 'idiot proof' as possible within the usual constraints of time and money. Various checks and balances can be built in to any system and the ability to make the type of mistake above can be overcome to a large extent by programming the computer to alert the operation when any deletion is about to happen, e.g. a message might appear on the VDU, 'YOU ARE ABOUT TO DELETE ROSSI'S FILE. ARE YOU SURE? (TYPE Y OR N)'. This allows users to consider their actions before all is lost!

Security procedures will involve the *Auditor* who will be concerned to see that the computer is programmed correctly, that there are satisfactory internal checks built in to the system, and that there is proper security of, and checks upon, the data being fed in so that the eventual results represent a 'true and fair view' of the organisation.

Dependency

If the accounts are computerised what happens if the system 'goes down', i.e. there is a power cut or some inexplicable systems failure? In order not to become too dependent on the computer a business should have contingency plans to cope with such hitches. These may include:

- an emergency manual system which can run until the system is recovered.
- a back-up computer facility perhaps through a time-share bureau
- stand-by equipment by prior arrangement with the manufacturer or dealer
- duplicate equipment. This is expensive but it may be essential on certain systems, e.g. real-time airline reservations

Inflexibility

Computer systems can be more difficult to change than manual ones. A minor change can involve time-consuming program modification and testing. Clearly it is worth thinking about the nature of and need for the various systems in the organisation before changes are made. At least the process of computerisation forces people to consider whether existing systems are outmoded or badly designed, and where change is most needed. Many manual 'systems' are a hotch-potch of requests whose usefulness has long since disappeared, but if the computer-based systems which replace them are carefully thought out and agreed upon, constant modifications, which interrupt the flow of work, can be avoided.

3.6 Steps in the creation of a working computer system

It should be no surprise that this procedure closely follows the management model outlined in Chapter 1. After all, the concern here is to manage a specific resource – the computer – , so this is a subsystem of the overall management model (see Figure 3.5).

Figure 3.5
Steps in the creation of a working system

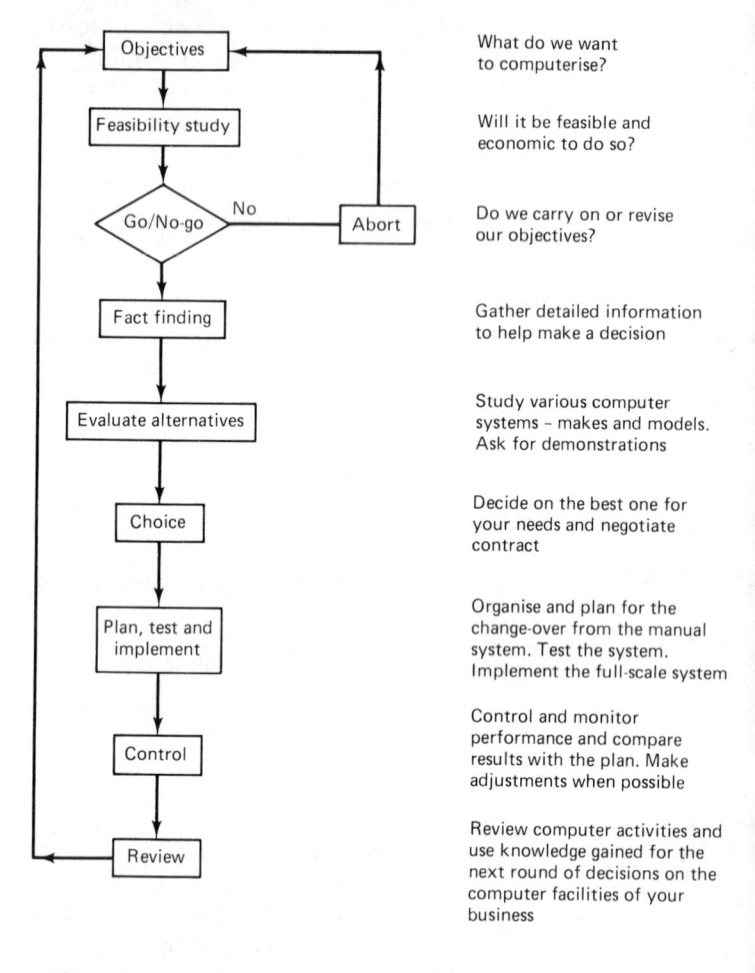

Objectives	What do we want to computerise?
Feasibility study	Will it be feasible and economic to do so?
Go/No-go (No → Abort)	Do we carry on or revise our objectives?
Fact finding	Gather detailed information to help make a decision
Evaluate alternatives	Study various computer systems – makes and models. Ask for demonstrations
Choice	Decide on the best one for your needs and negotiate contract
Plan, test and implement	Organise and plan for the change-over from the manual system. Test the system. Implement the full-scale system
Control	Control and monitor performance and compare results with the plan. Make adjustments when possible
Review	Review computer activities and use knowledge gained for the next round of decisions on the computer facilities of your business

There is no point in computerising an inefficient manual accounting system because the result will be faster errors and more headaches. Most examples of computer failures can be traced back to badly designed system and major rethinks (which upset many people because they involve change) are often necessary.

First of all there should be clear terms of reference so that the money and time available as well as the area(s) of work being considered for computerising are established. Some sort of feasibility study is necessary to ensure that the sort of job in mind could work on a computer. As mentioned, most accounting tasks have simple rules governing the way that data is handled which can easily be converted into the statements of a computer program. The study should screen out any bad ideas but those which pass will be subjected to a detailed fact-finding exercise and should reveal all the data which has to be put into the system, all the processing to be done with that input, what information is wanted out, and how to arrange the data into records and files for storage on disk or tape. How much data needs to be stored and how quickly it has to be processed will help to determine the size and type of system to buy, and the manufacturers' agents/suppliers/advertising etc. will influence the make. A checklist of factors which might influence the final choice for a small business system are given in Table 3.3. There is usually a program package which can be bought to do the job, or alternatively a programmer can be commissioned to write or amend one. Programs, especially those which have been specifically written,

Table 3.3 Checklist of selection criteria for buying a small business computer system

Price (£)	budget. Check whether this includes disk drive, printer, VDU, software, etc. (buying a system not a computer)
Memory size	internal capacity, type of operating system
Storage	capacity of floppy/hard disks
Languages offered	e.g. BASIC, COBOL
Keyboard type	number of keys, functions, 'professional' size
Display facilities	screen size (columns × rows), cursor control etc.
Graphics	optional feature
Interfaces	connections which can be made to the machine, e.g. teletext etc. Standard for printers and communications
Applications software	availability of general accounting, word processing packages
Manufacturing/ distribution base	home/overseas direct (mail order) microdealer shop national network proximity
Age of computer (years)	since prototype
Training	courses, manuals offered
Maintenance	after-sales service and back-up reliability
'Test drive'	try out the system (get a demonstration), contact local user groups
Documentation	read the manual
Popularity	number sold, tried and tested

will have to be tested, and then begins the work of transforming data and operations onto the computer. Once operational, it is essential to monitor the system carefully to see whether performance is as it was planned and whether any short-term amendments have to be made. As with any consumer durable it is useful to discuss the maintenance contract. After-sales service and guarantees are an important consideration when purchasing a computer system. It should be noted that the overheads in a computer project can be a very large proportion of total costs. Periodically, the system should be reviewed to assess its overall effectiveness and whether any major changes are needed.

Summary

This chapter has explained what a computer system is and how it can help the accountant. Some of the costs of computing were outlined, and it was emphasised how quickly costs have tumbled, so that computers are now economically feasible for the smallest of businesses. Most accounting tasks can be computerised and, with careful planning to avoid potential pitfalls, a computer system can lead to the production of cost-effective, relevant and up-to-date accounting information which satisfies external parties and enhances managerial decision making. Indeed, such information might otherwise be too costly or time-consuming to prepare using manual methods.

Assignments

3.1 An accounts department uses clerical labour and accounting machines to produce for management monthly departmental Profit and Loss Accounts and a company Balance Sheet. These monthly statements are ready on average 3 weeks after the month-ends.

(a) What possible advantages might result if the accounting system was computerised?

(b) Draw an outline chart which indicates the chief sources of information (data inputs) and the output to be produced by the computer system.

3.2 Many smaller businesses are now able to take advantage of computer-based systems to carry out their accounting tasks and provide management information. Unfortunately, many mistakes are made and there is much disappointment because of the lack of knowledge about computer systems among business people generally.

Write an outline for a leaflet for owners of small businesses advising them how best to plan, implement and develop a new computer-based business system.

Figure 3.6

Inputs	Processes
Files	Outputs

3.3 Many information processing systems, whether manual or computerised, can be described as in the diagram in Figure 3.6, a *systems outline*.

Give examples to illustrate the following statements.

(a) Data will be input to the system from a variety of sources and media.

(b) Information is required to be output for a variety of users inside and outside the organisation using the system.

(c) File processing is a central function of many information systems.

3.4 Discuss briefly the main stages in the creation of a working computer system. How might these stages overlap so as to minimise the total time devote to a project?

3.5 (a) What are the characteristics of business accounting systems which indicate that they are potentially suitable for transfer to computer?

(b) There is evidence to suggest that business data processing projects are often completed behind schedule and/or above *cost*. Why should this be so?

3.6 REALING COLLEGE of HIGHER EDUCATION

Memo from Ray Garnett

To: . . . .   Date   31 January 19-3

Subject: COMPUTER SYSTEM

I'm thinking of getting a computer for BTEC Administration and I'm looking for your help and advice. Would you prepare a report for me recommending a particular system, stating clearly the reasons for your choice? I'm not looking to spend more than £2,000.

Hints:
1. Look in Smith's computer retail outlets. Computer magazines in library/computer centre (eg WHICH MICRO etc) are especially geared to the comparative analysis of small business systems.
2. Try Yellow Pages, Thomsons, Teledata.
3. We love charts and diagrams (of the sort in Which Computer).

62 Accounting: A Practical Approach

4. We stop reading after 8 sides (excluding appended brochures/technical details, etc).
5. Be clear what the objectives are and what the output(s) should be.

We require:
a student record file
a staff record file:
   BTEC Number, name, address, telephone number, qualifications, mode, year, options, BTEC grade by subject, extensions, timetable
a word processing package for standard letters/notices
a staff file
   Name, Room Number, Telephone number, classes taught

Outputs
   Standard letter
   Circulation lists
   Staff teaching lists
   Exception reports
   Timetables (for staff and students)
   BTEC Course grades
   Residential weekends

3.7 Complete the spreadsheet below by writing formulae. Some answers are shown to help you along.

NB Formulae will be entered in column B and then replicated, i.e. copied across to the other columns.

		cell reference	formula
(a)	VAT	B8	B7*0.15
(a)	Price inc tax		
(b)	Price on road	B11	B9+B10
(c)	Total sales		
(d)	Grand Total		
(e)	Average cost		

	A	B	C	D	E	F
1			Arthur Daley Motors			
2			Car sales for August 19–9			
3						
4		Basic	Special	GTX	Turbo	Deluxe
5						
6						
7	Basic Price	5995.00	6995.00	9995.00	10995.00	15495.00
8	VAT					
9	Price inc tax					
10	Number plates	25.00	25.00	25.00	25.00	25.00
11	Price on road					
12						
13	Monthly sales	7	10	6	8	2
14	Total sales					
15						
16						
17	Grand Total					
18	Average cost					

4 The Valuation of Assets

When you have read this chapter you should be able to:
- appreciate the importance of stock and fixed asset valuation
- understand the common valuation methods for stock
- understand the reasons for and problems of deciding how to depreciate fixed assets
- calculate stock values and depreciation

4.1 Introduction

Both current and fixed assets are open to different valuations which can result in different accounting results. This chapter examines the more common valuation problems: those of stock and depreciation of fixed assets. Chapter 9 shows how the problem is further complicated by inflation and how accountants now cope with this. Profit (sales minus costs) is equivalent to the change in the net value of assets. Hence the way in which assets are valued will affect profit and if assets are not valued at historic cost the Profit and Loss Account must show this or different results will arise. Much of this valuation is based on personal opinion, and this is why the accounting profession has developed Statements of Standard Accounting Practice (SSAPs) – guidelines (house rules) to limit the scope for various opinions.

Asset valuation methods are of particular interest to management because the amount of profit reported depends largely on the method adopted. This, in turn, determines the amount of tax liability and influences management decisions on such matters as dividend policy, expansion plans etc. Clearly, decision making will be improved if these valuation procedures are understood and seen to be reasonably arrived at. Decisions can only be as good as the data on which they are based.

4.2 Stock

What is stock? At any moment most organisations, whether manufacturers or traders, will hold stock in some shape or form. Stocks can be very large in relation to profits and a small change in their valuation can lead to a significant variation in the profits reported.

Accurate profit measurement requires the *matching* of expenditure and related revenue. The cost of unsold/unused items is carried forward as stock. In this context the term stock will refer to raw materials, work-in-progress and finished goods.

Stock-taking

Stock-taking, the physical counting of items of stock, is necessary to check for fraud, theft etc. It can be a time-consuming and expensive business, particularly when stocks are large and there are lots of different items, so sample counts are often taken, compared with relevant records (invoice/computer report), and then grossed up (scaled up) to give an estimated total. This saves both time and money and is sometimes the only practical way of counting stock, particularly for audit checks.

How and why different stock valuation affect profit

Once these difficulties have been overcome there still remains the problem of *valuing* items of unsold stock.

Example Consider a small wine shop. At the end of last year it had several hundred bottles in stock which were valued at £3,000. During the present year it bought a further £12,000 worth and sold wine for a total sales revenue of £20,000. Again at the end of the year several hundred bottles were in stock and the higher the value given to these the higher the profits will be (because the cost of wine actually sold will be lower). Table 4.1 takes closing stock values of £2,000 and £4,000 to show this. Notice that the difference in the profits is the same as the difference in the value of closing stocks.

Table 4.1

	£000	£000	£000	£000
Sales		20		20
Opening stock	3		3	
Purchases	12		12	
Available for sale	15		15	
Less: Closing stock	2		4	
Cost of sales		13		11
Gross profit		7		9

Now assume, for simplicity, that all stocks are cleared in the second trading period prior to a refitting and reopening as a Wine bar.

	£000		£000	
Sales		4		4
Opening stock	2		4	
Purchases	—		—	
Available for sale	2		4	
Less: Closing stock	—		—	
Cost of sales		2		4
Gross profit		2		—

Notice that over the life of the shop total profits will be the same whatever the method of stock valuation chosen; it is the timing/pattern of profits reported that will be different. In our simple example £9,000 profit is made overall but you can see that the timing differs. This has important implications for tax (which is based on profits) and consequently dividend and working capital needs. Hence the choice of asset value has an important impact on profits and business worth.

4.3 Stock valuation

There are many ways of valuing stock and, as with depreciation, there is a good deal of judgement needed. Clearly different interpretations can produce different results in the final accounting statements, although in general a conservative attitude prevails, i.e. the lowest value for stock is reported.

The latest accounting standard on stocks (SSAP 9) reinforces the traditional emphasis on historic cost conservatism by requiring stock to be stated at:

'Cost, or, if lower, at net realisable value (NRV)'.

This emphasises the lowest value of assets and in a period of rising prices, cost will usually be below NRV. The new edict on inflation accounting recommends that *current replacement costs* should be used in the supplementary current cost statements (see Chapter 9).

Key problems of stock valuation

- should stock be valued at cost or selling price?
- in times of changing prices, when stock may be bought in at different prices, which value should be selected?

What is NRV? NRV is the effective selling price (net income from sales). For example, if a TV is sold through the small ads for £40 and £2.50 has to be spent to advertise it, then the NRV would be £40 − £2.50 = £37.50. More generally, NRV is the estimated selling price less any costs which relate to the marketing, sale or distribution of the product.

4.4 Cost bases

Current replacement cost The cost of using an item of stock is what will have to be paid to replace it. If this method is used then current purchase prices or finished stock of materials are matched with present selling prices and unsold stocks will be valued at current purchase prices. These may have to be estimates and so some objectivity may be lost, but this should be outweighed by the advantage of valuing stocks at today's rather than yesterday's prices. This method is recommended in the inflation accounting guidelines (SSAP 16) and will be explained in more detail in Chapter 9.

Historic cost Historic cost will be the purchase price (or production cost for a manufacturer) plus any allied costs incurred (e.g. delivery charges and storage) to put stock in a saleable condition.

As stated, historic cost is the usual basis for stock valuation because the lower the value given to stock the lower the profits. It accords with present professional attitudes towards objectivity and conservatism – embodied in the statement 'cost or net realisable value – whichever is the lower'. Historic costs are facts, not opinions; and can therefore be said to be objective although they might be unrealistical because they are out of date.

When to use NRV
- when goods can only be sold at a lower price than the cost

A loss on sale is likely to occur when stocks are marked down because they are:

- end of season lines (e.g. fashion sales)
- end of product lines (obsolescence)
- damaged/shop soiled (display items)
- under a guarantee/patent which has expired (e.g. camera film)
- perishable (e.g. end of date-stamped fresh food items, cf. above)
- slow moving (market demand less than expected)

The Valuation of Assets 67

Hence NRV will be used in limited circumstances when it is going to be lower than cost.

What is cost?

Cost means any expenditure incurred in bringing the product to its 'present location and condition'. Of course 'cost' presents little problem to traders who only need to account for purchase price. This might include: material costs, handling charges etc. For a manufacturer, 'cost' is more complicated and will include the purchase price of materials, any direct labour costs and expenses, and a proportion of the production overheads, such as factory heat and light which has been allotted to the product on some agreed basis.

Therefore, organisations will generally use historic cost; but goods in stock might not have been bought at the same time for the same price, and hence a method of cost must be selected for use when prices are changing.

Example The various methods of historic cost valuation are now illustrated using the following example and assuming conditions of rising prices (inflation):

Gladys Gill Ltd.
Purchases
10 items @ £5 each   (Batch A)
 6 items @ £7 each   (Batch B)

Sales
12 items @ £9 each

First in, first out (FIFO)

This method assumes that the stock bought first is the first to be sold. This roughly represents the actual physical flow of goods in a business. Taking our example, Gladys Gill Ltd., we can see that items were bought in at different costs. Of the total of 16 items, 12 are later sold for £9 each. The results using the FIFO method are shown in Table 4.2a. Using a FIFO system stock will be valued on the principle that the 12 items sold consist of Batch A and 2 items are from Batch B, leaving stock as 4 items at £7 each. Thus closing stock is valued at the most recent purchase cost (£7 per item). This value might be close to replacement cost if turnover is fairly rapid and prices do not change too frequently.

Last in, first out (LIFO)

This method assumes that the stock purchased most recently is the first to be sold. In our example all Batch B items are sold along with 6 items of Batch A, leaving stock as 4 items at £5 each. Consequently closing stock is carried forward at the earlier purchase price and in a period of inflation LIFO tends to depress profits, which is why it is not considered suitable in the UK by the taxman or SSAP 9 (the accounting standard on stock and work-in-

Table 4.2a FIFO

	Units	Price	£	£
Sales	12	@ £9		108
Purchases				
Batch A	10	@ £5	50	
Batch B	6	@ £7	42	
Stock for sale	16		92	
Less: Unsold stock	4	@ £7	28	
Cost of sales	12			64
Made up of				
Batch A	10	@ £5	50	
Batch B	2	@ £7	14	
Total	12		64	—
Trading profit				44

Table 4.2b LIFO

	£	£	Units	Price	
Sales	108				
Purchases					
Batch A		50			
Batch B		42			
Stock for sale		92			
Less: Unsold stock		20	4	@ £5	
Cost of sales	72				
Made up of					
Batch A		42	6	@ £7	Batch B
Batch B		30	6	@ £5	Batch A
Total	—				
Trading profit	36				

progress), although it is acceptable in certain other countries. The usual accounting practice is to treat stocks on the FIFO basis. However, in times of inflation this method gives a higher profit (compare Table 4.2a with 4.2b), which is why the taxman prefers it.

The Valuation of Assets

Average cost–weighted average

This method avoids the problem of changing prices. All stock acquired during a given period, at whatever price, is reduced to a single representative average cost. This can be done continuously after each purchase or at the period end. The average cost is simply calculated by dividing total cost of stock by the number of items:

$$\frac{\text{Total cost of stock}}{\text{Number of items}}$$

You can see the results, using our example again (Table 4.2a).

$$\text{Unit cost} = \frac{£92}{16 \text{ items}} = £5.75 \text{ per item of stock}$$

and £5.75 is used in the stock valuation below.

	Units		Price		£
Sales	12	@	£9		108
Purchases					
Batch A	10	@	£5	= 50	
Batch B	6	@	£7	= 42	
Stock for sale	16				92

$$\text{Unit cost} = \frac{£92}{16} = £5.75$$

Less: Unsold stock	4	@	£5.75	23	
Cost of sales	12	@	£5.75		69
Trading profit					39

Adjusted selling price

If there are practical difficulties in ascertaining cost, it is permissible to take the current selling price and deduct the normal gross profit margin to arrive at a cost price stock value. This method, which should only be used if others are too difficult to implement, is used mainly in the retail trade.

Look at three departments from the top peoples' store, Thomas Whitehead's:

Department	Sales value of stock unsold £000	Mark-up %
Bedding	20	150
Lingerie	7	100
Food (delicatessan)	5	25

Closing stocks will be valued as follows:

Department		Estimated cost Price value £
Bedding	$20{,}000 \times \dfrac{100}{250} =$	8,000
Lingerie	$7{,}000 \times \dfrac{100}{200} =$	3,500
Food	$5{,}000 \times \dfrac{100}{125} =$	4,000

Clearly if these values are grossed up by their mark-ups the sales values will result. Note that the mark-up is a percentage of cost price *not* of selling price which is known as the margin.

For information, the profit margins for the three departments are:

Department	Selling price £000	Cost price £000	Profit margin %
Bedding	20	8	$\dfrac{12}{20} \times 100 = 60$
Lingerie	7	3.5	$\dfrac{3.5}{7} \times 100 = 50$
Food	5	4	$\dfrac{1}{5} \times 100 = 20$

4.5 Choosing the final figure

Recall that stock is usually valued at the lower of cost or net realisable value, but even if the method has been decided on the final figure is still open to interpretation because:

aggregate (total) stock at cost can be compared with aggregate stock at net realisable value

categories of stock (say by department) can be compared and the lower figure taken for each grouping

comparison can be made *article-by-article* (i.e. individual items of stock)

A simple example should demonstrate.

Example Alexei Sayle, used car dealer, has the following stocks:

Car type	Cost £	NRV £
Morris 1100	500	450
Morris Traveller	800	1,000
Datsun	2,800	3,400
BL	2,000	1,900

aggregate	£6,100 (cost)	£6,750 (NRV)
category	£1,300 + 2,800 + 1,900	= £6,000
article	£450 + 800 + 2,800 + 1,900	= £5,950

Taking the stock as a whole (*aggregate* method) the stock valuation would be £6,100 (the sum of the values at cost).

Valuation by *category* (Morris, Datsun, BL) gives a figure of £6,000 (the sum of the lowest group values).

Valuation by *article*, + summing the lower figures for each individual car, gives a stock value of £5,950.

Clearly the choice of final figure will depend on the size and variety of stocks held. There is less excuse nowadays for valuing stock collectively just to avoid detailed calculations, particularly where stock systems are computerised.

Summary

This section has considered some of the problems of stock valuation. There are many different ways of valuing stock. There are at least:

- three possible bases
   (a) net realisable value
   (b) replacement cost
   (c) cost
- four possible cost methods
   (a) FIFO (first in, first out)
   (b) LIFO (last in, first out)
   (c) weighted average
   (d) adjusted selling price
- various methods of treating overheads (see Chapter 12)

- three methods of choosing the final figure
  (a) aggregates
  (b) categories
  (c) articles

Computerised stock-taking can do much to relieve the problems of immense and varied stock-holdings but there still remains the problem of choosing a value. Generally organisations opt for the historic cost basis (although replacement cost is preferred under inflation accounting) and choose one of those methods.

4.6 Depreciation of fixed assets

This section examines:

- the nature of and reasons for depreciation
- the problem of deciding the correct method and rate
- the main methods of depreciation

What is depreciation?

Statement of Standard Accounting Practice 12 (SSAP 12) defines depreciation as 'the measure of wearing out, consumption or other loss of value of a fixed asset' ... due to obsolescence, wear and tear or the passing of time.

Spending on fixed assets, the things we mean to use and keep in the business, is an example of *capital expenditure*. Fixed assets usually last for more than 1 year and have a long-term influence on the profit-making capacity of the business.

Suppose an organisation buys a mini-computer for £10,000 and expects it to last 4 years. By then it will probably be obsolete (if not worn out), but suppose that it can then be sold to the local further education college for £1,000. They are therefore estimating an overall 'loss' of £9,000 over the 4 year period; how should this be reflected in profits?

The precise 'loss' will not be known until the computer is actually disposed of, so should the organisation wait for 4 years and make the necessary adjustments in the year of sale? If no allowance is made for the 'loss' until the asset is sold or scrapped (when the precise loss will be known with certainty) then the profit and Balance Sheet figures will be distorted. This seems to be unfair and in any case contravenes the matching principle outlined in Chapter 2.

The normal practice, therefore, is to trade off the need for precision and objectivity by making a provision for the cost, i.e. an estimate of the likely loss, and spreading it over the asset's useful life by reducing the profit each year by an amount related to the decline in the value of the asset during the year. This is known as 'depreciation' and in this case it might be sensible to deduct £2,250 each year (£9,000/4). This annual cost allocation, or instalment plan, satisfies the matching principle and leads to a more even flow of profits as well as more realistic Balance Sheet asset valuations.

It seems reasonable to select some systematic way of writing down the value of a fixed asset so that the cost is spread fairly over the entire period that it is in use (which is likely to be several accounting periods), thereby making the reported profits figures over this time span more realistic.

Depreciation is an application of the matching principle in that accountants are attempting to match depreciation 'expenditure' with the benefits or service which the asset provides during a given period. Assets are recorded in the books at purchase price value or current valuation and this value is reduced over the life of the asset by allocating, as an expense, a portion of it to each accounting period involved. The written-down value remaining is treated as an asset and appears on the Balance Sheet.

Reasons for depreciation

Assets can lose value for a number of reasons:

Wear and tear Many assets, such as machinery and vehicles, deteriorate over time due to rust, corrosion, friction, and general damage and decay. This obviously impairs their usefulness and therefore reduces their value. Wear and tear may often be linked with the rate of usage and could be stated in some measure of use, e.g. machine hours or car mileage. (Production and corrosion experts can often give useful advice here.) The value of 'wasting' assets (e.g. mines) is directly governed by extraction or consumption.

Obsolescence Assets can become out-of-date and superseded by improved models which do the job more efficiently. For example, each new generation of computers tends to be much more cost-effective in terms of performance and price; they can do more things for the same money. It is also possible for an asset to become redundant if demand disappears for the product or service which it is helping to provide. This shows that fixed assets have 'derived demand' – they are only of value because of what they can do. If the machine has no other use then it will have to be scrapped even if it is in full working order. Of course, organisations hope that there is some other use (an 'opportunity cost') for their assets, or parts, so that some of the costs can be reclaimed.

Passage of time Some assets lose value just because of time passing. The most obvious examples are leasehold property and patents where the agreement or law will state how long they will run for. Depreciation in this sense is a function of time and is often known as amortisation.

Expected useful life

An asset's useful life is not easy to predict. 'Life-expectancy' will depend on the type of asset involved and, in some cases, e.g. leases or patents, can be predetermined by agreement or governed by the rate of extraction (e.g. a coal mine). Usually, useful life is dependent on the extent of use or physical deterioration and obsolescence. Such uncertainties have led many organisations to set standard time periods based on experience and general knowledge for writing off asset types. Table 4.3 shows appropriate extracts taken from a company's accounts. They show asset and life expectancy along with possible reasons for such assessments.

Table 4.3 *Extract from company accounts*

Asset	Life Assessment	Estimated life (years)*
Cars/motor vehicles	Replacement policy, pattern of running costs	3
Computers	Obsolescence	4
Machine tools	Wear and tear, physical deterioration	10
Office equipment	Notional	15
Buildings	Wear and tear, physical deterioration	50
Mine/quarry	Extraction rate	Variable
Freehold land	No loss in value	Endless–open
Leasehold land	Length of lease	Variable

* Typical asset lives.

Most British companies depreciate assets over a shorter period than the probable life, erring on the conservative side, thus reflecting the prudence concept outlined in Chapter 2.

To determine the correct method and rate of depreciation the following information is required:

- cost (or valuation when an asset has been revalued)
- the type of asset and its expected useful life
- the estimated residual value

Cost

Fixed assets are initially recorded at their purchase price, which normally includes any costs such as installation charges (e.g. connecting the power supply) and other associated expenses.

Generally there are no problems in valuation although certain qualifications should be made:

- later on it can be difficult to distinguish capital expenditure on

the asset (which adds to asset worth) from revenue expenditure on asset maintenance and overhaul
- when assets are revalued, procedures, by definition, become more subjective and discretionary

Residual value

An asset will probably be worth something to somebody, either as sale or scrap, at the end of its period with the organisation. Such a value is extremely difficult to estimate, particularly for assets which are scheduled to last for a number of years.

Often the residual value is likely to be so small relative to original cost (say a scrap value) that it is permissible to regard it as zero for practical purposes.

4.7 Methods of provision for depreciation

Once the information has been gathered organisations still have to decide on the correct method for providing for depreciation; they have to settle on a sensible basis for allocating the cost of an asset over its estimated service life.

Although there are a large number of ways of depreciation assets most of them are based on the two most popular methods examined here. The others will be outlined once the main ones have been explained.

Before choosing the method the objectives of the cost allocation have to be defined. Essentially the choice rests on whether depreciation is treated as a separate expense or as one of several associated costs, such as repairs and maintenance, which can be related to a given fixed asset. The two most common methods in general use, the straight-line and the reducing-balance methods, both allocate the same total amount for depreciation and will therefore arrive at the same final total. It is the timing of the costs which differs.

Straight-line depreciation

The straight-line method aims to spread the amount to be written off evenly over the service life of the asset by allocating an equal annual instalment. The asset is seen as providing an equal service each year with maintenance costs either constant or insignificant.

The formula for determining annual depreciation is:

$$\frac{\text{Original cost (or revaluation)} - \text{Residual value}}{\text{Useful life (years)}}$$

For example a machine is bought for £10,000. It is estimated it will last for 4 years when it will be sold for £2,000.

Applying the formula we get:

$$\frac{10{,}000 - 2{,}000}{4} = £2{,}000 \text{ per year}$$

The results are given in Table 4.4 and can be shown graphically as in Figure 4.1.

Table 4.4

Year end	Net value (£)	Depreciation (£) Annual	Cumulative
Start	10,000		
1	8,000	2,000	2,000
2	6,000	2,000	4,000
3	4,000	2,000	6,000
4	2,000	2,000	8,000

Figure 4.1
Straight-line and reducing-balance methods of depreciation

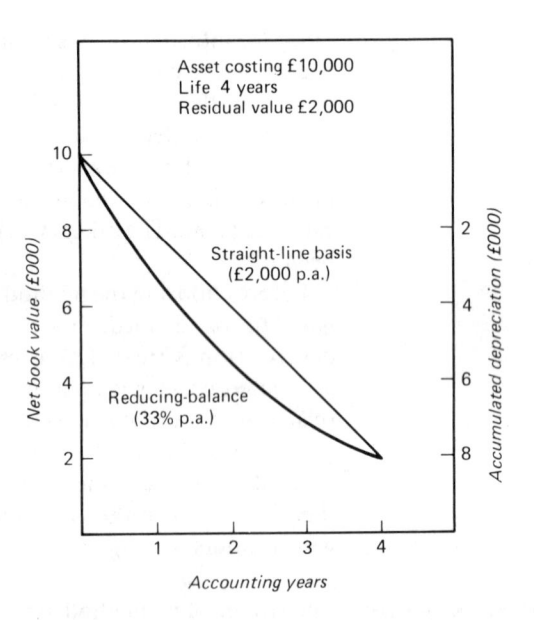

The written-down value gives a straight line (hence the name) as depreciation is an equal amount each year. The straight-line method is particularly appropriate to assets such as leases on land and buildings and patents where depreciation is a function of time. It can also be applied to assets where maintenance costs are small in proportion to the cost of the asset. This method is easily the most popular one in the UK mainly because it is easy to calculate but also because so much uncertainty surrounds the pattern of depreciation that equal apportionment is as 'fair' as any other method.

Reducing-balance method

The depreciation rate for this method is a fixed percentage of the written-down value of the asset, thereby allocating costs on a diminishing sliding scale as time goes by. The formula for reducing-balance is:

$$\text{Rate of depreciation} = 1 - n\sqrt{\frac{\text{Residual value}}{\text{Cost}}} \times 100$$

where n is the useful life in years. (You will be relieved to know that most examiners give the rate!) Taking data from our machine example we can apply the formula:

$$\left(1 - 4\sqrt{\frac{2{,}000}{10{,}000}}\right) \times 100 = 33\%$$

The result is given in Table 4.5

Table 4.5

| | | Depreciation | |
Year end	Net value	Annual	Cumulative
Start	10,000		
1	6,700	3,000	3,000
2	4,500	2,200	5,500
3	3,000	1,500	7,000
4	2,000	1,000	8,000

(Rounded to the nearest £100)

Note: The depreciation figure is based on a percentage of the net value of the asset not its original cost.

Again refer to Figure 4.1 for the graphical representation. Note how this method allocates a larger proportion of the cost in the early part of the asset's life.

The reducing-balance method attempts to account for the fact that:

- assets can lose their second-hand value more quickly in early life (e.g. cars) and a Balance Sheet value which reflects this is more realistic
- some assets tend to earn higher profits early on when they are new (think back to the matching principle)
- as assets get older many of them become more expensive to repair and maintain

Figure 4.2 shows that the reducing-balance method aims to even

Figure 4.2

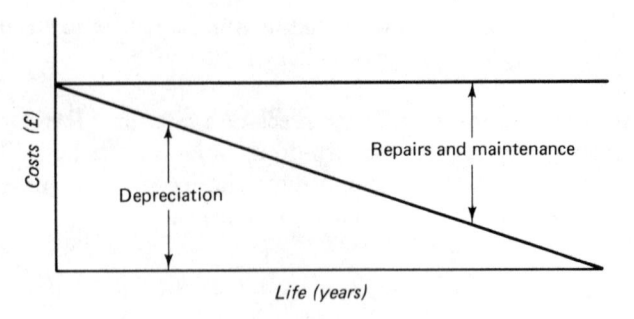

[Graph showing Costs (£) on y-axis and Life (years) on x-axis, with a declining line showing Depreciation below and Repairs and maintenance above, summing to a constant total cost]

out an asset's total running costs, which include depreciation. The decline in the depreciation provision is counterbalanced by the increases in repair and maintenance costs as the asset becomes older. This results in an equal cost each year and therefore there is a more even flow of profits over the asset's useful life.

Other methods

These will be mentioned in outline as they are used less often than the other two.

Sum of the years digits (SYD) This is really a variant of the reducing-balance method and likewise aims to show a higher depreciation charge in the early years of an asset's life. Similar comments apply. For example;

Cost of asset £12,500
Scrap value £500
Estimated useful life 4 years
Sum of digits = 4+3+2+1 = 10

The digits are, effectively, the weights. So, for example, depreciation in year 1 will be 40% ($\frac{4}{10}$) of the estimated total.

Year end	Value £
$1 = \frac{4}{10} \times £(12,500 - 500)$	4,800
$2 = \frac{3}{10} \times £12,000$	3,600
$3 = \frac{2}{10} \times £12,000$	2,400
$4 = \frac{1}{10} \times £12,000$	1,200
Total depreciation	12,000

Depreciation based on output or usage The aim here is to express the estimated useful life of an asset in terms of output or usage, rather than in terms of accounting period, e.g. technical experts might estimate that a machine's life is so many working hours.

Example The useful life of a company's van is estimated to be 100,000 miles after which it will be replaced.

Cost of van	£9,750
Trade-in value	£2,000
Depreciation	£7,750

The depreciation will be based on its usage (mileage) rather than time. Let us suppose that the following mileage profile occurred:

| Year | 1 | 2 | 3 |
| Mileage | 55,000 | 32,000 | 13,000 |

Hence depreciation charges will be:

Year		£		£
1	$\frac{55,000}{100,000} \times £(9,750-2,000)$	= 4,262.5	≃	4,250
2	$\frac{32,000}{100,000} \times £7,750$	= 2,480	≃	2,500
3	$\frac{13,000}{100,000} \times £7,750$	= 1,007.5	≃	1,000
Total				7,750

The advantage of this method is that depreciation is based on usage (in our example mileage) rather than time. Where there is variable use of the asset over time it could be argued that this method satisfies the matching concept better.

Choosing the method

The choice of method and the rate of depreciation therefore depends on the type of asset and how it benefits the organisation over its active life. It should be noted, however, that the Inland Revenue lay down maximum permitted rates of depreciation for tax purposes. Where assets provide a similar service each year of which no accurate estimate can be made, the straight-line method is preferable. If profits or costs (or both) can be shown to vary then a reducing-balance method should be chosen.

Revising estimates or methods

Market changes or unforeseen asset obsolescence may sometimes force a readjustment in the mid-life of an asset. SSAP 12 says take the present book value (historical cost less depreciation) and write off over the revised remaining life. Similarly, if the method is changed, it should be applied to the present book value. If the book value is regarded as too high it should be written down immediately but if the asset is likely to remain in use longer than at first anticipated the accountant is usually less bothered about

Revaluation of fixed assets

making adjustments; it might be written off but still in use (this is the conservative concept at its extreme!).

Of course not all assets lose their value, particularly in inflationary times. Indeed the current values may well be in excess of their net book value. Companies, if they choose to, are permitted to depart from the historic cost convention and revalue their assets (usually property). The increase over the book value is credited to a reserve account (see Chapter 9 for further details).

Summary

Profit can be significantly affected by the method or rates of depreciation but there is no effect on cash flow. Nor does depreciation automatically provide funds for replacement. Many fixed assets – assets which are kept in the business and have a long life – lose their value for a variety of reasons, e.g. time, obsolescence, use. Accountants attempt to predict this loss and must decide upon a method and rate for depreciation which should present a 'true and fair view' of the company. There are problems involved because accurate information on cost, useful life and residual value is hard to obtain and all these will affect depreciation decisions. The main methods of depreciation were outlined along with the book keeping requirements.

Assignments

4.1 (a) 'Stock should be valued at the lower of cost or net realisable value'. Explain what this statement means and comment on the significance of stock valuation to the annual accounts of a business.

(b) A retailer who specialises in three products has presented you with the following purchases and sales records for the second half of 198–. He commenced trading on the 1st July, 198–.

	Purchases			Sales	
Item	Month	Units	Unit price	Month	Units
A	July	90	2.30	Sept	45
	Oct	120	2.85	Nov	95
B	July	340	3.40	Oct	245
	Aug	265	3.75	Dec	280
C	Sept	1240	0.85	Nov	1180
	Oct	2520	1.05	Dec	2020

The net realisable value of the stock at 31st December, 198– is estimated by the retailer to be: Item A £3.20; Item B £3.65; Item C £1.25.
Ascertain the value of the closing stock at 31st December, assuming that
1. Stock is valued on the first in, first out basis
2. Stock is valued on the last in, first out basis.
Briefly comment on your results.

4.2 Engineers Ltd. provides depreciation on its plant at the rate of 10% p.a., on cost. Provision is made on new purchases from the date of acquisition, but no provision is made in the year of sale. The following items are relevant.

Balance Sheet date 30th June each year

Purchases:	30.9.–5	Lathe A	£2,400
	31.1.–6	Drilling machine B	£3,600
	1.11.–6	Press C	£6,000
	28.2.–7	Lathe D	£1,200

Sales & Disposals 7/8 Machine B was sold for cash £560. Lathe A was part-exchanged for Lathe E on 1.5–8. Cost of Lathe E was £3,000 and part-exchanged value of Lathe A was £1,600.

8/9 Press C was involved in a fire. Insurance proceeds were £800; a new press to replace was purchased 31.5.–9 for £7,200.

Write up:
(a) Plant Account
(b) Provision for Depreciation Account
(c) Disposals Account
Show balances on (a), (b) and (c) at the end of each year.

4.3 Kim and Don own the following machines on 31st December, 19–8.

Identification	A	B	C
Cost	£40,000	£60,000	£80,000
Date of purchase & first due	1st January, 19–6	30 June, 19–7	1st January, 19–8

Up to and including 31st December, 19–8, the business had depreciated its machines at the rate of 25% p.a. using the reducing-balance method. However, from 1st January, 19–9, it decided to adopt the straight-line method of depreciation in calculating future depreciation charges, on the basis that each machine has an estimated useful life of 4 years and an estimated residual or trade-in value of 10% of its cost.

On 30th June, 19–9 the organisation paid Plant Supplies PLC a cheque as follows:

New Machine D (in use from 1st July)	100,000
Replacement engine – machine B	5,000
	105,000
Trade-in allowance – machine A	15,000
Cheque	90,000

Kim is concerned that the company had to negotiate a large bank overdraft to fund the replacement of the machine and suggests that the depreciation rates must be inadequate.

Required:

(a) Prepare a schedule showing the net book value of each machine in the Balance Sheet on 31st December, 19–8

(b) Prepare the relevant ledger accounts for the year to 31st December, 19–9 (showing separately 'cost' and 'accumulated depreciation')

(c) Draft a concise note discussing the point raised by Kim and suggesting possible ways of resolving the problem

(d) Explain how the application of accounting concepts influences the charge for depreciation in the Profit and Loss Account.

4.4 Stan and Gladys Ltd. was established on 1st January, 19–3, to manufacture a single product using a machine which cost £400,000. The machine is expected to last for 4 years and then have a scrap value of £52,000. The machine will produce a similar number of goods each year and annual profits before depreciation are expected to be in the region of £200,000. The financial controller has suggested that the machine should be depreciated using either the straight-line method or the reducing-balance method. If the latter method is used, it has been estimated that an annual depreciation rate of 40% would be appropriate.

Required:

(a) Calculate the annual depreciation charges and the net book values of the fixed asset at the end of 19–3, 19–4, 19–5 and 19–6, using:
  1. the straight-line method
  2. the reducing-balance method

(b) Discuss the differing implications of these two methods for the financial information published by Stan and Gladys Ltd. for the years 19–3 – 19–6 inclusive. You should also advise management which method you consider more appropriate, bearing in mind expected profit levels.

Note: Ignore taxation.

4.5 (a) What method of depreciation would you choose for the following items? Give reasons for your answers.
1. Daisy-wheel printer
2. Sales representative's car
3. Microcomputer
4. Packing machine
5. Photocopier
6. Lease on land and buildings

In what ways would you seek advice on useful lives and residual values?

(b) What particular stock problems might be faced by a manager in a:
1. Supermarket
2. Department store
3. Fashion boutique
4. Construction company
5. Wholesaler
6. Delicatessen?

Recommend an appropriate stock valuation method in each instance.

4.6 Douglas Taylor, Managing Director of Woofta Ltd., returned from the 19–1 Earls Court Trade Exhibition with a large number of orders for his firm's new range of perfumes, but he was happier still to win the UK agency rights for the famous French fragrance house 'Giraffe', purveyors of the best-sellers, Fleur and L'essence de Giraffe. This acquisition tied in nicely with Taylor's diversification plans.

Sales of Woofta's products were mainly directed through representatives as well as 'down-market' outlets, so the marketing of the high-class Giraffe range required a different selling and distribution organisation. Hence a separate company, Giraffe (UK) Ltd. was founded to handle sales and to develop a marketing strategy through department stores, beauty salons etc. At the end of 19–1 the new company had completed only 3 months trading but to keep in line with the parent company's accounting year, Final Accounts were prepared. Stocks held on 31st December were 10,000 perfume packs valued at £4 each, the buy-in price. A summary of the working capital position on 31st December, 19–1 was:

Giraffe (UK) Ltd.

Current assets
Stock	40,000	
Debtors	20,000	
Cash	5,000	65,000

Less: Current liabilities
Creditors, tax		30,000
Net working capital		35,000

About a year later, in early November, 19–2, Taylor examined the sales and stock position of the company. It appeared that sales for the whole of 19–2 would reach 80,000 units with a selling price of £8 each. Purchases from France and the prices paid by Giraffe (UK) Ltd for each delivery in 19–2 were:

	Number of packs (000)	*Unit cost (£)*
March	30	4
June	20	5
September	40	6

The current price (early November, 19–2) was still £6 per pack. The year-end accounts will shortly have to be prepared for 19–2 and Taylor calculates that there will be 20,000 packs in stock on 31st December.

But Wellies, the Chemist, have just put in a large order for 15,000 packs for delivery in time for December Christmas shopping. The delivery dates were no problem, but Taylor was concerned that stocks might fall too much. Should he order more packs from France now, or should he wait until January, 19–3, and put in an appropriate order then? Taylor considered that the 19–2 profits and working capital position might be adversely influenced if stock was purchased now. However, before making a decision he asked Woofta's accountant, Mr Osgerby, for an estimated profit statement for 19–2, to help him make up his mind. Osgerby found it quite straight forward to complete a profit statement, but was unsure about which method of stock valuation to use. Although Woofta's had always used the average cost method, it seemed to him that the FIFO method was more realistic for Giraffe (UK) Ltd. So he produced both as shown below.

Giraffe (UK) Ltd.
Provisional profit statement 19–2

	FIFO		Average cost
	£000	£000	£000
Sales (80,000 units at £8 each)		640	640
Opening stock (10,000 units at £4 each)	40		40
Purchases 30,000 units @ £4 = £120,000			
20,000 units @ £5 = £100,000	460		460
40,000 units @ £6 = £240,000			
Available for sale	500		500
Less: Closing stock			
20,000 units @ £6 (FIFO)	120		100
@ £5 (Average cost)			
Cost of sales		380	400
Gross profit		260	240
Less: Operating expenses		100	100
Net profit		160	140
Tax (50%)		80	70
Profit after tax		80	70

Working capital summary 31st December, 19–2

Current assets	FIFO		Average cost	
	£000	£000	£000	
Stock	120		100	
Debtors	25		25	
Cash	10	155	10	135
Less: Current liabilities				
Creditors	30		30	
Tax position	80	110	70	100
Net working capital		45		35

Required:

(a) Which method of stock valuation should Osgerby adopt for Giraffe (UK) Ltd. Give reasons for your answer.
(b) Should Mr Taylor order 15,000 packs now (November) or in January? Show what effect this would have on profits.
(c) What effect does the choice of stock valuation method, FIFO or average cost, have on working capital?
(d) Why do you think Woofta's use the average cost method?

5 Final Accounts of Partnerships

When you have read this chapter you should:
- understand how profits or losses are shared by people in a business partnership
- be familiar with the accounts necessary to record the transactions relating to each partner
- to able to prepare Profit and Loss Accounts and Balance Sheets in good style

5.1 Introduction

You should already be familiar with the Final Accounts of one type of business organisation, namely, the sole trader. Although this type of organisation tends to predominate in the service sector of the economy, it has two main drawbacks:

1. The long-term capital of the organisation is supplied by one person and is therefore limited by that person's own financial circumstances. This in turn will limit the amount that can be borrowed from other sources.
2. The development of the organisation and its success or failure depends on the entrepreneurial skills of the owner.

One possible solution to these drawbacks is for two or more traders to combine their resources and skills and form a partnership. The Partnership Act, 1890, limits the number of partners to twenty, although with professional partnerships (e.g. firms of solicitors and accountants) this limit is set aside.

In preparing the Final Accounts of a partnership, due recognition should be given to the following:

- two or more people are interested in the performance and financial position of the organisation and will want to know how they are personally affected

- the accounting provisions of the Partnership Act, 1890 may need to be implemented

These points are developed in the following sections.

5.2 The partnership agreement

On the formation of a partnership, the business relationships between the partners is often set down in a partnership agreement. The information it contains does not follow a set pattern, but is likely to cover the following points:

Capital

This will specify the amount of capital that each of the partners has agreed to contribute, either at the start of the partnership or at some later date. A reserve of capital may therefore be called upon as and when it is required.

Division of profits/losses

This will specify how the profits or losses of the partnership will be apportioned between the partners. It should reflect the contribution made by each partner in relation to:

- capital
- specialist skills and knowledge
- involvement in day-to-day management

Salaries

Partners sometimes agree that in return for performing certain duties for the organisation, they will be allowed a salary out of the profits earned. The agreement will also specify how the salary is to be paid, e.g. by regular monthly payments or as a lump sum at the end of the financial period. Such an arrangement is normally in recognition of the fact that some partners are more involved in the running of the partnership than others.

Interest charges and allowances

In many partnerships, the capital contributed by each partner varies and other things being equal, the return on their investment should vary in the same way. In order to achieve this, the partners agree to allow interest on capital at some specified rate. By the same token, there is sometimes an agreed limit on drawings so that as much profit as possible is retained in the business. Any partner exceeding the drawings limit is penalised by being charged interest on the excess. This interest represents additional revenue for the organisation as a separate entity from the people who own it.

It is important to note that despite the usage of terms such as salaries and interest, they still represent different forms of profit sharing by the partners and are not charged as business expenses. Their proper treatment is explained later in the chapter.

In the absence of a partnership agreement, the provisions of the Partnership Act, 1890 will apply. These are now summarised:

- profits and losses will be shared equally between the partners
- there will be no salaries
- there will be no interest charged in drawings
- interest will be allowed at 5% on any investment in the partnership in excess of the agreed capital

5.3 The personal accounts of partners

Since there are two or more people interested in the performance of the organisation, a record should be kept of their personal financial standing in relation to the partnership. The most common practice is to maintain two personal accounts for each partner:

- a *capital account* providing a record of how much capital has been invested or withdrawn by the partner
- a *current account* providing a record of the profit share and drawings of the partner

There is an important link between the partners' current accounts and the Profit and Loss Account, a point which is developed in the next section.

5.4 The profit and loss account

This will comprise three main sections:

- the trading section
- the profit and loss section
- the appropriation section

Although the first two sections should already be familiar a brief outline of all three is now given, followed by a comprehensive example.

88 Accounting: A Practical Approach

The trading section The key figure to emerge from this section is the gross profit, i.e. the difference between sales proceeds and the cost of goods sold. The analysis of changes in profits and profitability will initially be focused on this part of the account.

The profit and loss section The key figure revealed by this section is net profit, i.e. the difference between gross profit (plus non-trading) revenue and the overhead expenses incurred in running the organisation. The main problem in preparing this section is the correct matching of relevant costs and revenues. Most errors of profit measurement occur in this section.

The appropriation section The main purpose of this section is to show how the profits or losses generated by the partnership are divided between the partners. The section will clearly show the breakdown between salaries, interest and profit share.

The structure of the Profit and Loss Account is now explained in more detail by considering a comprehensive example.

Comprehensive example I. Jones and I. Davies have been in partnership for a number of years, trading as Cray TV and Audio. A formal agreement was drawn up when the partnership was formed and the relevant provisions of this are as follows:

(a) Interest is to be allowed on capital at 10% p.a.
(b) Davies is entitled to a salary of £2,000 p.a. before profits are divided.
(c) Profits and losses are to be shared between the partners as follows: Jones–2/3 and Davies–1/3
(d) Interest is charged on drawings above the monthly allowance at the rate of 10% p.a.

The following *trial balance* was extracted from the books of the partnership as at 31st December, 19–1.

	Debit £	Credit £
I. Jones		
Capital A/c, 1st January, 19–1		20,000
Current A/c, 1st January, 19–1		1,860
Drawings	9,000	
I. Davies		
Capital A/c, 1st January, 19–1		16,000
Current A/c, 1st January, 19–1		940
Drawings	7,500	
Leasehold premises, at cost	45,000	
Equipment at cost	4,000	
Motor vehicles at cost	16,000	

Final Accounts of Partnerships 89

	Debit £	Credit £
Provisions for depreciation at January, 19–1		
Premises		18,000
Equipment		1,600
Motor vehicles		9,600
Stock, 1st January, 19–1, at cost	12,140	
Purchase and sales	119,440	182,160
Returns	940	760
Carriage out	140	
Discounts	470	220
Trade debtors and creditors	16,500	12,670
Bad debts	840	
Rent and rates	6,400	
Wages and salaries	18,560	
Light and heat	1,970	
General expenses	420	
Bank	4,490	
	263,810	263,810

The following information is also available:
  (a) Stock at the 31st December, 19–1 was valued at the lower of cost and net realisable value – £10,860.
  (b) Debts to the value of £320 have been outstanding for some time and are considered to be doubtful. These are in addition to bad debts actually written off.
  (c) There is £60 owing for carriage out and general expenses paid in advance amounting to £40.
  (d) There is a ten-year lease on the premises.
  (e) Depreciation is provided on fixed assets on the straight-line basis as follows:

  Equipment   10%
  Motor vehicles   20%

  (f) In addition to the cash drawings shown in the trial balance, the partners have also taken goods from stock valued at cost as follows:

  I. Jones   £450
  I. Davies   £740

  (g) Interest on drawings has been calculated as follows:

  I. Jones   £47
  I. Davies   £23

The Profit and Loss Account is now shown together with the explanatory notes.

Cray TV and Audio
Profit and Loss Account for the year ending 31st December, 19-1

	£	£	£	Explanatory notes
Sales		182,160		
Less: Sales returns		940		1
Net sales			181,220	
Stock 1st January 19-1		12,140		
Add: Purchases	119,440			
Less: Purchase returns	760			
		118,680		
		130,820		
Less: Drawings of stock		1,190		2
		129,630		
Less: Stock 31st December 19-1		10,860		
Cost of goods sold			118,770	
Gross profit			62,450	
Add: Discount received			220	3
			62,670	
Less: Provision for depreciation:				4
Leasehold premises	4,500			
Equipment	400			
Motor vehicles	3,200			
		8,100		
Carriage out	140			
Add: Owing	60			5
		200		
Discounts allowed		470		6
Bad debts		840		7
Provision for doubtful debts		320		
Rent and rates		6,400		
Wages and salaries		18,560		8
Light and heat		1,970		
General expenses	420			
Less: Prepaid	40			9
		380		
			37,240	
Net profit			25,430	
Add: Interest on drawings:				
I. Jones		47		
I. Davies		23		
			70	10
Net profit available for appropriation			25,500	
Salaries: I. Davies			2,000	
Interest on capital:				
I. Jones		2,000		
I. Davies		1,600		
			3,600	
Share of profits:				
I. Jones 2/3)		13,267		
I. Davies (1/3)		6,633		
			19,900	11
			25,500	

Explanatory notes

1 Sales returns or returns inwards will always appear in the trial balance as a debit balance. This is deducted from sales to obtain net sales. Purchases returns or returns outwards will always appear as a credit balance and this is shown as a deduction from purchases.

2 Drawings of stock by the partners is deduced at this stage since it should not be included in cost of goods sold. This figure will appear in the partners' current accounts as drawings.

3 Cash discounts are received from suppliers for the prompt settlement of their accounts. Although in effect, this is a cost saving, it is conventional to show it as an addition to gross profit.

4 Provisions for depreciation are calculated as follows:
   (a) Leasehold premises:

$$\frac{£45,000}{10 \text{ years}} = £4,500$$

   (b) Equipment: 10% of £4,000 = £400
   (c) Motor vehicles: 20% of £36,000 = £3,200

5 Although the amount owing for carriage out has not yet been paid, it is charged as an expense of this period and will subsequently appear on the Balance Sheet under current liabilities.

6 Cash discounts are granted to customers for the early settlement of their accounts.

7 Debts considered as irrecoverable are written off the sales ledger and charged to the Profit and Loss Account. In addition, some of this year's profit has been set aside as a provision for the debts which are doubtful and may prove to be bad in the next accounting period.

8 This figure does not include partners' salaries; these are shown in the appropriation section.

9 Prepaid expenses relate to the next accounting period and should therefore be charged to the Profit and Loss Account of that period. They will appear on the year-end balance sheet as a current asset.

10 Interest on drawings is charged to the individual partner but represents additional revenue to the organisation as a separate entity from the owners.

11 £19,900 is the profit balance remaining after appropriations for salaries and interest an capital.

5.5 The Balance Sheet

The purpose of the Balance Sheet for all business organisations is the same; to give a financial statement of the organisation from two viewpoints:

- The resources the organisation has at its disposal, subdivided between fixed assets and working capital
- The sources of the organisation's finance, subdivided between owners' capital and long-term loans

The Balance Sheet for a partnership is therefore very similar to that for a sole trader. The main differences occur in the second of the two sections mentioned above.

Since there are two or more people with an interest in the organisation, this section should specify the financial contributions of each partner. The Balance Sheet for Cray TV and Audio is shown below, together with explanatory notes. Before drafting the Balance Sheet, however, it is advisable to determine the balance of each partner's current account at the end of the accounting period. The most convenient way of doing this is shown below:

Partners' current accounts

	I. Jones	I. Davies		I. Jones	I. Davies
Drawings **(1)**	9,450	8,240	Balances b/d	1,860	940
Interest on drawings	47	23	Salaries **(2)**		2,000
Balances c/d	7,630	2,910	Interest on capital	2,000	1,600
			Share of profit	13,267	6,633
	17,127	11,173		17,127	11,173
			Balances b/d **(3)**	7,630	2,910

Notes

1 Drawings comprises cash and stock as follows:

Drawings	I. Jones	I. Davies
Cash	9,000	7,500
Stock	450	740
Total	9,450	8,240

2 If the salary had already been paid to Davies, it would not be credited to his current account. Otherwise, it would be double counted. However, the relevant entry is still made to the appropriation section of the Profit and Loss Account.

3 The closing balances appear on the Balance Sheet.

Cray TV and Audio
Balance Sheet as at 31st December, 19-1

	Cost £	Accumulated depreciation £	Net £	Explanatory notes
				1
Fixed assets				
Leasehold premises	45,000	22,500	22,500	
Equipment	4,000	2,000	2,000	
Motor vehicles	16,000	12,800	3,200	
	65,000	37,300	27,700	
Current assets				
Stock, at cost		10,860		
Trade debtors	16,500			2
Less: Provision for doubtful debts	320	16,180		
General expenses prepaid		40		3
Bank		4,490		
		31,570		
Current liabilities				
Trade creditors	12,670			
Carriage out owing	60	12,730		4
Working capital			18,840	
Capital employed			46,540	

Financed by:

Partners	Capital accounts	Current accounts	Total
I. Jones	20,000	7,630	27,630
I. Davies	16,000	2,910	18,910
	36,000	10,540	46,540

Explanatory notes

1 This is the neatest way of presenting information about the fixed assets of the organisation. The figures for accumulated depreciation are obtained by adding to the balance at the beginning of the year, the current year's provision.

2 Trade debtors are conventionally shown net of the provision for debts which are considered doubtful.

3 Although the expenses have been paid in this accounting period, the benefit will be consumed in subsequent periods. The item is therefore carried forward as an asset to be charged as an expense later.

4 The benefit of carriage out to the value of £60 has been taken by the organisation but no entry has yet been made for this in the accounting

records. However, the expense has properly been charged to the Profit and Loss Account and is carried forward as a current liability.

Summary

Although there is much in common with the final accounts of other types of organisation, partnerships present special problems which have to be overcome if adequate accounting records are to be maintained. The main distinguishing features can be summarised as follows:

1. The business relationship between partners is frequently set down in a partnership agreement and this information will be used in the preparation of the final accounts.
2. Profit and Loss Account has an additional section, called the appropriation section, which shows how the profits or losses of the partnership are shared between the partners. This information is sometimes given in a separate Appropriation Account.
3. Separate accounts are maintained for each partner, showing their financial interest in the partnership. It is a common practice for partners to have two accounts; a Capital Account, showing their long-term interest and a Current Account, showing their profit share and drawings.

Each of these features has been considered and a comprehensive example has been used in the chapter for illustration.

Assignments

5.1 You have received the following letter from a friend you met a few weeks ago:

>   19 Rookery Lane
>   Bromley
>   Kent
>   BR2 8HE
>
>   15th November, 19-0
>
> Dear Jo,
> You may recall that we spoke some weeks ago about the possibility of Steve Smart and I forming a partnership and going into business on a part-time basis. Although I am reasonably confident that we have enough experience and knowledge of the trade to earn a satisfactory income, I am a little worried about Steve's attitude to our rights and responsibilities in connection with the partnership. He is quite happy to leave on a verbal basis the tentative agreement we have reached on such

matters as our capital contribution, drawing rights and the ratio in which profits are to be shared. I am not happy with this arrangement at all and feel that we should have something more formal, set down in writing.

I get the feeling that he is willing to change his mind if he receives the right professional advice. If you would therefore write to me and let me have your recommendations about the partnership agreement between Steve and myself, I will pass the letter on to him. This will put my mind at rest, at least. I am, of course, quite happy to pay you the normal fee for this advice and look forward to hearing from you.

Yours sincerely,
Brian Bright

Required:

A letter to Brian giving the advice requested.

5.2 Brian and Steve decided to draw-up a formal partnership agreement, the relevant provisions of which are as follows:

(a) Interest is allowed on capital at the rate of 6% p.a.
(b) Steve is entitled to a fixed salary of £1,000 out of the profits.
(c) Profits and losses are to be shared in the ratio: Steve 1/3 and Brian 2/3.

The business has been running for a year and during this time they employed a part-time bookkeeper who has maintained proper records. The following balances have been extracted from the ledger at 31st December, 19-1:

	£	£
B. Bright		
Capital at 1st January, 19-1		2,500
Drawings during the year 19-1	1,850	
S. Smart		
Capital at 1st January, 19-1		2,500
Drawings during the year 19-1	1,750	
Equipment at cost	2,800	
Stock as at 1st January, 19-1	1,250	
Purchases and sales	7,686	21,050
Returns inwards and outwards	172	248
Carriage outwards	183	
Discounts	242	68
Salaries	1,260	
Sundry debtors and creditors	1,374	1,230
Bad debts	100	
Rent and rates	600	
Wages	3,827	
Light and heat	400	
General expenses	512	
Postage and stationery	300	
Bank	1,490	
Motor van	1,800	
	27,596	27,596

After investigating further, you discover the following information:
 (a) The van was estimated to be worth £1,200 at 31st December, 19–1.
 (b) A provision of £140 for doubtful debts is to be created.
 (c) The stock, as taken, was £1,540 on 31st December, 19–1.
 (d) Carriage outwards owing £60; general expenses in advance £40.
 (e) Equipment is to be depreciated at the rate of 20% p.a. on cost.

Required:

The Final Accounts of the partnership for the first year of trading (show the current accounts separately).

5.3 Mustoe, Rafferty and Morgan have been in partnership for some years, sharing profits and losses in the ratio of 50:25:25, respectively. They have a partnership agreement which provides for interest on capital and drawings at the rate of 10% p.a. It also states that Morgan is entitled to a fixed salary of £3,000 out of profits before the other matters are dealt with. Part of this salary is in respect of the maintenance of the financial records which Morgan learned about many years ago as a chartered secretary. The following trial balance has been extracted from the ledgers of the partnership as they stood at 30th September, 19–2.

	Debit £	Credit £
Motor vehicles, at cost	9,400	
Equipment, at cost	5,200	
Fixtures & fittings, at cost	18,100	
Stock, at 1st October, 19–1	7,280	
Purchases & sales	37,654	95,246
Debtors & creditors	1,540	4,821
Discounts	43	247
Returns	641	423
Motor expenses	2,436	
Wages & salaries (staff)	18,400	
Printing & stationery	240	
Rent & rates	8,430	
Light & heat	1,584	
General expenses	241	
Provisions for depreciation at 1st October, 19–1:		
Motor vehicles		4,700
Equipment		1,500
Fixtures & fittings		3,600
Bank		2,364
Capital:		
Mustoe £10,000		
Rafferty £5,000		
Morgan £5,000		20,000
Current accounts:		
Mustoe £1,564(cr)		
Rafferty £562(cr)		
Morgan £2,418(dr)	292	
Drawings:		
Mustoe £6,574		
Rafferty £7,658		
Morgan £7,188	21,420	
	132,901	132,901

As an independent accountant, assume that you have agreed to prepare the Final Accounts of the partnership and that you are going to take into account the following information:

1. Stock-taking has shown that on 30th September, 19–2, stock was valued on the usual basis at £8,245.
2. Rates in advance amount to £420.
3. An estimated amount for gas and electricity outstanding is £147.
4. Fixed assets are depreciated on the straight-line basis at the following rates: motor vehicles, 20% on cost; equipment, 10% on cost; fixtures & fittings, 5% on cost.

Required:
A draft of the Final Accounts for the year. Be prepared to answer any queries the partners might have about the way you have dealt with certain items.

5.4 Valerie and Tom started an antiques shop some years ago as a part-time venture. Over the years, the size of the business has grown and in order to commit all their time and effort to this business, they have both given up full-time jobs. Up to now, the business has operated as a partnership but they are beginning to wonder if they should form a limited company instead.

In order to help them make up their minds, they have asked you to look into the matter for them and give them some advice. In the first instance, they want you to prepare a written report with the idea of meeting at a subsequent date to discuss the findings.

5.5 Taylor, Clark and Hawkins have been in partnership for several years, sharing profits and losses equally. The three partners have been a little concerned by a fall in trade in the last few months and they have now received a letter from the bank requesting an urgent meeting to discuss their account. In preparation for this meeting, they have asked you to draft a set of accounts for the first eight months of the current financial year. The following trial balance has been extracted from the accounts of the partnership as at 31st August, 19–1:

	£	£
Capital accounts:		
Taylor		24,000
Clark		18,000
Hawkins		18,000
Current accounts:		
Taylor		1,464
Clark		242
Hawkins		782
Drawings:		
Taylor	8,500	
Clark	6,400	
Hawkins	6,800	
Premises, at cost	28,000	
Equipment, at cost	10,400	

	£	£
Fixtures & fittings, at cost	5,200	
Motor vehicles, at cost	15,400	
Purchases and sales	82,634	112,248
Wages and salaries	24,342	
Rates	1,200	
Light and heat	824	
Carriage inwards	623	
Discounts	340	280
Stock, at cost, 1st January, 19–1	8,946	
Provisions for depreciation, 1st January 19–1:		
Equipment		3,000
Fixtures & fittings		1,000
Motor vehicles		6,540
Debtors and creditors	3,642	9,546
Bank overdraft		8,695
Miscellaneous expenses	546	
	203,797	203,797

The following information is also available:

1. Stock at 31st August, 19–1 is valued at £7,864.
2. Fixed assets are depreciated on the straight-line basis at the following annual rates: equipment, 10% of £10,000; fixtures and fittings 5% of £5,000; motor vehicles, 20% of £14,600.
3. Light and heat owing has been estimated at £149.
4. Rates in advance, £100.
5. The partnership agreement provides for the profit and losses to be shared equally.

Required:

(a) A set of Final Accounts for the partnership.

(b) An analysis, for the benefit of the partners, of the financial state of the partnership as revealed by the accounts.

5.6 Hills and Knott began trading in partnership on 1st January, 19–1. At the end of the first year of trading, Hills, who has followed a short course in business book keeping, decided to prepare the Profit and Loss Account for the year as follows:

Profit and Loss Account as at 31st December, 19–1

	£		£
Sales	84,946	Purchases	61,428
Add: Loan from Smith	5,000	Net profit	28,518
	89,946		89,946
Overhead expenses	16,428	Net profit	28,518
Fixtures and fittings	7,540		
Motor vehicles	10,218		
Drawings	18,724		
		Gross loss	24,392
	52,910		52,910

	£		£
Share of loss:			
Hills	14,635		
Knott	9,757		
		Gross loss	24,392

Hills is a little worried since the Profit and Loss Account reveals a loss for the year when the business seemed to be doing very well throughout the year. You have been supplied with the following information:

1. The loan from Smith is at a rate of interest of 10%. This has not been paid or included in overhead expenses.
2. Stock, at 31st December, 19–1 is valued at £9,463.
3. The overhead expense figure does not take account of pre-payments of £462 and accruals of £156.
4. Fixtures and fittings will be used for about 10 years and then replaced. Their salvage value is estimated at £40.
   Motors, on the other hand, will be used for 5 years and then replaced. Their salvage value is estimated at £718.
5. There is no formal partnership agreement between Hills and Knott.

Required:

(a) Redraft the Profit and Loss account using normal accounting concepts and conventions.

(b) Explain the differences in the treatment given to each item by you and Hills.

6 The Final Accounts of Limited Companies

When you have read this chapter, you should:
- be familiar with the main sources of long-term company finance
- understand the significant features of the main types of share and debenture
- be able to prepare Profit and Loss Accounts and Balance Sheets in good style

6.1 Introduction

Limited companies differ from other types of business organisation in three distinct ways:

1. The liability of the owners is limited to the extent of the capital they have agreed to contribute, i.e. assets from their personal estates cannot be liquidated to settle the organisation's debts.
2. The capital of the organisation can be divided into shares of various types and values.
3. The administration of the organisation is governed by the provisions of the Companies Act, 1985.

In preparing the Final Accounts of this type of organisation, recognition must be given to these features and the structure outlined in the previous chapter must be adapted accordingly.

Although there are fundamental differences between Public and Private Limited Companies, they can be treated the same for final accounts purposes.

6.2 Sources of company capital

There are many sources of long-term capital for a limited company and this section will explain the main ones.

Share capital A company may issue share capital up to a specified limit. This is called the 'authorised share capital' and is detailed in the legal documents of the company, i.e. the Memorandum and Articles of

The Final Accounts of Limited Companies

Association. There are various types of share, each conferring different rights which may be attractive to different types of investor.

The nominal value of the shares actually issued is called the Issued Share Capital. These may be fully paid or partly paid for by investors. The amount that has been paid is referred to as the Called-up Share Capital and will be used in preparing the Balance Sheet.

Ordinary shares

Sometimes referred to as 'equities', holders of ordinary shares effectively own and control the organisation. Ordinary shareholders may vote at company meetings, the most important vote normally being in relation to the election of the Board of Directors. In theory, therefore, each shareholder may participate in the policy decisions of the company. In practice, however, the existence of institutional investors (insurance companies, pension funds, unit trusts) with block votes effectively nullifies the contribution of investors with small shareholdings.

Investors will acquire these shares for two basic reasons:

1. The expectation of receiving a share of the future earnings of the company, i.e. dividends.
2. The expectation of making a capital gain on the sale of the shares at some future date.

The annual dividend will be decided by the Board of Directors after considering a number of important factors. In practice, this can be an extremely complex matter, although in the first instance they must consider two fundamental factors:

(a) The level of profits the company has earned from which a dividend may be distributed.
(b) The availability of liquid funds from which the dividend can actually be paid.

Companies are under no obligation to propose an ordinary dividend if, in the view of the directors, it would be unwise to do so. The shareholders therefore take the risk of receiving no dividends at all in years when conditions are not favourable. This is, in fact, one of the key attractions of the ordinary share from the organisation's point of view. They are not committed to a fixed dividend payment when conditions do not justify it.

Preference shares

These differ from ordinary shares in two ways: −

1. The shares do not normally confer voting rights at company meetings.
2. Shareholders are entitled to a fixed rate of dividend.

Shareholders who do not welcome the risks associated with equities may prefer to invest in preference shares where their income is more secure. To avoid the restrictions imposed by the need to pay a fixed rate of dividend, companies may issue 'cumulative preference shares' instead. With this type of share, the dividend payment can be deferred to subsequent years.

A third variation of this type is the 'redeemable preference share', which gives the company more flexibility with its funding arrangements. Thus the company agrees to redeem the shares at some future date and they can therefore be used as a form of medium-term finance.

During the late 1970s when the government imposed dividend controls on shares, some companies issued bonus preference shares to their equity holders as an indirect form of dividend boosting.

Types of share issue

Shares are normally issued for cash, payable by instalments over a period of time. Applications for shares are invited from any individual or group interested. Sometimes, however, there are special types of share issue which do not follow this pattern. A 'rights issue', for example, gives existing shareholders first claim to a new issue of shares, usually at a lower price than would normally be expected from outsiders. If options are not taken up by existing shareholders, the shares are then offered to newcomers. A 'scrip issue', on the other hand, is a bonus issue of shares, free of charge, to existing shareholders. Since no cash changes hands with this type of issue, it is funded from the reserves instead.

Loan capital

Part of the longer term capital of a company may be funded by the issue of loan capital in the form of debentures. These are simply long-term loans redeemable at some future date and are often 'secured', i.e. a particular asset or group of assets is associated with the loan and in the event of a liquidation, the debenture holder has prior claim on the asset(s). Debenture holders are entitled to a fixed rate of interest each year regardless of the profits or liquidity of the company. One of the major advantages of the debenture is that the interest is allowable against profits for tax purposes.

Reserves

One of the major sources of capital for companies in the UK is 'ploughed-back profits' or 'retained earnings'. Instead of distributing all available profits to equity holders as dividends, companies reserve profits for a specific purpose or as a means of promoting the general capital growth of the company. The typical reserves a company may use are considered below.

Profit and loss balance Any undistributed profit remaining at the end of an accounting period may be transferred to a reserve or left as a balance on the Profit and Loss Account. This balance will be carried forward to the next period and a decision on its use made then.

General reserve Profits shown in this reserve are not ear-marked for a specific purpose and may be put to use in any manner the directors consider appropriate.

Fixed asset replacement reserve This reserve is used for the purpose of building-up funds which allow for the increased cost of replacing fixed assets during a period of rising prices. Thus, in addition to making the normal provision for depreciation, the organisation can set aside additional profits in this reserve.

Capital redemption reserve When a company has redeemable shares as part of its long-term capical, it should create this reserve to replace the shares at the time of redemption. In fact, companies are required by law to establish this reserve except in circumstances where a new issue of capital replaces the shares redeemed.

Reserves may also arise other than from a deliberate decision by the directors to reserve profits in the manner specified above. The two most common of these are as follows.

Revaluation reserve A company may decide to up-date the value of its fixed assets, most commonly, land and buildings, to show them at their current market value. The revaluation reserve will therefore show the increase in the value of the assets above their historic cost.

Share premium Shares may be issued at their nominal value (the face value of the share) or at a premium. If they are issued at a premium, the company will receive, for example, £1.50 for a share with a nominal value of £1. The excess payment is aggregated for all shares as the share premium.

6.3 The Profit and Loss Account

As for any form of business organisation, the Profit and Loss Account is one of the three main documents which represent the Final Accounts of a limited company. There are many similarities to the Profit and Loss Account of a partnership, and the same general concepts and conventions are applied in its preparation. At the same time, however, there are important differences that must be recognised. This is best explained by considering a specific example.

Example The following Trial Balance was extracted from the ledgers of Bromco Ltd. at 31 December, 19–2.

	Debit £	Credit £
Gross profit		94,650
Sundry expenses (e.g. rent, rates, salaries etc.)	27,460	
Directors' fees and salaries	19,470	
Auditors' fees	1,800	
Share Capital:		
Authorised issued		
300,000 200,000 £1 ordinary shares		200,000
50,000 40,000 £1, 8% preference shares		40,000
Preliminary expenses	4,600	
Freehold property, at cost	205,000	
Equipment, at cost	46,000	
Motor vehicles, at cost	25,000	
Trade debtors and creditors	28,650	15,000
Interim ordinary dividend paid	10,000	
Interim preference dividend paid	1,600	
10% debenture (19–6)		20,000
Provisions for depreciation as at 1st January, 19–2:		
Equipment		13,800
Motor vehicles		5,000
Stock (31st December, 19—2) at cost	46,170	
General reserve		12,650
Bank	6,800	
Debentures interest paid	1,000	
Retained earnings (1st January, 19–2)		22,450
	423,550	423,550

Example At a recent meeting of the Board of Directors, the following matters were agreed and should be taken into account when preparing the Profit and Loss Account and Balance Sheet.

(a) To write off the preliminary expenses.
(b) To make the following provisions:
   The final preference dividend.
   The debenture interest unpaid.
   The final ordinary dividend of 9%.
   Depreciation for the current year as follows:
      Equipment: 10% straight-line method.
      Motor vehicles: 20% straight-line method.
(c) To transfer £5,000 to the general reserve.
(d) Having taken the advice of a firm of chartered surveyors, to revalue the freehold premises to a current market value of £250,000.

The Final Accounts of Limited Companies 105

The Profit and Loss Account for Bromco Ltd. is now shown, followed by explanatory notes.

Bromco Ltd
Profit and Loss Account for the year ended
31 December, 19–2

	£	£	Explanatory notes
Gross profit		94,650	1
Sundry expenses	27,460		
Directors' fees	19,470		2
Auditors' fees	1,800		3
Debenture interest	2,000		4
Depreciation:			
Equipment	4,600		
Motor vehicles	5,000		
Preliminary expenses	4,600		
		64,930	
Net profit		29,720	5
Appropriations:			
Transfer to general reserve	5,000		7
Preference dividends	3,200		8
Ordinary dividends	28,000		9
		36,200	
		(6,480)	
Retained earnings at 1 January, 19–2		22,450	6
Retained earnings at 31 December, 19–2		15,970	10

Explanatory notes

1 The first figure given in the trial balance is gross profit. Therefore, the trading section has already been drafted. Its structure however, is exactly the same as illustrated for partnership in Chapter 5.

2 The fees and salaries of directors are treated as normal overhead expenses. This is different from partnerships where partners' salaries are treated as a form of profit sharing and shown in the appropriation section.

3 A legal requirement of the Companies Acts is that limited companies must have their accounts audited annually by an independent auditor. This is not a requirement for partnerships although it is obviously advisable.

4 Debenture interest is an expense and not an appropriation of profits. Since they are 10% debentures, the interest for a full year is £2,000 (i.e. 10% of £20,000). Only £1,000 has been paid so far so £1,000 is accrued and will be shown later under current liabilities on the Balance Sheet.

5 Having determined the net profit for the year, the remainder of the

Profit and Loss Account is the appropriation section. This specifies how the directors have decided to use the profits available.

6 Profits accumulated from earlier years are available for appropriation in the current year.

7 The directors have decided to build-up the capital base of the company by transferring £5,000 to the general reserve, rather than allow it to be distributed as dividends to the shareholders.

8 The preference shares have a fixed dividend of 8%. £1,600 has been paid as an interim dividend and the final dividend of £1,600 is accrued.

9 £10,000 has already been paid as an interim dividend. The final dividend proposed is 9%, i.e. 9% of £200,000 which is £18,000. This amount is accrued.

10 The directors have not made any decision regarding the remaining balance and this is taken forward to next year as retained earnings.

6.4 The Balance Sheet

Following the Profit and Loss Account, the Balance Sheet is prepared showing the financial position of the company at the end of the year. This will reflect the outcome of its trading activities throughout the year and the decisions taken by the directors in relation to the profit appropriations. The Balance Sheet is shown first followed by the explanatory notes.

Bromco Ltd
Balance Sheet as at 31 December, 19–2

	Cost or valuation £	Accumulated depreciation £	Net £	Explanatory notes
Fixed assets				
Premises	250,000		250,000	1
Equipment	46,000	18,400	27,600	2
Motor vehicles	25,000	10,000	15,000	
	321,000	28,400	292,600	
Current assets				
Stocks		46,170		
Trade debtors		28,650		
Bank		6,800		
		81,620		
Less				
Creditors: amounts falling due within one year				
Trade creditors	15,000			
Debenture interest	1,000			3
Dividends proposed	19,600			4
		35,600		
Net current assets			46,020	5

	£	£	£	
Total assets *less* current liabilities			338,620	
Less Creditors: amounts falling due after one year				
10% debentures (19–6)			20,000	9
			318,620	

Financed by
Capital and reserves
 Called-up share capital

	£	£	£	
200,000 £1 ordinary shares, fully paid	200,000			
40,000 £1 8% preference shares fully paid	40,000			
			240,000	
Reserves				
General		17,650		6
Retained earnings		15,970		7
Revaluation		45,000		8
			78,620	
			318,620	

Explanatory notes

1 Premises have been increased in value by £45,000. This represents an unrealised capital gain (i.e. a paper profit), and this is shown under reserves later in the Balance Sheet.
2 Accumulated depreciation is obtained by adding the provision from previous years to the provision for the current year, i.e. £13,600 plus £4,600.
3 This is the debenture interest accrued from the Profit and Loss Account and will remain a liability until it is paid.
4 Since the company is treated as a separate entity from the people who own it, the dividends proposed are shown as a current liability of the company until they are paid.
5 Working capital represents the liquid assets the company has at its disposal on which no claims are owing to creditors.
6 The general reserve was £12,650 and £5,000 has been added to it this year, making £17,650.
7 The retained earnings figure is taken straight from the Profit and Loss Account and represents the balance of profits remaining after all appropriations have been made.
8 The shareholders' interest is made up of issued share capital and reserves.
9 It is conventional to show both the interest rate and the redemption date associated with the debentures.

6.5 Published accounts

The Final Accounts shown above for Bromco Ltd. contain as much detailed information as permissible from the data extracted from the ledgers. If the accounts were being prepared for publication, i.e. made available to the general public, they would probably disclose only the minimum information required by law. The regulations governing published accounts are set-down in the Companies Acts. Since the information is available for public consumption, most companies like to protect as much information as possible from the gaze of say, competitors, who might gain some kind of advantage from the information supplied. Although the trend is towards greater public accountability and hence more detailed disclosure of trading information, serious consideration is still given to the likely impact of making 'inside information' public property.

Although a detailed understanding of the legislation governing published accounts is not a course requirement, it is worth obtaining the recent annual reports of a few public companies so that you may compare and contrast them with the examples given in this chapter. You will be surprised by the fact that some items do not have to be disclosed at all, whilst others have to be shown in considerably more detail than is possible from the information given about Bromco Ltd.

Summary

This chapter has shown how a set of Final Accounts may be prepared for a limited company from the source information contained in the ledgers. These accounts will reflect both the trading activities of the company for the period under review and the decisions made by the directors regarding the use or appropriation of profits. The basic concepts and conventions applied here are the same for any type of trading organisation.

In addition to the Profit and Loss Account and the Balance Sheet, SSAP 10 recommends that a third statement, the Funds Flow Statement, should also form an integral part of the Final Accounts of organisations with a gross income in excess of £25,000. The preparation of this statement is considered in Chapter 7.

Assignments

6.1 Cream Cakes Ltd
Two friends, Fred Bloggs and Joe Soap, decide that they want to go into business for themselves. Fred has had 20 years experience as a Master Baker whilst Joe is the proud recipient of the BTEC Higher in Business

Studies and, therefore, extremely knowledgeable in business matters. They determine to enter the baking trade and to sell high-class confections.

Seeking a discerning and affluent clientele they purchase three shops in the Hammersmith area, a pleasant suburb on the outskirts of London. Fred sells his house and his car which, together with his savings, means he can contribute £34,000 to the venture whilst Joe chips in with £26,000 he has managed to borrow from his family. They feel this will be sufficient and decide to call the new company Cream Cakes Ltd., with an authorised capital of 100,000 ordinary shares of £1 each.

They open a bank account and deposit their funds. Shortly afterwards they complete the purchase of their three shops for £80,000, half of which is paid for by raising a mortgage bond with an insurance company.

The three shops turn out to be something of an exception for the area in that they are rather tatty, and our intrepid traders decide that they must be renovated to promote their desired high-class image. After receiving many quotations they finally agree a contract whereby all three shops will be completed by 31 December, 19-7 for £10,000.

On the 1st January, 19-8 trading commences and Fred and Joe wait with some trepidation for the first week's figures. They have purchased some £2,000 worth of stock on credit and are delighted with figures of £2,600 in the first week. All unsold stock is deemed to be stale and unsaleable and is, therefore, donated to the canteen of the local college. Fred and Joe have employed three assistants for their shops and pay them at the end of the week. These wages, with other cash outlays, total £200.

During the rest of the year to 31st December, 19-8 the following transactions take place in total:

Stock purchases £110,000 (£107,000 paid by year end)
Cash sales £141,000 (all stocks cleared)
Wages and salaries £12,000
5% interest paid on mortgage (assume 20 year mortgage, interest paid on opening balance)
Credit purchase, delivery van, £3,000
Overheads £2,000
Provision for depreciation on equipment £2,000

Required:

Prepare the year-end accounts for this company. State all assumptions made.

6.2 The following is an extract from the most recent balance sheet of Superbyte Ltd, a company which specialises in the retailing of microcomputer equipment. There has been a dramatic increase in turnover in the last six months and the company want to capitalise on this.

Balance Sheet as at 31st December, 19-1

	£	£
Fixed assets		
Net book value		64,200
Current assets		
Stocks, at cost	27,600	
Debtors	8,600	
Bank	2,300	
	38,500	

Balance Sheet as at 31st December, 19-1 (continued)

	£	£
Current liabilities		
Creditors	16,700	
Working capital		21,800
Capital employed		86,000
Financed by:		
Ordinary share capital		60,000
Undistributed profits		26,000
		86,000

The Company are currently considering plans for expansion which will involve raising further capital to finance additional premises and working capital. The amount involved has been estimated at £40,000 and they have come to you for advice regarding what form the financing, if available, should take. They are considering the issue of shares or debentures but are not clear about the implications.

Required:

In the form of a brief report, outline the options open to Superbyte, the factors they must take into account when making a decision of this kind, and the likely benefits and drawbacks of the options.

6.3 After the accountants of Unsure PLC had prepared the draft Profit and Loss Account for the year ended 30th June, 19-1, the following balances remained on the books.

	£000	£000
£1 ordinary shares		2,000
£1, 9% preference shares		500
10% debentures		400
Net profit for 19-1		300
Undistributed profit		1,200
General reserve		800
Premises, at cost	1,500	
Equipment, at cost	150	
Motor vehicles, at cost	60	
Provisions for depreciation:		
Equipment		60
Motor Vehicles		12
Stocks, at cost	2,410	
Debtors and prepayments	840	
Bank	962	
Creditors and accruals		650
	5,922	5,922

The draft accounts were presented to the Board of Directors for their consideration and the following proposals were made by them:

1. To pay an ordinary dividend of 15%.
2. To pay the preference dividend for the year.
3. To capitalise part of the reserves by means of a scrip issue of one bonus ordinary share for every two currently held. Undistributed profits are to be used for this purpose.

Required:

(a) Prepare the appropriation account for the year and a Balance Sheet at 30th June, 19–1, taking into account the above matters.

(b) What factors would the directors have taken into account when deciding on the dividend for the year?

(c) Why did the directors make no proposal regarding the debenture interest?

(d) How are existing shareholders affected by the scrip issue?

6.4 (a) From the following information prepare a Profit and Loss Account for the year 19–2 and a Balance Sheet as at 31st December, 19–2.

Tayhawk PLC
Trial balance as at 31st December, 19–2

Authorised	Issued		£	£
200,000	140,000 ordinary shares @ £1 each fully paid			140,000
70,000	20,000 9% preference shares @ £1 each fully paid			20,000
	Gross profit			89,600
	Sundry Profit and Loss expenses		17,000	
	Rates paid for 5 quarters to 31st March, 19–3		2,000	
	Provision for depreciation			34,000
	Bad debts		3,000	
	Sundry fixed assets (plant)		212,000	
	Ordinary dividends		5,600	
	Preference dividend		900	
	12% debentures			15,000
	Investments in X Ltd 10,000 £1 shares at cost price		12,000	
	Bank		3,050	
	Sundry current assets		37,300	
	Debenture interest		900	
	Sundry current liabilities			10,000
	General reserve			3,500
	Undistributed profits			6,000
	Provision for doubtful debts			2,000
	Auditor's fees		650	
	Director's salaries		35,500	
	Sale of investments			9,800
			329,900	329,900

The directors have recommended that the following adjustments are made when the final accounts are prepared:

1. Provide for a proposed final dividend of 6% on the ordinary shares for the year.
2. Transfer £1,000 to the General Reserve.
3. Provide for the current year's depreciation on plant (equipment, buildings etc.) at $7\frac{1}{2}$% on the reducing balance method.
4. £9,800 represents the proceeds from the sale of 6,000 shares in X Ltd. No other entries have yet been made in the accounts for this transaction.
5. The provision for doubtful debts should be £1,600.

(b) At a subsequent meeting of the company, the accountant was asked the following questions by a confused shareholder:

- Why is it necessary to have a provision for doubtful debts? If the debtors fail to pay up next year, we can deduct the loss from next year's takings.
- What is the difference between the general reserve and undistributed profits? Both represent cash which could be paid in dividends if we wanted it so why show them separately?
- If accounts should be drawn up on a consistent basis, what is the point of providing for depreciation using the reducing-balance basis? This means that depreciation goes down each year.

Required:
Briefly reply to the points made by the shareholder.

6.5 Prepare the Profit and Loss Account for the year to 31st March, 19–1, and a Balance Sheet as at that date from the information relating to Wye Ltd. The Authorised Capital is £200,000.

Trial Balance 31st March, 19–1

	£	£
Issued share capital 115,000 £1 ordinary shares, fully paid		115,000
Share premium		1,500
Plant at cost	12,960	
Office equipment at cost	11,580	
Vehicles at cost	14,400	
Accumulated depreciation:		
Plant		1,290
Office equipment		1,150
Vehicles		7,860
Stock, at cost	15,900	
Purchases and sales	105,660	208,200
Salaries	18,000	
Vehicle expenses	2,060	
Rates and insurance	970	
Light and heat	660	
Advertising	1,670	
10% debentures		10,000

	£	£
Debenture interest	500	
Directors' salaries	15,000	
Provision for doubtful debts		700
Debtors and creditors	14,650	6,800
General reserve		14,500
Profit and Loss Account Balance		8,700
Interim dividend paid	2,300	
Bank	9,320	
Freehold land and buildings	110,000	
Wages	40,070	
	375,700	375,00

Further information:

1. Transfer £2,000 to the general reserve.
2. Provide for depreciation at the following annual rates on cost:
   (a) plant, 10%; (b) office equipment, 10%; (c) vehicles, 20%.
3. Stock 31st March, 19–1 is £17,200
4. The provision for doubtful debts is to be maintained at 5% of debtors.
5. Provide for the following expenses, accrued but not paid at 31st March, 19–1:
   (a) wages £670; (b) light and heat, £30.
6. Provide for a final dividend of 5%.

6.6 The Balance Sheet of Sharp Ltd., at 31st March, 19–1, is given below:

	£		£	£
		Fixed assets		
Ordinary share Capital (£1) shares	150,000	At cost		95,000
		Less aggregate depreciation		34,600
				60,400
Undistributed profits	27,500			
Creditors	16,900	*Current assets*		
		Stocks, at cost	74,000	
		Debtors	32,400	
		Bank	27,600	
				134,000
	194,400			194,400

Unfortunately, since the Balance Sheet was prepared, the following discoveries have been made:

1. Stocks included items valued at cost as £2,600 which are reckoned to have a net realisable value of only £800. In addition, items were

included in the stock valuation of the company that had been sent by suppliers on a sale or return basis. These were valued at £3,600.
2. Equipment costing £10,000, purchased for use by the company, was listed in the purchases day book and treated as stock in trade. It is company policy to provide for depreciation on all equipment at a rate of 10% p.a.
3. The debtors balance includes debts owing from customers who have been discovered to be bankrupt. There is little prospect of recovering the £4,500 owing.
4. During the year, the company made a scrip issue of one ordinary share for every ten currently held. No entries have yet been made in the books for this.
5. New staff were recruited during the year and the bill for the advertising has only just been received, amounting to £1,200. This had been overlooked when the accounts were prepared and no entry has been made in the accounts.

Required:

(a) Prepare a statement showing the corrections to the undistributed profits balance necessitated by these discoveries.

(b) Prepare the corrected Balance Sheet at 31st March, 19–1.

7 Funds Flow Statements

When you have read this chapter you should:
- understand the importance of the concept known as funds flow
- understand how a flow of funds can be measured
- be able to prepare Funds Flow Statements in good style

7.1 Introduction

From working through the earlier chapters of this book, you should already know that working capital is defined as the excess of current assets over current liabilities. One of the advantages of the vertical Balance Sheet is that the amount of working capital is shown as one of the major items. It represents the liquid assets supplied by people with a long-term interest in the organisation and will be continually changing in form in the process of earning profits. Maintaining an appropriate level of working capital is a matter of judgement, with the organisation having to strike a balance between two extremes.

Relatively high levels of working capital

The risk here is that assets are wasted and not put to their most efficient use. At the same time, valuable short-term finance may be going to waste. The efficient use of assets is one of the major determinants of profitable trading and, in brief, means that the organisation should pursue a policy which includes the following:

(a) Not overstocking so that items remain on the shelf for a long time before they are utilised or sold. Care must also be exercised over the choice of stock lines so that funds are not tied up in unsaleable stock.

(b) Ensuring that customers settle their accounts within a reasonable time by the wise use of reminders and cash discounts for early settlement.

(c) Carrying the minimum cash balance necessary to satisfy their day-to-day requirements. Cash in a current account earns no profit for the organisation and is therefore an idle asset which should be minimised.

(d) Making prudent use of credit facilities offered by suppliers. This source of finance should be used to the extent that the level of trading will enable repayments to be made at the specified times.

Relatively low levels of working capital

The risk here is that current assets are predominantly financed by short-term credit and any difficulties in making repayments when they fall due could jeopardise the financial viability of the organisation. Over-reliance on short-term credit could also mean that:

(a) The level and variety of stock is less than it should be, with trading opportunities lost as a result.
(b) Credit facilities cannot be used as an added attraction to customers.
(c) There could be difficulty in repaying suppliers, resulting in a lowered credit rating.

There are, however, no hard and fast rules as far as working capital is concerned. The level of working capital will depend on a number of factors; the type of organisation, its recent history, the skill and attitude and management, and its future trading prospects are just a few of them. Many companies can and do operate very successfully and profitably with very low levels of working capital, as can be witnessed from the recent published accounts of the major high-street retailers. Many appear to have utilised the major sources of short-term finance fully and remain financially sound.

7.2 Measuring working capital

Working capital should be viewed as a continuous circular flow of funds into and out of the organisation so that, at the completion of a cycle, a profit is earned which can either be reinvested to increase the size of the flow or reimbursed to the owners as their reward for supplying the long-term funds of the organisation.

Monitoring the size, composition and change in this flow over a period of time is extremely important to the assessment of both the past performance and future prospects of the organisation. Flow of funds statements, therefore, have a crucial role to play and there are two different types which are designed to highlight different aspects of the changes which have taken place:

1. The Sources and Applications of Funds Statement.
2. The Cash Flow Statement.

7.3 The sources and applications of funds statement

This statement deals with the changes in working capital as a whole and will show how its size and composition has changed or will change over a financial period. The Accountancy Profession recognises the importance of this statement by recommending its inclusion in the Final Accounts of all but the smallest companies. This recommendation comes in SSAP 10, which sets down broad guidelines for its preparation.

As a general rule, this statement contains three main sectors:

Section 1
Sources of funds

Under this heading is given a list of the sources of funds which have flowed into the organisation over the stated time period. The list may include:

Funds from operations Basically, this is net profit before tax with any non-cash expenses added back. The main non-cash expense is normally depreciation. Although depreciation is an expense of the period and as such should be charged against income, no funds have flowed out of the organisation which stem from this charge. The outward flow occurs when the fixed assets are acquired and this is dealt with separately in the statement.

The issue of capital for cash This covers the issue of shares and debentures by companies and the injection of capital by sole traders and partners. Bonus issues of shares do not count because funds do not flow into the organisation as a result. A transfer from one account to another of this kind does not constitute a flow of funds.

The sales of fixed assets The actual amount of cash received or receivable is shown and not the book value or cost of the assets involved.

Section 2
Applications of funds

Under this heading is given a list of the funds that have flowed out of the organisation over the period. These are simply the reverse of the sources given above:

1. A negative amount for funds from the operations, which could occur if the organisation has made a net loss.
2. The redemption of capital for cash.
3. The purchase of fixed assets.

In addition, two other items are likely to occur:

4. Tax paid.

5. Dividends paid (this means drawings for sole traders and partnerships).

Note carefully that it is the amounts paid during the period and not the amounts provided for at the end of period that are shown and counted. The year-end provisions will not actually involve funds flowing out of the organisation until the next accounting period and will therefore be shown then.

Section 3
The reconciliation section

The difference between the totals for Sections 1 and 2 shows whether working capital has increased or decreased. The purpose of this third section is to verify this difference and to specify the change in each item which comprises working capital.

Example The following are the summarised Balance Sheets of BIS Ltd. at 31st December, 19–0 and 19–1:

	19–0 £	19–0 £	19–1 £	19–1 £
Fixed assets				
Freehold property, at cost		24,000		45,000
Plant and machinery, at cost	12,000		14,500	
Accumulated depreciation	4,800		5,450	
		7,200		9,050
		31,200		47,050
Current assets				
Stocks, at cost		9,680		10,700
Trade debtors		4,260		5,100
Bank		2,870		
		48,010		69,850
Issued capital				
Ordinary shares (£1)		25,000		40,000
Reserves				
Share premium				3,000
Profit and loss		2,890		8,490
Loan stock (12%)	6,000		2,000	
		33,890		53,490
Capital employed				
Current liabilities				
Bank overdraft				1,460
Trade creditors		4,650		5,140
Corporation tax		4,470		5,760
Dividends proposed		5,000		4,000
		48,010		69,850

The following information is also available about the year ended 31st December, 19–1:

1. The ordinary shares were issued for cash.
2. A machine costing £2,000 which had been held for 4 years at 31st December, 19–0, was sold for £800 on the 1st March, 19–1.
3. The company provides for depreciation at the rate of 10% p.a. on cost, for assets held at the end of the accounting period.

Solution

Sources and Applications of Funds Statement for the year ended 31st December, 19–1

	£	£	Explanatory notes
Sources of funds			
Net profit before tax	15,360		1
Items not involving a movement of funds			
Depreciation	1,450		2
Loss on disposal of machinery	400		3
Funds from operations		17,210	
Sales of machinery		800	4
Issue of shares at a premium		18,000	5
		36,010	
Applications of funds			
Purchase of freehold property	21,000		
Purchase of plant and machinery	4,500		6
Redemption of loan stock	4,000		7
Corporation tax paid	4,470		8
Dividends paid	5,000		
		38,970	
Change in working capital		(2,960)	9
Increases/(decreases) in working capital			10
Increase in stock		1,020	
Increase in debtors		840	
Decrease in bank		(4,330)	
Increase in trade creditors		(490)	
		(2,960)	

The statement clearly shows how the working capital of BIS Ltd. has changed over this period and the items which have been affected. An analysis of the effects of these changes can proceed on a much sounder footing, with this statement providing some of the important information that would be used as a basis.

Explanatory notes

1 Net profit before tax is calculated as follows:

	£
Change in profit and loss balance as per balance sheets (£8,490−£2,890)	5,600
Corporation tax liability for 19−1	5,760
Dividends proposed for 19−1	4,000
Net profit before tax	15,360

2 The depreciation policy of the company is to provide for 10% on the cost of assets held at the year end, i.e. 10% of £14,500 = £1,450. This has been charged as an expense to the Profit and Loss Account in arriving at the net profit figure of £15,360. However, no funds have actually flowed from the business as a result of this expense.

3 The machine sold has been held for 4 years. The loss arising from the sale is calculated as follows:

	£	£
Cost of machine		2,000
Provision for depreciation (4 years × £200 p.a.)	800	
Cash received	800	
		1,600
Loss		400

Again, this would be quite properly shown in the Profit and Loss Account but has not involved a flow of funds in 19−1. The £400 can also be viewed as an under provision for depreciation for which an adjustment has to be made when the machine is sold.

4 The amount received when the machine was sold, not its book value nor its cost.

5 The nominal value of share capital has increased by £15,000 but there is also a share premium of £3,000

6 Plant and machinery:

	£
Balance at 1st January, 19−1	12,000
Less: Sale of machine	2,000
	10,000
Add: Purchase of machine	4,500
Balance at 31st December, 19−1	14,500

7 Loan stock has decreased from £6,000 to £2,000.

8 The tax and dividends paid during 19−1 are the amounts provided in 19−0 and are shown on that year's Balance Sheet under current liabilities.

9 Working capital has decreased by £2,960 overall as a result of the transactions of 19−1.

10 This part of the statement verifies the reduction in working capital of £2,960 by stating the effect of the change in each item comprising working capital. It is useful to remember two simple rules here:

- Increases in current assets increase working capital while decreases will decrease working capital.
- Increases in current liabilities decrease working capital while decreases will increase working capital.

7.4 The Cash Flow Statement

This statement deals specifically with the change in the cash/bank balance over a period of time. A commonly held misconception is that profit is synonymous with cash and that a period of profitable trading cannot result in a falling bank balance. One way that this apparent anomaly can be resolved is by means of a cash flow statement.

The statement contains two main sections:

Section 1
Sources of cash

This section lists the main sources of cash for the organisation which will include all the items previously shown as sources of funds. In addition, there are other sources of cash which stem from changes in items of working capital:

1. A reduction in stock represents a source of cash since a cash outlay is saved by not replacing stock which is sold.
2. A reduction in trade debtors provides cash either as a result of a tightening in credit control or reducing credit sales in favour of cash sales.
3. An increase in trade creditors saves a cash outlay on stock replacement and therefore can be seen as another source of cash.

Section 2
Applications of cash

In addition to the items previously listed as applications of funds, other applications of cash are the reverse of items 1 to 3 in Section 1:

1. An increase in stock.
2. An increase in trade debtors.
3. A reduction in trade creditors.

Example The Sources and Applications of Funds Statement of BIS Ltd. for 19–1 showed that the bank balance had decreased by £4,330. This reduction is analysed by the following Cash Flow Statement:

Solution

Cash Flow Statement for the year ended 31st December, 19–1

	£	£
Sources of cash		
Funds from operations		17,210
Sales of machinery		800
Issue of shares at a premium		18,000
Increase in trade creditors		490
		36,500
Applications of cash		
Purchase of freehold property	21,000	
Purchase of plant and machinery	4,500	
Redemption of loan stock	4,000	
Corporation tax paid	4,470	
Dividends paid	5,000	
Increase in stock	1,020	
Increase in trade debtors	840	
		40,830
Reduction in bank		4,330

Summary

In order for business organisations to succeed, they must not only make profits but also ensure an adequate flow of working capital and cash. It is quite possible, for example, for an organisation to show an apparently healthy profit while at the same time plunging into an unhealthy deficit of cash. By the same token, it is possible to make a loss and yet maintain a positive cash balance. How these apparent contradictions can occur is clearly explained by means of Funds Flow statements, which rank with Profit and Loss Accounts and Balance Sheets as essential for monitoring the progress of organisations.

The two main types of Funds Flow statement considered have been:

1. The Sources and applications of Funds statement. This looks at changes in working capital as a whole over a period of time and is contained in the Published Accounts of limited companies.
2. The Cash Flow Statement. This looks at the changes in the cash balance over a period of time.

These can be used to review the past and to aid financial planning.

Assignments

7.1 Tom Fogg is a little concerned about the way his business has been going and comes to you for advice. On meeting with him, you ask him to explain carefully why he is worried and his reply is:

'The accountant has prepared the annual accounts for the business but unfortunately, I've mislaid the Profit and Loss Account. He seems to think that the business is doing quite well but I cannot understand how the business shows a profit of £18,900 for 19–2 but my bank balance has fallen by £2,800. Perhaps you could look into it for me and let me have your advice at some time'.

From the following information, prepare a suitable statement showing the change in the cash position of the business during 19–2. Enclose the statement with a letter to Tom, making any comments that clarify the position.

Balance Sheets as at 31st December

	19–1 £	19–1 £	19–2 £	19–2 £
Fixed assets*				
At cost		36,000		35,000
Less: Accumulated depreciation		6,000		9,000
		30,000		26,000
Investments				
Building Society				2,600
Current assets				
Stocks	7,800		11,800	
Bank	3,200		400	
	11,000		12,200	
Current liabilities				
Creditors	3,600		2,800	
Working capital		7,400		9,400
Capital employed		37,400		38,000
Capital				
Opening balance		27,400		31,400
Add: Net profit		13,800		18,900
		41,200		50,300
Less: Drawings		9,800		12,300
Closing balance		31,400		38,000
Loan		6,000		
		37,400		

* During 19–2, equipment costing £4,000 was sold for £1,800. The accumulated depreciation on this equipment was £1,600

7.2 The Profit and Loss account and Balance Sheet of Solid PLC have already been prepared and are given below:

Profit and Loss Account for the year ended 31st December, 19–2

	£000	£000
Sales		11,000
Cost of sales		6,000
Gross profit		5,000
Add: Profit on disposal of		
Investments		40
Interest received		15
		5,055
Less:		
Running expenses	2,400	
Depreciation of fixed assets	520	
Loss on disposal of fixed assets	12	
		2,932
Net profit before tax		2,123
Less: Taxation		750
		1,373
Less: Dividends paid		600
		773
Add: Balance as at 1st January, 19–2		1,642
Balance as at 31st December, 19–2		2,415

Balance Sheet as at 31st December

	19–1		19–2	
	£000	£000	£000	£000
Fixed assets				
At cost or valuation		4,700		6,200
Less: Depreciation to date		1,200		1,600
		3,500		4,600
Investments				
At cost		340		180
Current assets				
Stocks	1,347		1,542	
Debtors	640		920	
Bank	410		1,048	
	2,397		3,510	
Current liabilities				
Creditors	320		475	
Taxation	475		750	
Working capital		1,602		2,285
Capital employed		5,442		7,065
Ordinary share capital (£1 shares)		3,000		3,500
Reserves				
Undistributed profits		1,642		2,415
Revaluation reserve		—		400
Share premium		—		250
12% debentures		800		500
		5,442		7,065

When reviewing these accounts, the managing director of the company comments:

'I can see that there has been a substantial increase in working capital in 19–2 but I'm not really sure how this has come about. Is there some way that this could be clearly explained to me?'

Required:

Prepare an appropriate accounting statement to explain the changes in working capital in 19–2 and attach this to a memorandum which outlines its main features. The following information should be taken into account:

(a) The revaluation reserve arises from the revaluation of freehold premises to a current market value.

(b) Fixed assets were disposed of during the year for £24,000. These had originally cost £156,000.

(c) The debentures were redeemed at par (face value) and the shares were issued at a premium of £0.50 per share.

7.3 Jim Keen is considering buying some of the ordinary shares of a private limited company, OK Ltd., from one of the major shareholders, Bill Dizzy. Unfortunately, when Jim asks to have a look at the latest Balance Sheet of the company, Bill says that he has mislaid it. However, the accounts he does have available are as follows:

Balance Sheet as at 30th June, 19–1

	£ Cost	£ Accumulated depreciation	£ Net
Fixed assets			
Freehold premises	48,000	—	48,000
Machinery and equipment	18,000	7,200	10,800
Motor vehicles	15,000	9,000	6,000
	81,000	16,200	64,800
Current assets			
Stocks, at cost		24,000	
Debtors		7,400	
Bank		11,200	
		42,600	
Current liabilities			
Creditors	16,000		
Taxation	7,000	23,000	
Working capital			19,600
Capital employed			84,400
Financed by			
Ordinary share capital			
(£1, fully paid)			40,000
Preference shares (£1, 8% fully paid)			15,000
Undistributed profits			9,400
10% debentures			20,000
			84,400

Sources and Applications of Funds Statement for the year ended 30th June, 19–2

	£	£
Sources of Funds		
Net profit before tax	29,500	
Add: Depreciation	5,600	
	35,100	
Less: Profit on disposal of motor vehicle	900	
Funds generated from operations		34,200
Sale of motor vehicle		4,200
Issue of debentures		12,000
		50,400
Applications of Funds		
Purchase of equipment	8,000	
Purchase of motor vehicle	9,500	
Redemption of preference shares	15,000	
Taxation paid	7,000	
		39,500
Increase in working capital		10,900
Increases (decreases) in working capital		
Increase in stocks		7,200
Increase in debtors		4,700
Decrease in bank		(5,600)
Decrease in creditors		4,600
		10,900

As well as the information contained in these accounts, Bill can also remember that the following events took place during the year to 30th June, 19–2:

1. The freehold property was revalued on 1st April, 19–2, to a current market value of £72,000.
2. The preference shares were redeemed on the 1st July, 19–1.
3. The motor vehicle disposed of had originally cost £8,400.
4. The tax liability for the year to 30th June, 19–2, was estimated at £9,200.

Jim has asked you to prepare the Balance Sheet as at 30th June, 19–2, in as much detail as possible and you have agreed, with certain reservations.

Required:

Prepare the Balance Sheet and explain your reservations.

7.4 (a) The balance sheet of SAF Ltd. as at 31st March, 19–1, is given below:

	£		£
Ordinary share capital	25,000	Plant and equipment at cost	78,000
Undistributed profits	31,000	*Less*: Depreciation to date	27,000
			51,000

	£		£
Creditors	14,000	Stocks	18,000
Taxation (due 1st January, 19–2)	5,000	Debtors	9,000
Dividends	5,000	Bank	2,000
	80,000		80,000

The company are in the process of preparing their financial budget for the following year and have already collated the following information:

	£
Sales	150,000
Purchases	96,000
Operating expenses (excluding depreciation)	37,000
Taxation	7,000

The directors of the company expected to propose a dividend of 20% for the year. By the end of the year, stocks will be equivalent to 3 months' purchases, creditors equivalent to 2 months' purchases and debtors equivalent to 1½ months' sales. The provision for depreciation is estimated at £9,000, which allows for the fact that equipment costing £15,000 will be acquired during the year.

So that the directors can get a clearer idea of the financial implications of these plans, prepare the budgeted Profit and Loss Account, Balance Sheet and Sources and Applications of Funds Statement for the year ended 31st March, 19–2. Add any comments that might help to clarify the position.

(b) On receiving your memorandum with the accounts, one of the directors comments:

'I'm still not really sure why the company's cash position is expected to change in the manner shown by these accounts. Is it possible to explain the movements of cash in some other way?'

Required:

Prepare a statement that should help to sort out this confusion, making brief comments about what it reveals.

7.5 The directors of Acctwo Ltd. are reviewing their financial plans for the year to 31st December, 19–2:

1. The budgeted data already prepared is as follows:

	£
Sales	480,000
Purchases	388,000
Operating expenses	72,000
Depreciation	5,000
Taxation	24,000

2. Credit periods from suppliers and granted to customers are expected to be the same as in recent years, i.e. 1½ months from suppliers and 1½ months to customers. Stocks will be built-up to £67,000.

3. In order to retain as much profit as possible, no dividends will be

proposed. However, a rights issue of 1 ordinary share for every 2 currently held is expected to be taken up. The nominal value of the shares will be £1, issued at a premium of £0.70 per share.
4. Equipment costing £18,000 will be acquired during the year.
5. The debenture interest has not yet been paid or allowed for in the above estimates.

The Balance Sheet of the company as at 31st December, 19–1, is given below:

		£	£
Fixed assets			
Freehold premises			27,000
Equipment, at cost		28,000	
Less: Depreciation to date		8,400	
			19,600
Current assets			
Stocks		38,900	
Debtors		42,600	
Bank		4,700	
		86,200	
Current liabilities			
Creditors	18,400		
Taxation (due 1st October, 19–2)	16,300		
		34,700	
Working capital			51,500
Capital employed			98,100
Financed by			
Ordinary share capital			40,000
(£1 shares)			
Undistributed profits			32,100
12% debentures			26,000
			98,100

Required:

(a) Prepare a budgeted Cash Flow Statement for the year ended 31st December, 19–2.

(b) The directors of the company are considering a number of alternative strategies and have asked you to explain what effect they would have on the cash position of the business at 31st December, 19–2.

    1. Revalue the premises to a current market value of £48,000.
    2. Reduce the provision for depreciation to £4,000.
    3. Propose a final dividend of 5% on the ordinary shares.
    4. Reduce the credit period to customers by half a month.
    5. Reduce creditors by £6,000.

8 The Analysis of Financial Statements

When you have read the following chapter you should be able to:
- analyse and interpret a set of Published Accounts
- calculate ratios relating to profitability, liquidity and investment
- report on the significance of the results

8.1 Introduction

Although useful accounting information can be gleaned from the financial or trade press, or, in limited circumstances, from industry-wide surveys conducted by trade associations or specialist firms, most external interest groups use the annual Published Accounts as the main source of information from which to measure organisational performance. This chapter shows how the statements prepared (in previous chapters) for publication can be analysed and interpreted by means of ratio analysis.

A check back to Chapter 1 will remind you that there are various *groups* of people who are interested in the Published Accounts and each has certain needs. These are summarised in Table 8.1.

Table 8.1

Interest group	Main interest(s)
Managers	Decision making
	Planning and controlling operations efficiently
Employees	Security of job and income
Shareholders	Present and expected earnings, security
Creditors/banks	Future orders, security of payments
Customers (public)	Reliability and continuity of supply
Government	Economic and social planning, tax calculations
Competitors	Comparative performance measures

These users of accounts need to draw conclusions which will form the basis for decisions and much of this information can be gathered by calculating ratios. However, the limited amount of information disclosed in Published Accounts does not really indicate how a company is performing unless some yardstick is

provided. The basis for comparison may be:
- last year's results (a time-series or trend analysis)
- competitor's performance (inter-firm comparison)
- an industrial norm or average
- a combination of the above

These comparisons are known as accounting ratios and can be calculated in order to evaluate the performance of an organisation. They are a shorthand way of showing relationships between figures in the Profit and Loss Account, the Balance Sheet and the Funds Flow Statement.

Figures on their own have little meaning and ratios will have much more validity if they are placed in context over time and between companies. A profit of £1m seems impressive until you are told that the investment required to make that profit is £100m, giving a return of only 1%. Additionally, supposing you then discover that profits last year were £2m. Not only is there a poor rate of return but profits have actually fallen! This in turn looks even worse if we know that our competitors and the economy in general have done rather well over the year. This simple example is given to emphasise the fact that if accounts are to be properly analysed, then comparisons have to be made and we must have figures to compare with!

Relative figures (£1m/£100 = 1%) are much more revealing than absolute figures (£1m) standing in splendid isolation.

The form of ratios

Accounting 'ratios' are not necessarily ratios in the mathematical sense, but can be expressed in the form which conveys information in the best way to the user.

For example, if an organisation's sales in a year are £150,000 and the average value of debtors is £25,000 the relationship between the two can be expressed in a number of ways, for for example:

- ratio of sales to debtors 6:1
- average debtor collection periods in days:

$$\frac{25,000}{150,000} \times 365 = 61 \text{ days}$$

- percentage of debtors to sales

$$\frac{25,000}{150,000} \times 100 = 16.7\%$$

- annual sales per £1 of debtors = £6

Selecting ratios

The analyst must be careful to select the relevant and significant ratios from the many available. The most common ratios (there are many others) are explained in this chapter and are concerned with profit performance, liquidity and investment. A significant ratio is one which differs sufficiently from a previous or planned or external ratio to warrant further investigation. The magnitude of this difference will be predefined by management and might be expressed in monetary or percentage terms. For example, management might take a policy decision to treat any item which has changed by more than ±£500 or ±10% as significant and therefore requiring attention. This type of analysis is known as *exception reporting*. When you are analysing accounts learn to scan the figures and select only the exceptional items for analysis.

8.2 Analysis of accounts

A word of warning before we apply ratio analysis to a set of fictitious Published Accounts. Ratios should be used with caution; they are not ends in themselves, merely aids to decision making. They are intended to complement rather than replace the experience, judgement and common sense of the decision maker.

In the rest of the chapter, an imaginary set of Published Accounts of Eleri PLC for the year ending 31st December, 19–1, will be used to apply ratio and funds flow analysis to assess the organisation's performance.

Eleri PLC
Profit and Loss Accounts for the years ended 31st December

		19–0 £000		19–1 £000
Turnover (sales)		3,400		4,000
Cost of sales		3,100		3,500
Gross profit		300		500
Distribution costs	120		150	
Administration costs	40		50	
Interest paid	90	250	100	300
Profit on ordinary activities before tax		50		200
Tax		25		100
Profit for the financial year		25		100
Undistributed profits from last year		50		50
		75		150
Dividends		25		50
Transfers to reserves		50		100

Note: Employee's remuneration this year was £1,500,000 compared with £1,400,000 last year. The number of employers was 200 in both years.

Balance Sheet on 31st December

		19–0 £000		19–1 £000
Fixed assets				
Buildings		1,500		1,500
Plant and equipment		300		500
		1,800		2,000
Current assets				
Stock	500		650	
Debtors	400		500	
Cash	50		—	
	950		1,150	
Less: Current liabilities				
Creditors	400		500	
Tax provision	25		100	
Dividends payable	25		50	
Bank overdraft	—	450	50	700
Net working capital		500		450
Net assets employed		2,300		2,450
Financed by				
Issued share capital (£1 shares)		1,000		1,000
Reserves		400		400
Retained profits		50		100
Shareholders funds		1,450		1,500
Loans: debenture stock		850		950
		2,300		2,450

Note: Fixed assets are shown at net book value.

Statement of Sources and Applications of Funds Year Ended 31st December, 19–1 (£000)

Sources		
Profit before tax	200	
Adjustments for non-cash items		
Depreciation	150	
Funds from trading	350	
Loan capital	100	
Increase in creditors	100	
		550
Applications		
Expenditure on fixed assets	350	
Dividends paid	25	
Tax paid	25	
Increase in debtors	150	
Increase in stocks	100	
		650
Net reduction in cash balance		(100)

Financial ratios can be classified in several ways which can be reduced into 3 groups, namely:

1. profit
2. liquidity
3. investment

8.3 Profit ratios

The main objective of any management should be to ensure that the organisation's funds are efficiently employed. In the private sector, this is closely linked to the aim of making a profit and providing shareholders with a reasonable return. In the public sector other measures of success, which might include social or political objectives, may exist although an internal rate of return is often prescribed.

A main measure of success for a private sector organisation is known as the *primary ratio*. This is usually expressed as:

$$\frac{\text{Profit before tax and loan interest (bti)} \times 100}{\text{Net capital employed}}$$

This ratio is sometimes known as the *return* on capital employed. For Eleri Ltd. the figures will be:

	19-0	19-1
1. *Profit bti* %	$\frac{140}{2,300} = 6$	$\frac{300}{2,450} = 12$
2. Net capital employed		
Calculations		
Profit before tax	50	200
Add back interest	90	100
1. Profit bti	140	300

2. Net capital employed is equivalent to net assets employed

Tax and loan interest have been left out of the profit figure because they are not really relevant to management efficiency. This makes sense to the extent that external factors, such as monetary and fiscal policy, are outside management's control, so the figure of net profit before tax and interest should be a better measure of the management's ability to make profitable use of available resources.

The primary ratio, like all other ratios, is only meaningful when comparisons are made. It will be useful to check the ratio with other firms in the industry, or an industrial average, or, more generally, external yardsticks such as bank interest rates to gain some sort of perspective. The ratio in the case of Eleri PLC has increased by 6 percentage points which, in itself, is a step in the right direction, although as we shall see it is by no means exceptional for this particular industry.

The primary ratio can be broken down into many component or subsidiary ratios which may prompt further investigation if they prove to be significant (see Figure 8.1). The first step in this investigative process is to divide the primary ratio into the margin and asset turnover ratios, thus:

Primary ratio = Margin × Asset turnover

$$= \frac{\text{Net profit bti}}{\text{Net capital employed}}$$

$$= \frac{\text{Net profit bti}}{\text{Sales}} \times \frac{\text{Sales}}{\text{Net capital employed}}$$

You can see that when the two ratios are multiplied together sales cancel out to give the primary ratio.

Figure 8.1 Primary ratio – breakdown

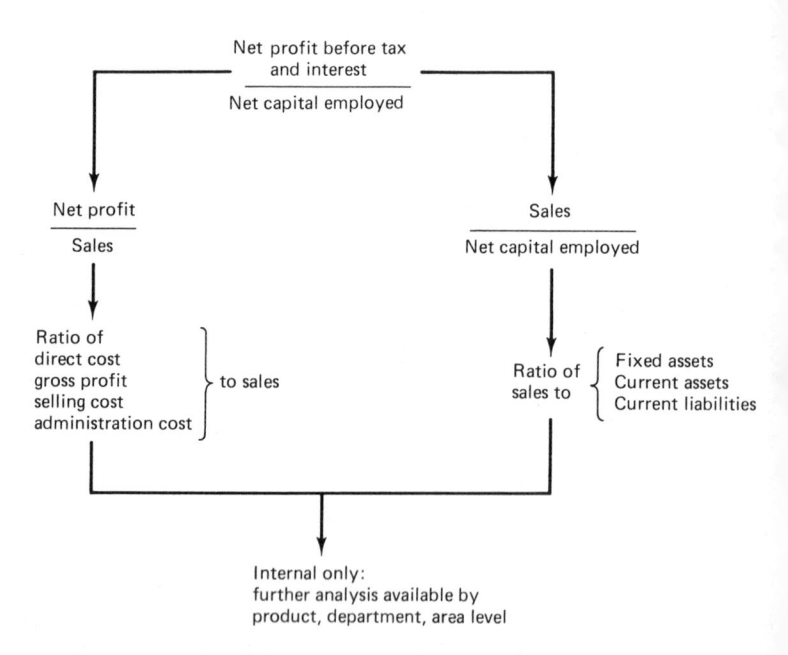

```
                    Net profit before tax
                       and interest
          ┌─────────────────────────────────────┐
          │         Net capital employed         │
          ▼                                     ▼
      Net profit                              Sales
      ─────────                       ─────────────────────
        Sales                         Net capital employed
          │                                     │
          ▼                                     ▼
   Ratio of                                                ⎧ Fixed assets
   direct cost                              Ratio of      ⎨ Current assets
   gross profit    } to sales               sales to      ⎩ Current liabilities
   selling cost
   administration cost
          │
          ▼
   Internal only:
   further analysis available by
   product, department, area level
```

The margin is the percentage profit made on each item sold. The asset turnover ratio indicates how efficiently the assets of the company are being used to generate sales. In simple terms the ratios show that there are two ways of making a profit: charge high margins on a few items (e.g. luxury goods) or low margins on many items (e.g. basic foods). In practice, of course, pricing strategy often contains elements of both. For example,

Eleri PLC
19–0 Margin × Asset turnover = Primary ratio

$$\left(\frac{140}{3400} = 4.1\%\right) \times \left(\frac{3400}{2300} = 1.48 \times\right) = 6\%$$

19—1 $\left(\dfrac{300}{4000} = 7.5\%\right) \times \left(\dfrac{4000}{2450} = 1.63 \times\right) = 12\%$

The margin is expressed as a percentage, and the asset turnover is expressed as the number of times by which sales exceed assets employed. For example, in 19–0 sales are 1.48 greater than assets.

Breaking down the primary ratio in this way enables a start to be made in identifying areas for further investigation (particularly from a management viewpoint). In this example, profit per £ of sales has increased to 7.5p whilst sales volume has increased only slightly relative to the value of the net assets. So the main reason for Eleri's improvement was the significant increase in the margin over last year. To discover the reasons behind this would require more detailed figures concerning prices and costs which Published Accounts do not usually show, although such data will be available for internal analysis and management decision making.

However, we can show the beginnings of margin analysis by looking at a sales breakdown as follows: This information can be extracted from the company's profit statement

	19–0 £000	%	19–1 £000	%
Sales	3,400	100	4,000	100
Employees (wages)	1,400	41	1,500	38
Other costs	1,700	50	2,000	50
Dividends	25	1	50	1
Tax	25	1	100	3
Distribution and administration costs	160	5	200	5
Interest	90	3	100	3
Retained profits	—	—	50	1

Percentages rounded to nearest whole number)

The reason for the increase in margin could be a straightforward price increase and/or an improvement in labour productivity. Sales value increased by 18%, whereas labour costs only rose by 7%. Perhaps a detailed internal analysis of sales and labour costs (by department/product) etc. would reveal causes and responsibilities.

8.4 Liquidity ratios

Liquidity refers to an organisation's ability to meet demands for cash. Not only should a business be profitable but it should also be

Current ratio (net working capital)

able to pay its debts when they fall due. Cash will be needed to pay suppliers' bills, workers' wages, tax demands etc. The easier it is to convert assets into cash the more liquid the asset will be and the cheaper the cost of the conversion. The cost of conversion could be discounts on sales or factoring of stock (selling off stock at a discount to a middleman). Cash in itself is an idle asset in that it earns no interest, so organisations will seek to keep their cash balances as small as possible. Rather there is the need to ensure that cash is ready as and when required. So attention is drawn to those current assets which can usually be converted into cash relatively cheaply and within a short time period. Two ratios are in common use and are of particular interest to an organisation's creditors.

This ratio indicates the extent to which short-term debts are covered by cash or 'near-money'. By definition current liabilities are repayable within a year, although in many cases the credit period may be a matter of months. Conversely, items such as bank overdrafts may be 'rolled over' to future years although technically they are repayable on demand. Current assets are those assets which will normally be converted into cash in the the near future. They are at some stage in the selling process (either stocks of some description, debtors) where the sale has been made but no money has been received, or cash itself. Clearly if the short-term debts exceed these near-cash items the organisation may not be able to meet such demands as they arise. Ideally, therefore, the relationship between current assets and current liabilities should be well above 1:1 (although this varies from industry to industry) so that any exceptional claims can be paid off. Of course, this need for liquidity should be traded off against the expense of holding cash or liquid items.

Eleri PLC *19–0* *19–1*

$$\text{Current ratio: } \frac{\text{Current assets}}{\text{Current liabilities}} = \frac{950}{450} = 2.11 \times \quad \frac{1150}{700} = 1.64 \times$$

The current ratio shows a decline in the liquidity position but this should not be a cause for concern because the ratio is still above 1:1.

Liquid ratio (acid test)

A tighter test of liquidity is the liquid ratio which excludes stock from the calculations on the assumption that it might not be sold quickly or at present values. This ratio might be applied in companies where stocks are high, or are mainly raw materials and work-in-progress which need further work before they can be sold off for cash.

19–0 *19–1*

$$\text{Liquid ratio: } \frac{\text{Liquid assets}}{\text{Current liabilities}} = \frac{450}{450} = 1 \times \quad \frac{500}{700} = 0.71 \times$$

The decline in this ratio is not a cause for concern in itself but the organisation should bear in mind that they have only 71p in near-cash for every £1 of bills due to be paid shortly.

8.5 Funds Flow analysis

The Funds Flow Statement in the accounts of Eleri PLC shows changes in the cash balance over the last year. The reduction in cash can be largely attributed to the £350,000 purchase of fixed assets during the year.

The funds resulting from a new issue of loan capital, trading and delayed payments to creditors cover this capital expenditure as well as tax and dividends but only part, 60%, of the increased working capital burden. Hence stocks and debtors are partly financed by an overdraft facility.

The number of days stock is held is:

$$\frac{\text{Stock}}{\text{Cost of sales}} \times 365 \quad \begin{array}{c} 19\text{-}0 \\ \frac{500}{3100} = 59 \text{ days} \end{array} \quad \begin{array}{c} 19\text{-}1 \\ \frac{650}{3500} = 68 \text{ days} \end{array}$$

Although the cost of sales increased by 13%, stocks held have gone up by 30% so that the organisation's stockholding costs might have increased disproportionately.

Similarly debtors are taking a little more time to pay thereby tying up further funds.

The average debtor collection (credit) period =

$$\frac{\text{Debtors}}{\text{Sales}} \times 365 \quad \begin{array}{c} 19\text{-}0 \\ \frac{400}{3,400} = 43 \text{ days} \end{array} \quad \begin{array}{c} 19\text{-}1 \\ \frac{500}{4,000} = 46 \text{ days} \end{array}$$

This has been offset by the slowing down of payment to creditors, however. So, apparently, credit policy is synchronised as far as customers and suppliers are concerned.

8.6 Investment ratios

The investment ratios chosen are those commonly quoted in Published Accounts or the financial press. They are of particular interest to shareholders and other investors both actual and potential.

138 Accounting: A Practical Approach

Return on equity This ratio shows the rate of return after all costs, including tax, have been met, on the funds provided by shareholders either as share capital or as retained profits.

Eleri PLC

	19–0	19–1
$\dfrac{\text{Net profit after tax}}{\text{Shareholders funds}}$	$\dfrac{25}{1,450} = 1.7\%$	$\dfrac{100}{1,500} = 6.7\%$

This indicates an increase in the *potential* payout; the directors will choose whether to distribute or retain earnings. The ratio can be expressed as earnings per share (EPS):

	19–0	19–1
$\text{EPS} = \dfrac{\text{Net profit after tax}}{\text{Number of shares issued}}$	$\dfrac{25}{1,000} = 2.5\text{p}$	$\dfrac{100}{1,000} = 10\text{p}$

So a holder of 1 share could receive a 10p dividend if the company were to pay all its profits over to the shareholders.

Dividend cover (c'vr) This is the number of times that profits cover the dividend payment. It represents the firm's ability to meet its dividends. In this sense it is similar to the liquidity ratios which indicate an ability to service short-term debts overall.

Eleri PLC

	19–0	19–1
$\text{Dividend cover} = \dfrac{\text{Net profit after tax}}{\text{Dividends}}$	$\dfrac{25}{25} = 1$	$\dfrac{100}{50} = 2$

Clearly there is a safety margin in 19–1 as profits cover dividends twice over.

Dividend yield (Y'ld Gr's) Gross dividend yield is obtained by dividing the dividend per share by the market price

	19–0	19–1
$\text{Dividend per share} = \dfrac{\text{Dividends}}{\text{Number of shares issued}}$	$\dfrac{25}{1,000} = 2.5\text{p}$	$\dfrac{50}{1,000} = 5\text{p}$
$\text{Dividend yield} = \dfrac{\text{Dividend per share}}{\text{Market share price}}$	$\dfrac{2.5}{1.10} = 2.3\%$	$\dfrac{5}{1.25} = 4\%$

Assume market share prices are given.

The return on equity showed the shareholder what might be received from earnings, but some of these are usually kept back for use within the business. The shareholders have little control over the amount paid out as dividends so they will want to know how much they might *actually* get if shares are bought at the current

Price/Earnings ratio (P/E)

market price. The real rate of return has improved to 4% as far as Eleri PLC is concerned.

This shows the number of years it will take to get an investment back. This payback period is expressed in years and is calculated as follows:

$$\text{P/E ratio} = \frac{\text{Market share price}}{\text{Earnings per share}} = \frac{£1.10}{2.5p} = 44 \text{ years} \quad \frac{£1.25}{10p} = 12.5 \text{ years}$$

So it will take about $12\frac{1}{2}$ years to earn the price paid for a share (£1.25) out of profits at the current rate. Bear in mind that the price of a share on the market depends as much on future expectations as on past performance. So the P/E ratio might be high if investors expect future earnings to increase.

The figures for Eleri PLC are now presented as if they were an extract from the Financial Times (FT) share information service showing stock exchange and company information on 31st December, 19—1. Reading from left to right, the first two columns show the high and low share price for the year. The name of the company together with the normal (par) value of the shares quoted is then given. When no amount is shown the nominal value per share is 25p. Next appears the closing market share price of £1.25 for the previous day and the change during the day, if any. The remaining four headings have been explained.

FT share information service

19–1 High	Low	Stock	Price	+ or –	Div* Net	C'vr	Y'ld Gr's	P/E
1.40	1.07	Eleri £1	125	+1	5	2	4	12.5

* Div net – net dividend, i.e. dividend per share.

Note: Cover and price/earnings are usually based on the latest annual report and accounts and, where possible, are updated on half-yearly figures.

Gearing

It is often useful to inspect the organisation's capital structure to find the extent of its reliance on outside funds. If a business uses loan finance it incurs an unavoidable fixed cost because of the interest it will have to pay. This means a greater degree of risk if the money subsequently proves to have been ill-spent.

The gearing ratio (broadly, loans compared with share capital) measures this level of risk. A company is said to be low-geared if the bulk of its finance is equity, which is the case with Eleri PLC. It therefore runs less risk because it can vary the dividend payout to shareholders according to profit levels (ordinary shares have a variable interest rate). In good years shareholders may be highly rewarded but in bad years (loss-making or start-up periods) the directors may decide to pay out little or nothing, keeping back any profits to finance operations. If a company has borrowed heavily, however, and is high-geared (i.e. debt exceeds equity), then there is a greater risk of default and possible bankruptcy. The gearing ratio (sometimes known as the debt to equity ratio) can be expressed in several ways, a popular approach being as follows:

$$\text{Gearing} = \frac{\text{Long-term borrowing}}{\text{Net capital employed}} \qquad \begin{array}{c} 19\text{-}0 \\ \frac{850}{2,300} = 37\% \end{array} \qquad \begin{array}{c} 19\text{-}1 \\ \frac{950}{2,450} = 39\% \end{array}$$

This shows debt as a percentage of net capital employed. There is no significant change in the structure of Eleri PLC, roughly 40% of its funds deriving from loan rather than share capital sources.

8.7 Employees

Increasingly, accounting reports feature information specifically related to the interest groups outlined in Table 8.1. Taking employees as an example, the accounts of Eleri PLC reveal the following:

	19-0	19-1
Total wages and salaries (£000)	1,400	1,500
Number of employees	200	200
∴ Average pay per employee (£)	7,000	7,500

A sales per employee figure can also be calculated:

Total sales (£000)	3,400	4,000
Number of employees	200	200
Sales per employee (£)	17,000	20,000

This suggests an increase in productivity by about 18%, well in excess of the wage rise. Indeed worker representatives could go further and examine company profits per employee and liquidity as a basis for wage claims. Clearly all this must take place within the context of comparable rates elsewhere as well as the general level of inflation.

8.8 Inter-firm comparisons

Once ratios have been calculated for Eleri PLC these might usefully be compared with other companies in the same industry. This will place them in context and indicate whether Eleri's performance is broadly in line with industry trends. There are particular problems with comparing figures across companies because definitions and classifications may differ. In addition, competitors may be quite different in terms of size and the products that they sell.

Valid comparisons can be made only if 'like is compared with like'. Occasionally a Trade Association may produce industry-wide comparisons based on individual submissions. There are also specialist firms, such as the Centre for Inter-firm Comparisons, which carry out this sort of work. The important point is that figures should be standardised and procedures agreed if the results are to be meaningfully compared. Not many firms are keen to provide extra information, even anonymously, and therefore most have to rely on the annual report and accounts.

Let us imagine that Eleri PLC goes through its three main competitors' accounts for the past five years and extracts the return on capital employed figures (the primary ratio). These are shown along with Eleri's in Figure 8.2. This is an example of ratio analysis over time and between companies; it combines the two.

As mentioned when the primary ratio was explained, Eleri's performance in the last year is a considerable improvement on 19-0, but the return on capital employed still lags behind Osgerby and the industrial average although it has just overtaken Muir. If the comparison is valid, i.e. the figures have been adjusted to account for any differences in reporting times and procedures, then this company is not particularly profitable within its own industry. Assume that further figures have been calculated and compiled from the appropriate annual reports. These are presented in the Performance League Table (Table 8.2). From this you can begin to see the possible reasons for Eleri's performance. The margin is below the industry norm and this seems to be because of high selling costs. Likewise fixed assets appear unproductive compared to the average, although working capital seems to have been well managed. Clearly only tentative conclu-

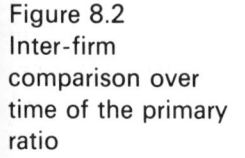

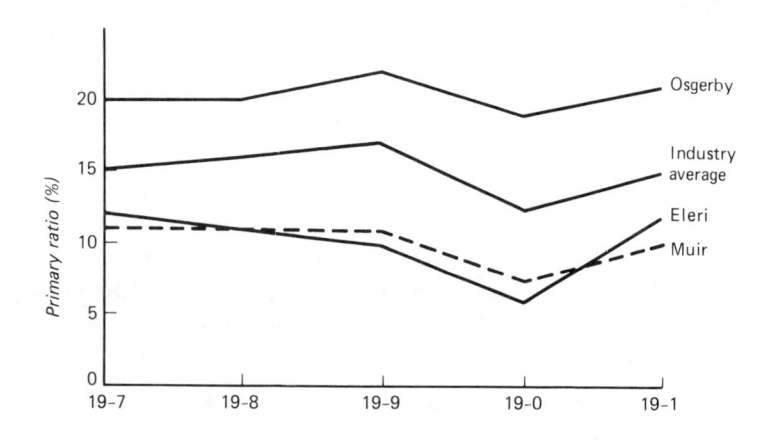

Figure 8.2
Inter-firm comparison over time of the primary ratio

Table 8.2 *Performance League Table*

Ratios for 19–1(%)	Osgerby	Eleri	Muir	Industrial average
Primary ratio	21	12	10	15
Margin	10	7.5	5	10
Asset turnover	2.1 ×	1.63 ×	2 ×	1.5 ×
Direct cost/sales	35	38	38	36
Selling costs/sales	17	30	20	15
Sales/fixed assets	3.2 ×	2 ×	1.67 ×	2.73 ×
Sales/current assets	6 ×	3.48 ×	2.5 ×	2.22 ×

sions can be drawn from such data but these factors may prompt further investigation to try to pinpoint cause and responsibility.

8.9 Problems with the use of ratios

A ratio is only as good as the data on which it is based and published accounting data has its weaknesses:

1. Only a legal minimum amount of financial data need be disclosed and this incomplete picture may give a distorted view of the true performance of the business.
2. Annual Published Accounts do not disclose short-term fluctuations between reporting dates. The reported figures may disguise underlying problems. An example of this 'window-dressing' would be paying off debts before the year-end only to borrow early in the new year.
3. Ratios based on this published data do not isolate the cause or the responsibility for any given problem; that is one of the functions of management and cost accounting.
4. Additionally, trends themselves may be misleading and should be considered in the context of the whole economy. Nor is there any guarantee that existing trends will continue (as before) although forecasts will often be based on a sensible appraisal of past performance.
5. Further, we have seen how certain figures (stock, fixed assets) are estimates based on subjective judgement and it follows from this that there are various ways of measuring profit and valuing assets. This problem is compounded by the possible effects of inflation on income and net worth measurement. Ratios based on these figures are consequently open to question.

Inter-firm comparisons present further difficulties as organisations in any given industry may be quite different in terms of size and product mix. Worse still, different definitions and classifications may be used as well as various costing systems and year-end dates. All these make a valid comparison of 'like with like' that much more difficult even at a basic level.

The natural reluctance of firms to standardise procedures and pool information means that only a relatively small number of businesses can use inter-firm comparisons without making major assumptions about the accounting procedures of their competitors. Where industry-wide studies exist they are normally compiled by trade association or the Centre for Inter-firm Comparisons (CIC). At best, ratios for a number of years can be set against competitor figures and ranked in a Performance League Table (see Table 8.2).

In spite of all the drawbacks mentioned, ratios, if handled cautiously, can be a useful aid in the interpretation and analysis of accounting data. They are not ends in themselves but can point to aspects of the business which might usefully warrant further research.

Summary

This chapter has demonstrated the use of both ratios and funds flow analysis for the purposes of measuring organisational performance. An imaginary set of Published Accounts were produced and interpreted in terms of profitability, liquidity and investment.

An example of how accounting information can be adapted for specific needs (in this case workers) was outlined and it was also shown how ratio analysis can be used to make comparisons between companies. Finally, some of the problems with using ratios were outlined.

Assignments

8.1 (a) Write a letter to a company asking them for a copy of their latest annual accounts. Get your colleagues to write to other companies (see below).

(b) Obtain copies of published accounts for three companies in the same line of business (e.g. food retailing).

(c) For the three companies calculate the:
1. Return on net capital employed
2. Working capital ratio, and any other ratios which you feel are significant.
3. Say which, in your opinion, is the most successful company.
4. Where appropriate draw comparison charts and diagrams to highlight particular strengths and weaknesses.
5. Be sure to point out any reservations you may have about making inter-firm comparisons.

8.2 The following figures are taken from the recently Published Accounts of Luckie Mucklebackit PLC for the year ended 31st March, 19–2. The preceding year's figures are given for the purposes of comparison:

Balance Sheet as at 31st March

		19–2 £000			19–1 £000
Ordinary share capital		300			300
Retained earnings		50			40
10% debentures		380			180
		730			520
Fixed assets					
Buildings	340			180	
Plant and machinery	310	650		140	320
Current assets					
Stock	240			200	
Debtors	160			120	
Bank balance	—			40	
	400			360	
Current liabilities					
Creditors	290		160		
Bank overdraft	30	320	80	—	160	200
		730			520

Profit for the year ended 31st March, 19–2, before taxation amounted to £66,000 and for the year to 31st March, 19–1, it was £63,500.

Required:

(a) Calculate a ratio for each year which indicates the firm's return on net capital employed and suggest reasons for any change that has occurred in this ratio.

(b) Calculate *ratios* for each year which indicate the company's liquidity and discuss the significance of any changes that have occurred in these ratios.

(c) Discuss the importance of *adequate working capital* in the financial management of a business.

8.3
Clive Eastwood PLC:
Summarised Balance Sheet (as at 31st December, 19–1)

		£000
Fixed assets		
Less: accumulated depreciation		2,600
Current assets		
Stock	600	
Debtors	900	
Cash	100	
	1,600	
Less current liabilities	800	
Working capital		800
		3,400
Financed by		
Ordinary share capital		1,200
Retained earnings		800
Loans		1,400
		3,400

Summarised Profit and Loss Account
(Year ending 31st December, 19–1)

	£000
Sales	6,000
Profit after depreciation etc. but before interest and taxation	340
Loan interest	74
Pre-tax profits	266
Taxation	106
Profit available for shareholders	160

The industry's average performance ratios are:

1. ROCE — 16%
2. Current ratio — 2.2 times
3. Debtors collection period — 50 days
4. Acid Test ratio — 1.0 times
5. Net profit as a % of sales — 7%
6. Sales to net assets ratio — 4.5 times

Required:

(a) From the above information you are required to calculate for Eastwood PLC the relevant ratios to compare with the industry's average performance. Each result should be followed by your comment on the company's performance in relation to that being achieved by the industry.

(b) Assume the following information for 19–2:

Company	Myers £000	Longson £000
Ordinary share capital (£1 shares)	2,000	1,000
Reserves (average figure for 19–2)	1,500	1,000
15% debentures repayable 19–5 – 19–0	500	4,000
Profit for 19–2 before deducting loan interest	600	900

The companies are engaged in the same kind of business, which is cyclical, and from past experience profits before deducting loan interest are liable to fluctuate up to 50% above or below the 19–2 level.

Contrast the effect of these potential profit variations from the viewpoint of shareholders and management. Be sure to explain gearing and its effects.

8.4 Martin Holt is interested in obtaining shares in Green Ltd. and is at present examining financial data in respect of the past three years, derived from Published Accounts.

Before acquiring shares he approaches you for assistance in obtaining the answers to the following questions concerning the trend over the period.

1. Is the company more able to pay its creditors?
2. Do the shareholders gain any advantages from financial leverage?
3. Are debtors settling their accounts quickly?
4. Are the total debtors increasing?
5. What has happened to the price/earnings ratio over the period?
6. Are the earning per share increasing?
7. What trend can be seen in the movement of the market price of the company's shares?
8. What movement is there on the level of stock held?

Required:

Answer each of the above questions, using the following data, giving reasons for your answer.

Green Ltd

Selected financial data for the years	19–6	19–5	19–4
Sales trends (as percentages)	120	107	100
Stock turnover	4.7 times	5.3 times	6.4 times
Dividend per share	Unchanged over the three-year period		
Yield	5%	4%	3%
Dividend payout ratio	35%	45%	55%
Debtors turnover	8.3 times	9.1 times	10.0 times
Return on total assets	6.3%	5.6%	5.2%
Acid test ratio	0.5:1	0.7:1	1.2:1
Return on shareholders capital employed	7.6%	5.5%	4.4%
Working capital ratio	2.4:1	2.1:1	1.7:1

(*IAS*)

The Analysis of Financial Statements   147

8.5 Using the accounts of Eleri PLC from this chapter, or any published annual report which you have obtained, answer the following question.

(a) In which ways might the analysis of annual reports using ratios help the following people?
   1. A supplier thinking of doing business with the company.
   2. A job applicant.
   3. A potential investor wondering whether to buy shares.
   4. A bank manager evaluating a term loan to this company.
   5. A manager of a competitor assessing the company's efficiency.

(b) Check the Auditors' Report, notes, 5 to 10 year Summary and the Chairman's/Director's Reports. What do these sections of the Annual Report show?

(c) Can you suggest any other sources of information which might help the individuals mentioned make their decisions?

8.6 Malcolm Rennard and Neil Massie are steelworkers who have just been made redundant and decide to set up in business on their own. Their severance pay amounts to £20,000 and to this they can add their joint savings of £15,000. They are looking at three possible schemes which are summarised below:

	Scheme 1 (£000)		Scheme 2 (£000)		Scheme 3 (£000)	
Income Statements						
Sales		100		150		200
Variable costs	40		100		70	
Fixed costs	55	95	44	144	120	190
Net profit		5		6		10
Balance Sheets						
Fixed assets		20		30		60
Current assets	8		10		20	
Current liabilities	3	5	5	5	12	8
Net capital		25		35		68

Notes
1. The figures represent the expected averages over the first operating year for each of the three options.
2. Costs include an allowance for salaries and depreciation but exclude interest payable on existing savings or any extra long-term borrowing.

Required:

Analyse and compare the three schemes by using appropriate financial ratios. Comment on your results. Which scheme would you recommend they take up?

8.7 X, Y and Z are small businesses in the same industry taking part in an inter-firm comparison scheme. As a consultant to firm X and in the light of information provided, highlight areas where you think there may be weaknesses.

Income Statements

	Business X % of sales	Business X £000	Business Y % of sales	Business Y £000	Business Z % of sales	Business Z £000
Sales	100	1,250	100	1,500	100	1,200
Cost of sales						
Direct Labour	25	312.5	18	270	15	180
Direct materials	20	250	21	315	20	240
Variable overheads	11	137.5	11	165	11	132
Fixed overheads	16	200	13	195	14	168
Selling expenses	9	112.5	12	180	12	144
Admin and financial expenses	13	162.5	13	195	14	168
Net profit before tax	6	75	12	180	14	168

Balance Sheets

	X £000	Y £000	Z £000
Fixed assets			
Land and buildings	200	180	270
Plant and machinery	100	150	100
Motor vehicles	150	100	120
	450	430	490
Current assets			
Work-in-progress	100	100	90
Stocks	400	200	180
Debtors	250	190	160
Cash at bank	300	80	70
	1,050	570	500
Less current liabilities			
Trade creditors	180	200	140
Bank overdraft	220	—	—
Tax due	30	72	67
Proposed dividend	50	60	60
	480	332	267
Net working capital	570	238	233
Net worth	1,020	668	723
Financed by			
Issued share capital	600	400	500
Reserves	120	168	73
Loans	300	100	150
	1,020	668	723

9 Current Cost Accounting

When you have read this chapter you should:
- be familiar with the main principles of current cost accounting
- be able to calculate simple current cost adjustments
- be able to prepare current cost Profit and Loss Accounts and current cost Balance Sheets in good style

9.1 Introduction

Up to now, all of the accounting statements you have met in this book have been prepared using the historic cost concept. This means that in the Profit and Loss Account, for example, expenses are charged at the amounts paid in the past. In the Balance Sheet, assets are shown at their cost when acquired in the past. Unfortunately, in a period of rising prices, some major distortions can occur as a result of applying the traditional historic cost concept:

1. Net profit will be overstated by the failure to recognise that fixed assets and stock must be replaced at higher prices than those paid in the past.
2. The net assets employed by the organisation (capital employed) will be understated in value since their current or replacement value is higher than their historic cost, unless the assets were acquired fairly recently.

The accountancy profession has considered for many years the distorting effects of price inflation and the need for a system of inflation accounting. After much discussion and disagreement over the course of the 1970s, it was finally proposed to implement a system of Current Cost Accounting (CCA). An agreed accounting standard, SSAP 16, was issued on 31st March, 1980, for immediate implementation. In spite of this, CCA continued to arouse strong feelings both for and against and, after a trial period of three years, many organisations began to drop Current Cost Statements from their Published Accounts. This trend has continued and a recent survey has suggested that less than 5% of companies still produce these statements in spite of the fact that the standard remains in operation.

9.2 The main features of current cost accounting

SSAP 16 recommends that all quoted companies (those whose shares are quoted on the stock exchange) and other large companies which satisfy two of three criteria should include in their final accounts:

1. A current cost Profit and Loss Account.
2. A current cost Balance Sheet.

These criteria are as follows:

1. A turnover of £5,000,000 or more p.a.
2. A balance sheet total at the beginning of the accounting period of £2,500,000 or more. This total includes the net book value of fixed assets, investments and current assets.
3. An average number of employees in the UK of 250 or more.

These current cost accounts are additional to the historic cost statements normally found, although companies can adopt current cost as their basic accounts if they wish to do so. Although the main thrust of CCA has been directed towards large companies, the need to adjust accounts to cater for price changes applies to organisations of all types and sizes.

9.3 The Current Cost Profit and Loss Account

The first figure shown in this statement is normally the net profit before interest and tax obtained from the historic accounts. Four adjustments are then made to this figure, which the following outline example illustrates.

Example

Current cost Profit and Loss Account for the year ended 30th June, 19–0

	£000	£000
Net profit before interest and tax as per historic accounts		1,650
Less: Current cost adjustments		
Depreciation	120	
Cost of sales	260	
Monetary working capital	40	

	£000	£000
Current cost operating profit		420
		1,230
Add: Gearing adjustment	90	
Less: Interest payable	30	
		60
Current cost profit before tax		1,290

The remainder of the statement will show the appropriations for tax, dividends and transfers to reserves in the normal way, (see Chapter 6). The main principles of the four current cost adjustments shown in this statement are as follows:

The depreciation adjustment

One of the main recommendations of SSAP 16 is that provisions for depreciation should be based on the current value of the asset to the business or its replacement value during the period of use. In a period of price inflation, this will be higher than the historic cost and *the difference between depreciation based on historic cost and replacement value is the depreciation adjustment for the period*. It is important to note that the adjustment refers only to one year, i.e. the current year for which the accounts are being prepared. The additional depreciation which should have been provided in earlier years is called *backlog depreciation*.

The replacement value of assets at any given time can be obtained from a number of sources, for example:

(a) Local surveyors and valuers for land and buildings.

(b) Suppliers' price lists for plant and equipment, fixtures and fittings, motor vehicles and stock.

(c) Price indices published by the Central Statistical Office for use with CCA.

(d) Specific price indices prepared by individual organisations.

Example A company purchased machinery on 1st January, 19–1 for £9,000. It provides for depreciation at a rate of 10% p.a. on the straight-line basis. It has decided to produce, for the first time, current cost accounts for the year ended 31st December, 19–4. A relevant price index has been found which revealed the following information:

	Price index
1st January, 19–1	150
1st January, 19–4	225
31st December, 19–4	250

Calculate the depreciation adjustment for 19–4.

Solution

Historic cost depreciation for 19–4 = $£9,000 \times \dfrac{10}{100} = £900$

Replacement value of machinery at 1st January, 19–4 =
$£9,000 \times \dfrac{225}{150} = £13,500$

Replacement value of machinery at 31st December, 19–4 =
$£9000 \times \dfrac{250}{150} = £15,000$

The average replacement value for 19–4 = $\dfrac{£13,500 + £15,000}{2}$
= £14,250

Depreciation charge based on average replacement value =
$£14,250 \times \dfrac{10}{100} = £1,425$

Depreciation adjustment = Depreciation based on average replacement value – Depreciation based on historic cost
= £1,425 – £900 = £525

The cost of sales adjustment (COSA)

Using the historic cost concept to measure profit, the revenue from the sale of an item of stock is matched against a purchase price paid some time in the past. For example, if a trader bought an article for £2 in March and sold it for £5 in May, profit using the historic cost concept would be £3. If however, the replacement value of the item at the time of sale was £2.20, the profit according to current cost principles is only £2.80 (£5 – £2.20). *The difference of £0.20 is the cost of sales adjustment, and represents the amount of profit retained to cover the additional cost of replacing the stock.*

Ideally, therefore, the cost of sales adjustment for the year should be obtained by recording, where necessary, a small adjustment each time a sales transaction takes place, and then aggregating these adjustments at the end of the year. With computer-based accounting systems, this can be built-in as one of the routines of, say, a strock control package. However, the prospect of recording a large volume of these transactions manually is horrendous. As a much simpler alternative, it is possible to obtain an approximation for this adjustment by applying relevant index numbers. The following example illustrates this.

Example The following is an extract from the Profit and Loss Account of an organisation:

Current Cost Accounting 153

	£000	£000
Sales		1,590
Opening stock	220	
Purchases	860	
	1,080	
Closing stock	240	
Cost of goods sold		840
Gross profit		750

The following are some relevant price index numbers:

Index when opening stock was bought	120
Index when closing stock was bought	140
Average index for the period	130

Calculate the cost of sales adjustment.

Solution

First, the current cost of sales is calculated by converting all stock to mid-year values using the index numbers as follows:

		£000
Opening stock	$220 \times \dfrac{130}{120}$	238
Purchases		860
		1,098
Closing stock	$240 \times \dfrac{130}{140}$	223
Current cost of sales		875

The cost of sales adjustment is then calculated as follows:

	£000
Current cost of sales	875
Historic cost of sales	840
Cost of sales adjustment	35

The monetary working capital adjustment (MWCA)

In simple terms, *monetary working capital is defined as the difference between trade debtors and trade creditors*. The adjustment to it is designed to allow for the additional finance which is needed to maintain the real value of monetary working capital during a period of rising prices. It can be calculated in a similar fashion to COSA by using relevant index numbers.

Example The following information has been extracted from the sales and purchases ledgers of an organisation:

	1st January, 19–1 £	31st December, 19–1 £
Trade debtors	28,400	35,600
Trade creditors	15,600	18,400

Index numbers showing the changing values of monetary working capital are given below:

	Index
1st January, 19–1	110
31st December, 19–1	130
Average index for the year	120

Calculate the monetary working capital adjustment.

Solution

First, calculate the real change in monetary working capital by converting all items to mid-year values using the index numbers as follows:

Monetary working capital at 1st January, 19–1 = £28,400 − £15,600 = £12,800

$$\text{Converted to mid-year values} = £12,800 \times \frac{120}{110} = £13,964$$

Monetary working capital at 31st December, 19–1 = £35,600 − £18,400 = £17,200

$$\text{Converted to mid-year values} = £17,200 \times \frac{120}{130} = £15,877$$

The *real* change in monetary working capital is therefore:

£15,877 − £13,964 = £1,913

The total change in monetary working capital is £17,200 − £12,800 = £4,400

The change due to price increases in therefore £4,400 − £1,913 = £2,487. This is the monetary working capital adjustment and represents the profits necessary to maintain the real value of monetary working capital.

The gearing adjustment

The three adjustments explained so far have shown how it is possible to adjust net profit to allow for the effect of specific price changes. However, what has been overlooked in these calculations is the way in which the organisation is financed. Most organisations obtain some of their long-term funds by borrowing rather than by issuing shares and this is particularly advantageous during a period of inflation when the value of the assets financed by the borrowing is rising while the liability to the lender remains fixed. In order to adjust the profit of the organisation to allow for this sort of gain, an appropriate proportion of the current cost adjustments already calculated is added back to net profit. This amount depends on the proportion of net assets which are financed by borrowing. The greater the amount of borrowing, the greater the adjustment.

Current Cost Accounting

Example An organisation is in the process of preparing current cost accounts and the following information has been put together:

	1st January, 19–1 £000	31st December, 19–1 £000
Net operating assets (i.e. net assets employed)	2,780	3,460
Net borrowing (i.e. loans)	800	600

Note: The net operating assets are shown at their current replacement values.

The current cost adjustments calculated so far:

	£000
Depreciation	186
Cost of sales	174
Monetary working capital	59

According to the historic cost accounts, net profit before interest and tax is £1,462,000 and interest amounts to £65,000.

Required:

Calculate the gearing adjustment and then show the current cost Profit and Loss Account.

Solution

The *gearing proportion* is calculated from the following formula:

$$\frac{\text{Average net borrowing}}{\text{Average net operating assets}} \times \frac{100}{1}$$

$$= \frac{\left(\frac{£800 + £600}{2}\right)}{\left(\frac{£2{,}780 + £3{,}460}{2}\right)} \times \frac{100}{1}$$

$$= \frac{£1{,}400}{£6{,}240} \times \frac{100}{1}$$

$$= 22\%$$

Therefore, the gearing adjustment, i.e. the amount to be added back to net profit, is:

$$(£186 + £174 + £59) \times \frac{22}{100}$$

$$= £92$$

The current cost Profit and Loss Account can now be drafted:

Current cost Profit and Loss Account for the year ended 31st December, 19–1

	£000	£000
Net profit before interest and tax as per the historic accounts		1,462
Less: Current cost adjustments:		
Depreciation	186	
Cost of sales	174	
Monetary working capital	59	
		419
Current cost operating profit		1,043
Add: Gearing adjustment	92	
Less: Interest payable	65	
		27
Current cost profit before tax		1,070

9.4 The Current Cost Balance Sheet

You should see from the following example that the current cost Balance Sheet is exactly the same in structure as the historic one with which you should already be familiar. The major distinguishing features are explained below the example:

Current Cost Balance Sheet as at 31 December, 19–1

	£000	£000	£000
Fixed assets, at replacement value			5,940
Accumulated depreciation			1,782
			4,158
Current assets			
Stocks, at replacement value		940	
Trade debtors		590	
Bank		47	
Cash		5	
		1,582	
Creditors: amounts falling due within one year			
Trade creditors	470		
Dividends proposed	200		
Corporation tax	180		
	—	850	
Net current assets			732
Total assets less current liabilities			4,890
Less			
Creditors: amounts falling due after one year			
12% Secured debentures			600
			4,290

Financed by	£
Called-up share capital	
3,000,000 £1 ordinary shares, fully paid	3,000
Reserves	
Current cost	720
Retained earnings	570
	4,290
Loan capital	
12% secured debentures	600
	4,890

Notes

Fixed assets These are shown at their replacement value at the Balance Sheet date and the accumulated depreciation is also based on this replacement value.

Stocks These are also shown at their replacement value at the Balance Sheet date. All other current assets and current liabilities are shown at the same values as those given in the historic cost Balance Sheet.

The current cost reserve This is crucial to the current cost accounting system since it is the means by which double-entry principles can be maintained when adjustments are made to the Profit and Loss Account and Balance Sheet. Without this reserve, to which counterbalancing entries can be put when the adjustments are made, the current cost Balance Sheet would not balance. Its use is illustrated more fully in the comprehensive example which now follows.

A comprehensive example The following are the summarised final accounts of CCA Ltd., prepared using the historic cost concept:

Profit and Loss Account for the year ended 31st December, 19–2

	£000	£000
Sales		31,200
Stock, 1st January, 19–2	750	
Purchases	23,405	
	24,155	
Stock, 31st December, 19–2	850	
Cost of goods sold		23,305
Gross profit		7,895
Running expenses	3,750	
Interest	120	
Depreciation	1,440	
		5,310
Net profit		2,585

Balance Sheet as at 31 December, 19–2

	£000	£000
Fixed assets, at cost		14,400
Accumulated depreciation		8,640
		5,760
Current assets		
Stocks, at cost	850	
Trade debtors	2,360	
Bank	842	
	4,052	
Creditors: amounts falling due within one year		
Trade creditors	2,240	
Net current assets		1,812
Total assets *less* current liabilities		7,572
Less		
Creditors: amounts falling due after one year		
10% Debentures		1,200
		6,372
Financed by		
Called-up share capital		3,000
Retained earnings		3,372
		6,372

The following information is also relevant:

1. There were no acquisitions or disposals of fixed assets during the year. At 31st December, 19–2, the assets are 6 years old. Depreciation is provided at the rate of 10% p.a. using the straight-line method.
2. There have been no changes in share or loan capital during the year.
3. At 1st January, 19–2, trade debtors and creditors amounted to £1,846,000 and £1,750,000 respectively. The bank balance was £745,000.
4. Relevant index numbers are given below:

Fixed assets	Index
When acquired	100
1st January, 19–2	120
31st December, 19–2	140

Stocks and monetary working capital	
When opening stock was acquired	220
1st January, 19–2	230
Average for 19–2	240
When closing stock was acquired	245
31st December, 19–2	250

Current Cost Accounting

Required:

A current cost Profit and Loss Account for the year ended 31st December, 19–2, and a current cost Balance Sheet also at the date.

Solution

The required statements are now shown, followed by explanatory notes. These should be referred to as you progress through the statements.

Current cost Profit and Loss Account for the year ended 31st December, 19–2

	£000	£000	Explanatory notes
Net profit before interest and tax as per the historic accounts		2,705	1
Less: Current cost adjustments			
Depreciation	432		2
Cost of sales	85		3
Monetary working capital	9		4
		526	
Current cost operating profit		2,179	
Add: Gearing adjustment	24		5
Less: Interest payable	120		
		96	
Current cost profit before tax		2,083	

Current Cost Balance Sheet as at 31 December, 19–2

	£000	£000	Explanatory notes
Fixed assets, at replacement value		20,160	5
Accumulated depreciation		12,096	
		8,064	
Current assets			
Stocks, at replacement value	867		5
Trade debtors	2,360		6
Bank	842		6
	4,069		
Creditors: amounts falling due within one year			
Trade creditors	2,240		
Net current assets		1,829	
Total assets *less* current liabilities		9,893	
Less			
Creditors: amounts falling due after one year			
10% Debentures		1,200	6
		8,693	

Financed by
Called-up share capital £3,000   6
Retained earnings 2,870   7
Current cost reserve 2,823   8

£8,693

Explanatory notes
(all calculations shown are in £000)

	£000
1 Net profit	2,585
Interest	120
	2,705

The interest will be shown as a deduction later in the statement, together with the gearing adjustment.

2 *Fixed assets*

Replacement value at 1st January, 19–2 = £14,400 × $\frac{120}{100}$

= £17,280

Replacement value at 31st December, 19–2 = £14,400 × $\frac{140}{100}$

= £20,160

Average replacement value for 19–2 = $\frac{£17,280 + £20,160}{2}$

= £18,720

£000

Depreciation based on average replacement value

= £18,720 × $\frac{10}{100}$ = 1,872

Depreciation based on historic cost = 1,440
Depreciation adjustment = 432

3 Cost of sales using mid-year values is as follows:

£000

Stock, 1st January 19–2 = £750 × $\frac{240}{220}$ = 818

Purchases = 23,405

24,223

Stock, 31st December, 19–2 = £850 × $\frac{240}{245}$ = 833

Current Cost of sales = 23,390

Cost of sales adjustment = Current cost of sales – Historic cost of sales

= £23,390 – £23,305
= £85

Current Cost Accounting

4 The total change in monetary working capital:

	£
Monetary working capital at 1st January, 19–2	
= £1,846 – £1,750	= 96
Monetary working capital at 31st December, 19–2	
= £2,360 – £2,240	= 120
Increase in monetary working capital	24

The real change in monetary working capital:

1st January, 19–2 = $£96 \times \dfrac{240}{230}$ = 100

31st December, 19–2 = $£120 \times \dfrac{240}{250}$ = 115

$\underline{15}$

	£
Total change in monetary working capital	24
Real change in monetary working capital	15
Monetary working capital adjustment	9

5 The gearing proportion is calculated from the current cost values at the beginning and end of the year:

At 1st January, 19–2 £000
Fixed assets at replacement value (see note 1) 17,280
Accumulated Depreciation = 5 years × £1,728 p.a. 8,640
 8,640

Stocks, at replacement value = $£750 \times \dfrac{230}{220}$ = 784

Monetary working capital (see note 4) 96
Net operating assests 9,520

Net borrowing
Debentures 12,00
Less: bank 745
Net borrowing 455

Therefore, the gearing proportion at 1st January, 19–2, is:

$= \dfrac{£455}{£9,520} \times \dfrac{100}{1} = 5\%$

At 31st December, 19–2 £000
Fixed assets at replacement value (see note 1) 20,160
Accumulated depreciation = 6 years × £2,016 12,096
 8,064

Stock, at replacement value = $£850 \times \dfrac{250}{245}$ 867

Monetary working capital (see note 4) 120
Net operating assests 9,051

Net borrowing
Debentures 1,200
Less: Bank 842
 358

Therefore, the gearing proportion at 31st December, 19–2 is:
$$\frac{£358}{£9,051} \times \frac{100}{1} = 4\%$$

Therefore, average gearing proportion for 19–2 is:
$$\frac{5\% + 4\%}{2} = 4.5\%$$

$$\text{Gearing adjustment} = £526 \times \frac{4.5}{100} = £24$$

6 As per the historic accounts

	£000
7 Undistributed profits as at 31st December, 19–2	3,372
Less: Net profit for 19–2	2,585
	787
Add: Current cost profit	2,083
	2,870

	£000
8 Increase in net value of fixed assets = £8,064 − £5,760	2,304
Increase in value of stocks = £867 = £850	17
Current cost adjustments	
Depreciation	432
Cost of sales	85
Monetary working capital	9
	2,847
Less: Gearing adjustment	24
	2,823

Summary

This chapter has shown that in order to adjust for the effects of inflation, a system of current cost accounting has been developed which requires the preparation of a current cost Profit and Loss Account and Balance Sheet. The purpose and calculation of the main current cost adjustments has been explained and a comprehensive example given to illustrate the fundamentals of the system in its entirety. The net result of the use of this system is that a more realistic view of the operating performance of the organisation (in terms of profits and profitability) and its financial standing is given than is the case with accounts prepared using the historic cost concept.

Assignments

9.1 An organisation bought plant and machinery on the 1st January, 19–1, for £40,000 when the relevant price index was 100. As a policy, the organisation provides for depreciation at a rate of 10% p.a., on the straight-line basis. Given that the index number showed values of 120 on the 31st December, 19–1, and 150 on the 31st December, 19–2, show the entries that would appear in the balance sheets on these dates if the principles of CCA are observed. Calculate the depreciation adjustment for each year.

9.2 The managing director of your organisation has recently been presented with a draft of the current cost profit statement for the last financial period. Since he is not familiar with the principles of CCA, he has asked you to prepare a memorandum, explaining clearly the four current cost adjustments shown in the statement. He is particularly concerned about their financial implications for the shareholders of the company. The statement is given below.

Current cost profit statement for the year ended 30th June, 19–1

	£	£
Net profit as per historic accounts		146,540
Less: Current cost adjustments		
Cost of sales	11,482	
Depreciation	5,896	
Monetary working capital	2,409	
		19,787
Current cost operating profit		126,753
Plus: Gearing adjustment		2,272
Current cost profit before tax		129,025

9.3 The final accounts of LBB PLC for the year ended 31st December, 19–4, prepared on the historic cost basis, are given below:

Profit and Loss Account Year ended 31st December, 19–4

	£000	£000
Sales		8,400
Opening stock	400	
Purchases	4,200	
	4,600	
Closing stock	800	
		3,800
Gross profit		4,600
Operating expenses	3,790	
Depreciation	150	
		3,940
Net profit		660

Balance Sheet as at 31st December, 19–4

	£000	£000
Fixed assets		
At cost	1,500	
Depreciation to date	600	
		900
Current Assets		
Stocks	800	
Bank	420	
		1,220
		2,120

	£000		£000
Ordinary share capital			860
Profit and loss balance			1,260
			2,120

The following additional information is available:
  (a) Purchases and sales are made on a cash basis only
  (b) The fixed assets were purchased on 1st January, 19–1, and are being depreciated at 10% on cost p.a.
  (c) Stocks held on 31st December are normally acquired during December.
  (d) Index numbers showing the movement in the price of certain assets are as follows:

	Stock	Fixed assets
1st January, 19–1		150
Average for December, 19–3	120	
31st December, 19–3	122	175
Average for 19–4	125	190
Average for December, 19–4	127	
31st December, 19–4	130	200

Required:

(a) Calculate the cost of sales adjustment and the depreciation adjustment and then draft the current cost Profit and Loss Account for the year.

(b) Draft the current cost Balance Sheet for 31st December, 19–4.

9.4 The final accounts of Righton PLC, prepared on a historic cost basis, are given below

Profit and Loss Account Year ended 31st December, 19–6

	£000	£000
Sales		47,486
Cost of sales		31,247
Gross profit		16,239
Operating expenses	14,575	
Depreciation	400	
Debenture interest	240	
		15,215
Net profit		1,024

Balance Sheets as at 31st December

	19–5 £000	19–5 £000	19–6 £000	19–6 £000
Fixed assets				
At cost	4,000		4,000	
Depreciation	2,000		2,400	
		2,000		1,600
Current assets				
Stocks	2,140		2,390	
Debtors	3,210		3,710	
Bank	370		235	
		5,720		6,335
		7,720		7,935
Called-up capital		2,000		2,000
Profit and loss balance		971		1,995
Debentures (12%)		2,800		2,000
Current liabilities				
Creditors		1,949		1,940
		7,720		7,935

The following information is available:

(a) Fixed assets were aquired on the 1st January, 19–1, and are being depreciated at 10% p.a. on cost.

(b) Stocks and monetary working capital at 31st December accrue evenly during December.

(c) Price indices showing the movement in certain items are given below:

	Stock and monetary working capital	Fixed assets
1st January, 19–1		200
Average for December, 19–5	150	
31st December, 19–5	150	400
Average for 19–6	170	460
Average for December, 19–6	180	
31st December, 19–6	180	500

Required:

(a) Calculate all relevant current cost adjustments and prepare the current cost Profit and Loss Accounts for the year ended 31st December, 19–6.

(b) Prepare the current cost Balance Sheet as at 31st December, 19–6.

10 Preparing Accounts from Incomplete Records

When you have read this chapter and completed the assignments at the end, you should:
- understand why accounts must sometimes be prepared from incomplete records
- be able to prepare Final Accounts from incomplete records
- have revised some important accounting principles

10.1 Introduction

Chapters 5 and 6 have shown how it is possible to prepare Final Accounts when a full set of accounting records has been maintained. Ideally, these records are based on sound double-entry principles. This means that at the end of the accounting period, Final Accounts are normally prepared in the following manner:

- the balances on the accounts in the ledger are extracted and a preliminary trial balance is drafted
- corrections and period-end adjustments are made to these balances
- the adjusted figures are then used to prepare the final accounts

Even when records have been maintained properly, many hours can be spent checking and adjusting the ledger accounts before they are used for final accounts purposes. This task is lengthened considerably when full records are not available.

However, the main aim of this chapter is to demonstrate that with a sound knowledge of double-entry book keeping and the concepts and conventions which guide the accountant's work, it is possible to prepare a set of Final Accounts from incomplete records.

10.2 The reasons for incomplete records

There are a number of reasons why organisations may not have a complete set of accounting records from which to work. The first is where records have been kept but have been partly lost or destroyed. This certainly does happen but is less frequent than is suggested by the number of assignments and examination questions based on this assumption. Most organisations maintain duplicate records, particularly where the accounting system is maintained by computer and records are easier to damage. The second is where full accounting records have not been kept by the organisation, either because of ignorance of the need for such records or because the process of maintaining a full system is considered troublesome, time-consuming and unnecessary. It is quite true that with small organisations, where there are none or few credit transactions, an analysed cash book, ruled in the appropriate manner, can provide an adequate record of business transactions and be kept with the minimum of effort. Preparing accounts from these records is relatively easy.

Finally, incomplete records exist where organisations assess their future financial plans by preparing and analysing budgeted final accounts. These can only be prepared on the basis of projected future transactions and how they would be dealt with by the accounting system. Of course, budgeted accounts are based on a number of assumptions that may not hold in reality. This whole area of accounting is covered in Chapter 15 of the book.

10.3 Final accounts from incomplete records

This section explains how a set of Final Accounts can be prepared by considering an example of a small organisation.

Example Mrs A. Morgan has a retail shop from which glass and china are sold for cash and on credit. You have been asked by her to prepare Final Accounts for the year ended 30th June, 19-1, and you have obtained the following information:

1. A friend of Mrs Morgan, who is training to be an accountant, had agreed to prepare her accounts last year but had left them unfinished when he discovered that he could be barred from membership of the profession as a result. From the work he had done, you are able to ascertain that on 30th June, 19-0, business

assets and liabilities were as follows:

	£
Equipment, at cost	5,800
Equipment, depreciation	1,740
Stock, at cost	2,560
Debtors	2,980
Rent prepaid	400
Creditors	1,290
Light and heat owing	120

2. Mrs Morgan has kept an analysed cash book from which you have extracted the following summary:

	£	£
Balance, 1st July, 19–0	750	
Cash received	33,620	
Cash paid to creditors		19,440
Rent		4,640
Rates		1,200
Wages		5,260
Sundry expenses		680
Light and heat		970
Balance, 30th June, 19–1		2,180
	34,370	34,370

The cash received is mostly cash sales and receipts from debtors. However, when you query this figure you are told that £3,000 of this amount represents a loan from a friend who has agreed to accept a rate of interest of 15% p.a. This has not been paid. In addition, Mrs Morgan has taken £7,500 for her personal use and paid sundry expenses of £170 from cash receipts. These have not been recorded. Otherwise, all payments and receipts have been through the business bank account.

3. From further checking of the records, such as they are, you have been able to obtain the following information about the financial position of the business at 30th June, 19–1:

(a) Debtors from credit sales are £1,970.
(b) Creditors for goods applied are £1,520.
(c) £300 is owing for rates.
(d) Sundry expenses include a payment of £75 for an advertisement in a local paper that will appear in the middle of July, 19–1.

4. There have been no additions or disposals of equipment during the year.

5. From stock sheets prepared by Mrs Morgan, the value of stock at 30th June, 19–1, is £2,150. This is a cost valuation and includes items totalling £420 which have been damaged and are unlikely to fetch more than £95.

6. Mrs Morgan expects to use the equipment for 10 years.

Preparing Accounts from Incomplete Records

Solution

The Final Accounts of Mrs Morgan's business, i.e. Profit and Loss Account, Balance Sheet, and a Sources and Applications of Funds Statement, are now shown together with explanatory notes. You are advised to work through the statements systematically, making reference to the notes where appropriate.

A. Morgan
Profit and Loss Account for the year ended 30th June, 19–1

	£	£	Explanatory notes
Sales		37,280	1
Stock, 1st July, 19–0	2,560		
Purchases	19,670		
	22,230		2
Stock, 30th June, 19–1	1,825		3
Cost of goods sold		20,405	
Gross profit		16,875	
Rent	5,040		4
Rates	1,500		5
Wages	5,260		
Sundry expenses	775		6
Light and heat	850		7
Loan interest	450		8
Depreciation	580		9
		14,455	
Net profit		2,420	

A. Morgan
Balance Sheet as at 30th June, 19–1

	£	£	£	Explanatory notes
Fixed assets				
Equipment, at cost		5,800		
Accumulated depreciation		2,320		10
			3,480	
Current assets				
Stock		1,825		
Debtors		1,970		
Prepayments		75		11
Bank		2,180		
		6,050		
Current liabilities				
Creditors	1,520			
Accruals	750			12
		2,270		
Working capital			3,780	
Capital employed			7,260	

Balance Sheet (continued)

Financed by
Capital

	£	Explanatory notes
Balance, 1st July, 19–0	9,340	13
Net profit	2,420	
	11,760	
Drawings	7,500	
Balance, 30th June, 19–1	4,260	
Long-term loan (15%)	3,000	
	7,260	

A. Morgan
Sources and Applications of Funds Statement for the year ended 30th June, 19–1

	£	£	Explanatory notes
Sources of funds			
Net profit	2,420		
Depreciation	580		
Contribution from trading		3,000	
Loan		3,000	
		6,000	
Applications of funds			
Drawings		7,500	
Decrease in working capital		1,500	
Increases/(decreases) in working capital			14
Decrease in stock		(735)	
Decrease in debtors		(1,010)	
Decrease in prepayments		(325)	
Increase in bank		1,430	
Increase in creditors		(230)	
Increase in accruals		(630)	
		(1,500)	

Explanatory notes and calculations

1

	£
Cash received	33,620
Less: Loan	3,000
	30,620
Add: Drawings	7,500
Sundry expenses	170
Debtors, 30th June, 19–1	1,970
	40,260
Less: Debtors, 1st July, 19–0	2,980
Sales	37,280

2

	£
Cash paid to creditors	19,440
Add: Creditors, 30th June, 19–1	1,520
	20,960
Less: Creditors, 1st July, 19–0	1,290
Purchases	19,760

3

Stock, at cost	2,150
Less: Write-down of damaged stock (£420–£95)	325
Stock at the lower of cost and net realisable value	1825

Remember that when there is a choice of asset valuations, the convention of *conservatism* or *prudence* should be observed, i.e. the value which understates rather than overstates profit should be chosen. In the case of the damaged stock, it is written down to its net realisable value, thus observing the recommendation of SSAP 9.

4

	£
Rent paid	4,640
Add: Rent prepaid at 1st July, 19–0	400
	5,040

5

Rates paid	1,200
Add: Rates owing at 30th June, 19–1	300
	1,500

6

Expenses paid	680
Add: Expenses not recorded	170
	850
Less: Payments in advance	75
	775

7

Light and heat paid	970
Less: Owing at 1st July, 19–0	120
	850

8 15% of £3,000   450

9 10% of £5,800   580

10

Accumulated depreciation: 1st July, 19–0	1,740
Add: Provision for the year	580
	2,320

11 The advertising paid for in advance

12

Rates	300
Loan interest	450
	750

13 Using the accounting equation:

Capital = Assets − Liabilities

the balance of capital at 1st July, 19–0, is calculated as follows:

Assets	£	£
Equipment, at cost		5,800
Less: accumulated depreciation		1,740
		4,060

	£	£
Stock		2,560
Debtors		2,980
Rent prepaid		400
Bank		750
		10,750
Liabilities		
Creditors	1,290	1,410
Light and heat owing	120	9,340
Balance as at 1st July, 19-0		

14 You will remember from Chapter 8 that this part of the statement can be a little tricky. You should therefore recall two important rules:

- Increases in current assets will increase working capital while decreases will decrease it
- Increases in current liabilities will decrease working capital while decreases will increase it

10.4 Budgeted Final Accounts

By necessity, these must be prepared from incomplete records because they relate to a future accounting period for which no actual transactions have taken place. Budgeted accounts are extremely important as they usually provide the basis for an initial evaluation of an organisation's plans. If the results revealed by these accounts are deemed to be unsatisfactory, then a number of alternative strategies can be evaluated.

The following is a typical example which illustrates this situation.

Example John Blunt plans to start business on 1st July, 19-1, by introducing capital of £20,000 which will be paid into a business bank account. He will make immediate payments of £10,000 for a lease on premises and £11,800 for equipment. In addition, he will buy stock, costing £4,800 on credit. Suppliers have agreed to give him two months' credit and he plans to maintain his stock at this level throughout the year. John has made some preliminary calculations and has put together the following estimates:

1. Sales are likely to be between £7,000 and £12,000 per month, depending on customer response and the reaction of his main competitors. All sales will be on credit and customers are expected to take a credit period of one month.

2. He expects to earn an average gross margin of 20%.

3. During the first year of trading, he will incur the following

expenses:

Rent and rates	4,000
Sundry expenses	2,000

These costs will remain fixed whatever the level of sales achieved. The lease is for ten years and the equipment will be used for five years, after which it will be scrapped for £1,800.

4. He intends to withdraw £800 per month from the business for his personal use.

Required:

In order to help him assess the viability of his plans for the first twelve months of trading, you are asked to prepare the budgeted Final Accounts for the period if sales average £7,000 per month.

Solution

As with the previous example, the required Final Accounts are shown, followed by explanatory notes. Refer to the notes as you proceed through the statements.

J. Blunt
Budgeted Profit and Loss Account for the year ended 30th June, 19–2

	£	£	Explanatory Notes
Sales		84,000	1
Cost of goods sold		67,200	2
Gross profit		16,800	
Rent and rates	4,000		
Sundry expenses	2,000		
Depreciation:			
Lease	1,000		3
Equipment	2,000		
		9,000	
Net profit		7,800	

J. Blunt
Budgeted Balance Sheet as at 30th June, 19–2

	Cost £	Accumulated depreciation £	Net	Explanatory Notes
Fixed assets				
Leasehold premises	10,000	1,000	9,000	
Equipment	11,000	2,000	9,800	
	21,800	3,000	18,800	

Budgeted Balance Sheet (continued)

	£	£	Explanatory Notes
Current assets			
Stock, at cost		4,800	4
Debtors		7,000	5
		11,800	
Current liabilities			
Bank overdraft	1,200		6
Creditors	11,200		7
		12,400	
Working capital		(600)	
Capital employed		18,200	
Financed by			
Capital			
Balance 1st July, 19–1		20,000	
Net profit		7,800	
		27,800	
Drawings		9,600	
		18,200	

Sources and Applications of Funds Statement for the year ended 30th June, 19–2

	£	£	Explanatory Notes
Sources of funds			8
Net profit	7,800		
Depreciation: Lease	1,000		
Equipment	2,000		
Contribution from trading		10,800	
Applications of funds			
Lease	10,000		
Equipment	11,800		
Drawings	9,600		
		31,400	
Decrease in working capital		20,600	
Increases/(decreases) in working capital			
Increase in stock		4,800	
Increase in debtors		7,000	
Decrease in bank		(21,200)	
Increase in creditors		(11,200)	
		(20,600)	

Explanatory notes and calculations

1 £7,000 × 12 months = £84,000.

2 With an expected gross margin of 20% of sales, cost of goods sold will be 80% of sales, i.e.

80% of £84,000 = £67,200

3 Straight-line depreciation of the lease over 10 years, i.e. £1,000 p.a.
The equipment cost £11,800 with an estimated salvage value of £1,800. The net cost is therefore £10,000, giving an annual depreciation provision of £2,000.

4 Stock of £4,800 is bought at the beginning of the year and it is maintained at this level until the end.

5 With one month's credit offered to customers, the money from sales in June will be outstanding at the end of June.

6 The closing balance at the bank is calculated as follows:

	£	£
Balance 1st July, 19–1		20,000
Receipts from debtors (£84,000–£7,000)		77,000
		97,000
Payments to creditors (£7,000 × 80% × 10 months + £4,800)	60,800	
Lease	10,000	
Equipment	11,800	
Rent and rates	4,000	
Sundry expenses	2,000	
Drawings (£800 × 12 months)	9,600	
		98,200
Balance, 30th June, 19–2		(1,200)

7 £7,000 × 80% × 2 months = £11,200.

8 The statement is drawn up on the assumption that the opening balances are:

Bank	£20,000
Capital	£20,000

Summary

There are three basic reasons why Final Accounts must sometimes be prepared from incomplete records:

- accounts have been lost or damaged
- accounts have not been kept because of ignorance or apathy
- Budgeted accounts are being prepared for a future period

With a sound understanding of double-entry bookkeeping and the conventional measurement and valuation concepts used by accountants, it should be possible to prepare a valid set of Final Accounts from basic information. This will typically include:

- A summary of cash payments and receipts

- a summary of expenses for the period, adjusted for prepayments and accruals
- valuations for fixed assets, current assets and current liabilities for the beginning and end of the period

It should be stressed, however, that the preparation of the Final Accounts is only the first stage in the accounting process. The information contained in these accounts must then be analysed and used in an appropriate manner.

Assignments

10.1 From the data given in Section 10.4 for J. Blunt:
(a) Prepare a set of budgeted Final Accounts, on the assumption that sales are £12,000 per month.
(b) On the basis of the two sets of accounts, prepare a brief financial report, outlining the owner's prospects for the first twelve months of trading.

10.2 R. Stornaway, a building worker, was made redundant in November, 19-5. He had, however, accumulated some savings and he also received some redundancy pay. On 1st January, 19-6, the total capital he held in cash was £5,800. On this day he was faced with two different propositions:
1. To place all his capital in a bank deposit account for the next twelve months at an interest rate of 10% p.a. In addition, he would take a job in a factory for a weekly wage of £100.00 throughout the year.
2. To stay in the building trade and run a jobbing business on his own account, using all his existing capital in his business venture.

He decided on the latter course and started business operations on 1st January, 19-6, with all of his initial capital in cash.

The following information was available on his business activities for the year ended 31st December, 19-6:

	£
Cash used for private purposes	3,000
Motor van bought for business use	750
Petrol and running costs	253
Cash receipts for work done for households	950
Amounts paid to creditors for materials used	6,890
Amounts received from building contractors for work done	9,050
Creditors for materials at 31st December, 19-6	740
Wages paid to casual labour	350
Payments for stationery and postage	35
A small stock of stationery existed at 31st December, 19-6	11
Audit charges not yet paid	25
Amounts owing to Stornaway at 31st December, 19-6 for work done for builders	1,750
Loose tools adquired	300
Sundries	90

Stornaway has decided to depreciate his motor van by 20% and his loose tools by 25%. All receipts and payments were in cash.

Required:

(a) A Profit and Loss Account for the year ending 31st December, 19–6.

(b) A Balance Sheet on that date.

(c) An analysis of whether Stornaway was wise to go into his own business or not.

(*University of London adapted*)

10.3 Sheriff Ltd. commences business on 1st July, 19–6.
1. Initial requirements are:
   Furniture and equipment £3,500   Stock of materials £2,800
   One month's credit is given by all suppliers. Material stocks are replaced during the month in which the material is used, with stock at the end of each month maintained at £2,800.
2. Goods are sold at 33⅓% above cost of materials and all customers are allowed two months' credit. Sales are £2,000 per month for the first three months and £3,000 per month after that.
3. Monthly expenses paid out in cash are £460, (exclusive of rates and insurance of £500 which is paid in July, and advertising of £950 paid for in August). Both of these payments are for the whole financial year.
4. Depreciation for the six month period is estimated at £300.

Required:

Prepare a Profit and Loss Account for the half year ended 31st December, 19–6, and a Balance Sheet at the same date, assuming that the opening share capital is £8,000 and any additional needs were met with the aid of a bank overdraft.

10.4 On 1st January last the Balance Sheet of J. Walsh was as follows:

	£	£
Fixed assets		
Equipment		2,500
Current assets		
Stocks	3,180	
Debtors	2,200	
Bank	920	
	6,300	
Less: Current liabilities		
Creditors	1,700	
Working capital		4,600
Net assets employed		7,100
Financed by		
Capital		6,000
Loan		1,100
		7,100

Business transactions for Walsh's last trading year can be summarised as follows:

	£
Payments to suppliers	27,250
Receipts from customers	39,725
Private drawings	5,000
Salaries and wages	6,500
Sundry expenses	1,660
Discounts allowed	740
Discounts received	480

All receipts and payments were paid through the bank account.

At the year end 31st December, the stock was valued at £3,578, sundry expenses paid in advance amounted to £90, trade debtors to £2,564 and trade creditors to £3,110.

Depreciation is at the rate of 10% p.a. on cost.

Required:

Prepare a Profit and Loss Account and Balance Sheet at the year end.

10.5 A. Bucket and J. Cloth started in business as Windowclean Ltd. on 1st January, 19-1, and contributed on initial capital of £8,000 each for 16,000 £1 ordinary shares.

A business bank account was opened and they acquired the lease on premises for £5,000, bought ladders and equipment for £2,000 and two small motor vans for £3,500 each. The remaining £2,000 provided working capital while the business expanded.

Unfortunately, neither Bucket nor Cloth had any knowledge of keeping business accounts and proper records were not maintained during the year. However, from their bank's statements, you have been able to ascertain the following:

Payments for the year:

	£
Rent	1,800
Rates	660
Light and heat	320
Motor expenses	3,440
Directors' salaries	16,000
Stationery and postage	240
Advertising and promotion	450
Receipts from customers	28,620

From discussions with Bucket and Cloth, you ascertain the following information:

1. Rent of £300 has been paid in advance.
2. Rates of £120 are owing.
3. There is a bill outstanding for advertising for £45.
4. Motor vans will be used for 5 years and then be replaced. The estimated salvage value for each is £500.
5. Equipment will be used for 10 years and have a residual value of £200.

6. The lease had 4 years left to run when it was acquired.
7. Customers owe the business £560.

Required:

Prepare the Final Accounts for 19–1, including a Profit and Loss Account, Balance Sheet and a Sources and Applications of Funds Statement.

10.6 Newbold Ltd. commenced trading on 1st January, 19–1, and the directors are reviewing their plans for the first twelve months of operation. Their bank has agreed to provide overdraft facilities on the condition that by the end of December, 19–1, the current ratio will be at least 2:1 and the liquid ratio will be 1.5:1. In order to meet this requirement, the shareholders have agreed to inject sufficient capital when required.

The estimates already prepared are as follows:

(a) There will be some variation in monthly sales but on average this will amount to £15,000. Two-thirds of the sales are on credit and by the end of the year, it is estimated that 1½ months' sales will be outstanding from customers.
(b) Gross profit margin will average 50% on sales, and stock holding will be equivalent to 3 months' sales by the end of the year. One months' credit will be received from suppliers.
(c) Running expenses have been estimated at £68,400, and in addition fixed assets costing £25,000 will be acquired at the beginning of the year. These will be used for 8 years and have no residual value.
(d) The bank balance will be consistent with this information.
(e) The shareholders have agreed not to take a dividend for the first two years of operation to allow the business a chance to 'get off the ground'.

Required:

Prepare the Profit and Loss Account for 19–1 and Balance Sheet at 31st December, 19–1, showing clearly the amount the shareholders will need to contribute.

10.7 Bill Brown acquired the business of Ted Pink on 1st January, 19–1. He took over all the assets and liabilities of the business as at that date and paid Pink the net book value. Unfortunately, Bill has lost all the records pertaining to this transaction but from discussion with him and Ted, you have ascertained the following information:

Balances as at 1st January, 19–1

	£
Fixed assets, at cost	19,000
Accumulated depreciation	8,600
Stocks, at cost	7,340
Debtors	2,680
Bank balance	750
Creditors	1,460

From cheque stubs, credit slips and an occasional bank statement he has kept, you have found that during the year takings banked amounted to £78,400, while payment for purchases amounted to £74,600. Other payments were as follows:

	£
Wages	4,630
Rent and rates	3,760
General expenses	1,480
Cash drawings	6,500
Fixed assets	2,600

Bill informs you that the drawings and £470 of the general expenses were paid out of the takings before the balance was banked. You have also been able to ascertain the following:

Balances as at 31st December, 19-1

	£
Stocks, at cost	5,140
Debtors	2,760
Creditors	1,320

Bill normally establishes his selling prices by using a mark-up on cost of 25%. However, because a fire destroyed some of his stock during August, he expects his overall profit margin to be lower than in previous years. However, due to his poor record-keeping, he has not been able to calculate the value of the stock he has lost.

Required:

Prepare a Profit and Loss Account for 19-1 and a Balance Sheet as at 31st December, 19-1. The Profit and Loss Account should show separately the loss of stock due to the fire. (Assume that it is appropriate to provide for depreciation at the rate of 25% on the reducing balance basis.)

11 Manufacturing Statements

When you have read this chapter you should be able to:
- understand the main elements and nature of costs
- prepare a Manufacturer's Operating Statement

11.1 Introduction

So far only trading organisations such as retailers and wholesalers have been considered. These firms act as middle men between the manufacturer and the end-customer. But what of those businesses which make things? We now turn to consider their accounting requirements which will include, in addition to the statements you have met, some sort of statement about their manufacturing operations. The aim of the present chapter is to introduce the main elements and divisions of costs and to show how manufacturer's Final Accounts are compiled. This should act as a prelude to more detailed work as production costs are closely linked with costing techniques which will be covered in later chapters.

11.2 Classifying costs

Before any detailed cost analysis can take place or decisions be made, management must know about the nature and behaviour of the costs involved. There are several ways of classifying the same costs, each of them looking at the same problem in a slightly different way, according to the reason why the information is needed.

Cost units and cost centres

Some materials, labour and expenses can be identified straight away with a particular cost unit, which means that those costs can be easily and precisely calculated, and directly linked to a specific unit of goods being made. Such *direct* costs, as they are known, belong to a unit of product or service. Examples of direct expenses include royalties, hire charges, production workers' wages and raw materials.

Other expenses, such as factory lighting, supervisors' wages, and rent, for example, can cover a number of different items of production. These costs are known as *indirect* costs or overheads and can often be identified with cost centres (see Chapter 12).

Cost behaviour at different levels of output

Some costs tend to be unaffected by variations in the level of output. They are therefore known as *fixed* costs. A good example is rent on factory premises under a lease agreement (see Figure 11.1)

Figure 11.1
Fixed cost

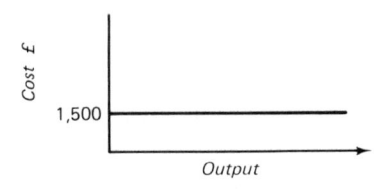

Figure 11.1 shows that the rent will be £1,500. Whatever the output, rent will have to be paid regardless of whether the works are closed or operating at full capacity. However, these costs may only be fixed over a set time period or range of output. Figure 11.2 assumes, for example, that the existing factory premises have a capacity of 5,000 units and therefore more space will be needed if demand exceeds this level. Hence there will be step-ups in rental costs for extra blocks of capacity (in this case floor space).

Figure 11.2
Stepped fixed costs

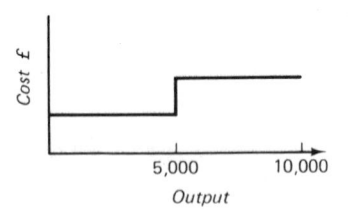

Some costs, however, vary directly with output. For example, raw material costs will depend on how many items are produced. As long as the unit price is constant the relationship can be shown as in Figure 11.3

Incidentally, it should be obvious to you that each unit of output

Manufacturing Statements 183

Figure 11.3 Variable costs

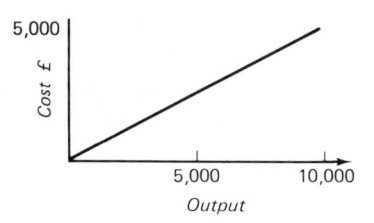

contains raw materials worth 50 p, i.e.

$$\frac{£5,000}{10,000 \text{ units}}$$

However, in the commercial world it often happens that discounts are available on bulk purchases. Figure 11.4 shows this situation but with a unit price reduction after 6,000 units. What is the discount price?

Figure 11.4 Variable cost decreasing

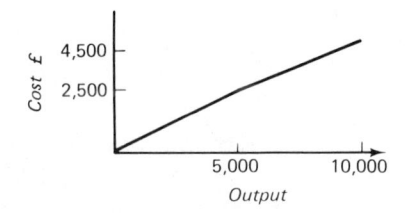

Orders of 5,000 units or less result in a unit price of 50p but anything over this level gains a discount of 10p. This can be seen from the diagram because the second 5,000 units cost only £2,000 (£4,500 − £2,500), i.e.

$$\frac{£2,000}{5,000 \text{ units}} = 40\text{p per unit}$$

Conversely, costs might shift upwards after a certain output level. Direct wage costs may be boosted by shift allowances or overtime once a certain production level has been achieved. Or, using our raw material example, unit costs may actually be larger as the firm pays penalty prices or market rates for a scarce resource. Figure 11.5 shows a position where a firm has to turn to a second (and

Figure 11.5 Variable cost increasing

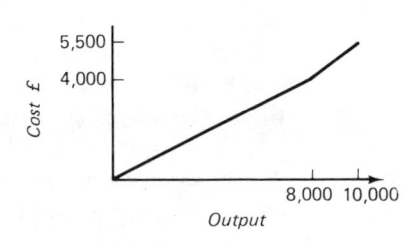

more expensive) supplier having exhausted its main allocation of 8,000 units. What is the spot price?

The extra 2,000 units cost £1,500 which means that a unit charge of £1,500/2,000 = 75p must be paid. This is 25p above the main supplier's rate.

Finally, there are some costs which are partly fixed and partly variable: these are known as semi-variable costs. For example, a sales person could be on a fixed basic salary plus commission once a certain sales level is reached. In Figure 11.6 commission would start to be earned on top of the £8,000 basic salary once 5,000 units had been sold. You can see that the basic salary could be doubled if 10,000 units per time period can be sold.

Figure 11.6 Semi-variable cost

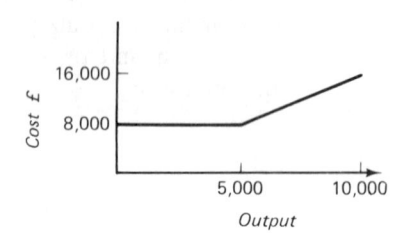

Amongst other things, the classification of costs into fixed, variable and semi-variable, provides a useful basis for break-even analysis and price–volume decision making (see Chapter 13).

Control of costs

A third way of looking at costs is from the management viewpoint of whether a cost is controllable or not. Some costs, such as a nationally agreed wage rate, an oil price rise or a change in VAT, are outside the control of business; they are *externally* imposed. On the other hand, certain costs should be within the direct control of management. The annual advertising budget is an example of a predetermined sum which should not be exceeded; although its component parts might vary, the overall total remains set. Similarly, cash limits can be set in other areas.

Obviously, it is much easier to plan costs which are present or are controllable because they are known with a reasonable degree of accuracy in advance. For planning purposes it makes sense to try and bring under control costs which were previously regarded as uncontrollable. For example, it may be possible to negotiate fixed-price contracts with suppliers of raw materials, thereby guaranteeing prices for the whole planning period. Alternatively materials could be bought at known prices for delivery sometime in the future (known as the futures market).

The nature of the item

A distinction can be made between labour, material and overhead costs, normally with a further subdivision of overhead costs by function (production, selling, administration, finance etc). Using this classification, the basic elements of cost are shown in Table 11.1

Table 11.1 *Classification of costs*

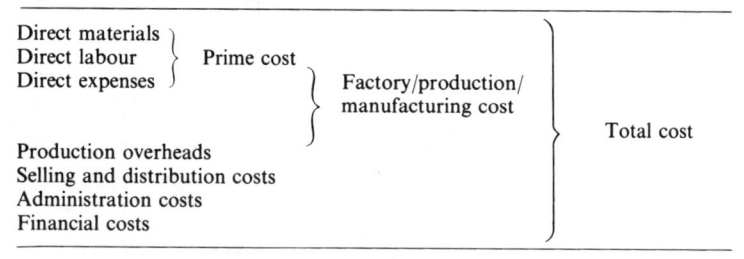

Direct materials ⎫
Direct labour   ⎬ Prime cost ⎫
Direct expenses ⎭   ⎬ Factory/production/ ⎫
⎭   manufacturing cost ⎬ Total cost
Production overheads   ⎭
Selling and distribution costs
Administration costs
Financial costs   ⎭

In effect, Table 11.1 represents a summary of the cost side of a Manufacturer's Operating Statement which we shall now develop in more detail. A general format is shown in Figure 11.7.

11.3 The manufacturing statement

We have already mentioned that direct costs can be identified directly with the product being made, and normally include raw materials which end up in the finished product (direct materials), and the wages paid to employees engaged directly in its manufacture (direct wages). Sometimes there are also direct expenses, which arise if, for example, the organisation pays royalties for the right to manufacture a particular product, or if the product is part-processed by another organisation (perhaps work is subcontracted out) which makes a charge for the work. Collectively these direct costs are sometimes known as *prime* costs.

Production overheads, also known as factory indirect costs, are costs which cannot easily be linked with individual units or batches of output and normally include such items as factory rent, machine maintenance and supervisory salaries. Many of them are fixed, in that they will be constant whatever the level of output. In practice, however, it is often difficult to distinguish between direct and indirect costs as items may contain elements of both (some of these problems will be resolved in the next chapter).

The Manufacturer's Operating Statement classifies costs under these headings, ending up with a production cost (prime + production overheads) for a given period. Normally, no attempt is made to calculate profit in this account. This is usually left until the next part, i.e. the trading account is prepared. We should already be familiar with this and the remaining sections as these were

186 Accounting: A Practical Approach

Figure 11.7
General format for a manufacturer's Operating statement

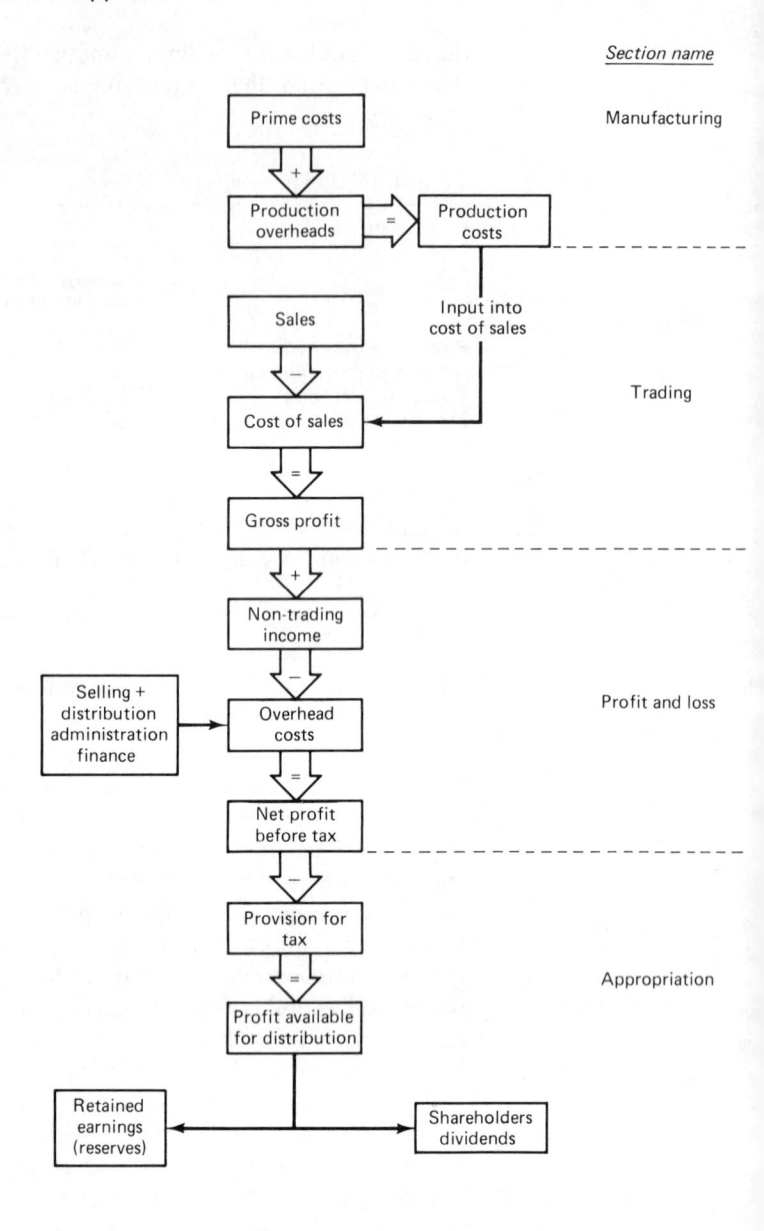

```
                    ┌──────────────┐
                    │ Prime costs  │                    Section name
                    └──────┬───────┘
                           + ↓                          Manufacturing
                    ┌──────────────┐    ┌──────────────┐
                    │  Production  │ =  │  Production  │
                    │  overheads   │──▶ │    costs     │
                    └──────────────┘    └──────┬───────┘
                                               │
                    ┌──────────────┐    Input into
                    │    Sales     │    cost of sales
                    └──────┬───────┘
                           − ↓                          Trading
                    ┌──────────────┐           │
                    │ Cost of sales│◀──────────┘
                    └──────┬───────┘
                           = ↓
                    ┌──────────────┐
                    │ Gross profit │
                    └──────┬───────┘
                           + ↓
                    ┌──────────────┐
                    │  Non-trading │
                    │    income    │
                    └──────┬───────┘
┌──────────────┐           − ↓
│  Selling +   │    ┌──────────────┐                    Profit and loss
│ distribution │───▶│   Overhead   │
│administration│    │    costs     │
│   finance    │    └──────┬───────┘
└──────────────┘           = ↓
                    ┌──────────────┐
                    │  Net profit  │
                    │  before tax  │
                    └──────┬───────┘
                           − ↓
                    ┌──────────────┐
                    │ Provision for│
                    │     tax      │
                    └──────┬───────┘
                           = ↓
                    ┌──────────────┐
                    │Profit available│                  Appropriation
                    │for distribution│
                    └──────┬───────┘
                           │
        ┌──────────────┐   │   ┌──────────────┐
        │   Retained   │   │   │ Shareholders │
        │   earnings   │◀──┴──▶│  dividends   │
        │  (reserves)  │       │              │
        └──────────────┘       └──────────────┘
```

covered in earlier chapters. It might be useful at this point to skip back over the elements of a trader's Profit and Loss Account to remind yourself of the format and the main concepts used. Some organisations obtain estimates of how much it would cost them to buy in, as finished products, the output they have manufactured themselves. By comparing this figure with their own manufacturing costs, a manufacturing profit or loss can be determined and the future of the organisation's manufacturing operations assessed.

Sometimes goods are transferred from the factory to the sales department at wholesale price or at a fixed percentage above cost in order to show a separate manufacturing profit.

This information will focus management attention on particular items of cost which will be subjected to more detailed analysis.

Example A Manufacturer's Operating Statement will now be compiled from the following base data. It will be shown in separate sections with notes for demonstration purposes.

The balances of J. D. Osgerby Ltd, a manufacturing company, are given below for the year ending 31st March, 19–7:

	£
Raw materials at 1st April, 19–6	5,980
Finished goods at 1st April, 19–6	6,250
Purchases: Finished goods	13,540
Raw materials	22,770
Delivery to customers	940
Delivery costs on components	1,220
Manufacturing: Wages	14,500
Royalties	250
Depreciation: Delivery vans	375
Machinery	530
Work-in-progress 1st April, 19–6	1,200
Discounts received	1,000
Interest from investment	200
Sales	101,250
Sales office salaries	13,740
Foreman's salary	12,500
Loose tools at start	600
Salespeople's commission	300
General expenses	13,000
Audit fee	275
Advertising	1,500
Provision for doubtful debts	100
Rates	749

Notes:
1. Stock at 31st March, 19–7: Raw materials £7,532, finished goods £5,360, loose tools £560, work-in-progress £1,060.
2. Bad debts amounting to £500 are to be written off and the provision for doubtful debts adjusted to £75.
3. Rates and general expenses are to be shared ¾ factory, ¼ administration.
4. Prepaid: Advertising £500.
    rates   £25.
5. Owing: General expenses £1,000.
    commission   £100.

Required:

1. Prepare a Manufacturer's Operating Statement and clearly show (a) prime cost, (b) factory cost, (c) cost of sales, (d) gross profit and (e) net profit.

2. Write a brief reply to the following:
During the year 50,000 units were manufactured. Another manufacturer, who has excess capacity, offers to supply these at £1 per unit. Would you accept the offer?

Solution

J. D. Osgerby Ltd
Manufacturing Statement – Year ending 31st March, 19–7

	£	£	Explanatory notes
Opening stock (raw materials)	5,980		
Plus: Purchases	22,770		
Plus: Delivery	1,220		1
	29,970		
Less: Closing stock (raw materials)	7,532		
Cost of materials used		22,438	
Manufacturing: Wages		14,500	
Royalties		250	
(a) *Prime cost*		37,188	
Depreciation (machinery)	530		
Foreman's salary	12,500		
Loose tools	40		
General expenses	10,500		
Rates	543		2
Factory indirect expenses		24,113	3
		61,301	
Plus: Opening stock (work-in-progress)		1,200	4
Less: Closing stock (work-in-progress)		1,060	
(b) *Factory cost of goods completed*		61,441	5

Explanatory notes

1. Opening stock is the unprocessed material brought forward from the previous accounting period. Although this stock was purchased and probably paid for in the previous period, it has been used in this period and will therefore count as part of the costs. Opening stock is added to the material purchases bought during the period which in this instance does not include delivery costs (sometimes called carriage in) which are shown as a separate item. The closing stock remaining at the end of the period represents unused stock that will be used next year. Therefore, it does not form part of this year's costs and is deducted.

2. Manufacturing wages and royalties are deemed to be direct costs and are therefore included in the *Prime cost* figure.

3. Depreciation on machinery, foreman's salary, loose tools, general expenses and rates are all examples of factory *indirect* expenses, some of which need further explanation. Note that for general expenses and rates $\frac{3}{4}$ are charges to the factory (see note 4). So rates will be

calculated as follows:

	£
Rates	749
Less: Prepaid (note 5)	25
	724

$\dfrac{724}{4} = £181$ to administration $\qquad 724 \times \tfrac{3}{4} = £543$ to factory

and

	£
General expenses	13,000
And owing (note 6)	1,000
	14,000

$\dfrac{14,000}{4} = £3,500$ to administration $\qquad 14,000 \times 3 = £10,500$ to factory

Loose tools (hammers, wrenches, screwdrivers etc.) were valued at £600 at the beginning of the period but at only £560 at the end (note 1). This could be due to pilferage, wear and tear, or many other things. It seems reasonable to represent the loss as a factory overhead expense.

4. Not only will manufacturers have stocks of unprocessed raw materials at the start and stocks of finished goods at the end, but also stocks of work-in-progress or partly finished products at various stages of completion along the way. These stocks are all treated in the same way (see note 1).

5. The production or factory cost figure will be plugged in to the next part of the trading account.

Trading account

	£	£	*Explanatory notes*
Sales		101,250	
Opening stock (finished goods)	6,250		6
Plus: Purchases	13,540		
Plus: Factory cost	61,441		
Less: Closing stock (finished goods)	5,360		
(c) *Cost of sales*		75,871	
(d) *Gross profits*		25,379	7

6. Notice that (as with raw materials and work-in-progress) adjustments have been made for opening and closing stocks of finished goods. This company is also buying in finished goods from outside (the purchases figure). This could be subcontract work to meet an extra order, for example.

7. The difference between sales revenue and cost of sales is, as we know, the gross profit. All businesses need to show a healthy profit at this stage because it is from gross profit that all non-manufacturing costs must be met. These are detailed in the Profit and Loss Account.

Profit and Loss Account

	£	£	£	Explanatory notes
Gross profit	25,379			
Plus: Discounts received	1,000			
Investment interest	200			
Decrease in provision for doubtful debts	25			8
			26,604	
Less: Selling and distribution expenses:				
Advertising	1,000			
Delivery	940			
Depreciation on vans	375			9
Sales office salaries	13,740			
Commission	400			
		16,455		
Administration expenses				
General expenses	3,500			10
Rates	181			
		3,681		
Financial expenses				
Bad debts	500			11
Audit fee	275			
		775		
Total expenses			20,911	
(e) *Net profit*			5,693	12

8. Non-trading income which includes discounts received (from suppliers) and investment interest is added on at this point. Note also that the level of doubtful debt provision has been reduced from £100 to £75. This is effectively a reduction in expenses of £25. Usually the adjustment is made in this section because the net effect of the reduction in doubtful debts is an increase in revenue (i.e. a cost reduction means bigger profits).

9. All selling and distribution expenses have been grouped together. Note that the advertising figure is net of the £500 prepaid for next year. Delivery costs to customers are transport expenses incurred in distribution and it seems reasonable to charge depreciation on vans to the selling section.

10. Administration expenses are fairly straightforward in this instance. The general expenses and rates calculations can be seen under note (3).

11. Bad debts and the audit fee have been placed in the financial expenses section. Arguably bad debts could feature in the selling and distribution section as they are a consequence of company sales and credit policy. This example serves to show that there are no hard and fast rules and that common sense should always prevail.

12. In sum, net profit is the difference between gross profit plus any non-trading revenues and all the non-manufacturing expenses incurred in running the business. These expenses will normally be divided into selling and distribution, administrative and financial expenses.

We now have an answer to part 1 of the question. The Manufacturer's Operating Statement has been compiled, albeit in sections so that components could be analysed and explained. We now turn to part 2.

If 50,000 units were manufactured during the year the unit cost would be

$$\frac{£61,441}{50,000 \text{ units}} = £1.23$$

Clearly therefore the buying-in price of £1 would result in a saving overall of £61,441 − £50,000 = £11,441. So, measured against external prices, Osgerby's manufacturing operations do not seem to be too efficient; there is a notional loss, particularly if the outside price includes a profit margin. Incidentally, some organisations use market values/buy-in prices as benchmarks by which to measure their own manufacturing profit or loss. These can also be used as transfer prices between departments (see the assignments).

This kind of comparative information can be used in make or buy decisions. Although the supplier is offering the goods at £11,441 less, the decision on whether to accept or not is by no means clear-cut. Clearly if the offer was accepted profits would rise by this amount and capital at present tied up in the business could be released for other purposes. But the potential saving may not outweigh factors such as undesirable unemployment and the loss of manufacturing status. Additionally, there is no guarantee that the arrangement is permanent. If the supplier finds alternative uses for his capacity he may switch supplies, or raise prices, in the future. This is likely if, for example, the £1 is an 'entry price' to gain a foothold in the market, or if it is an artificially low price, perhaps to off-load surplus stocks.

Summary

This chapter introduced the basic elements and nature of costs and various approaches to cost classification including:

- cost units and cost centres
- cost behaviour over different levels of output
- control of costs
- nature of the item

192 Accounting: A Practical Approach

An understanding of costs, how they behave and how they can be measured, is necessary for management to plan and control activity. Finally, some of this costing knowledge was used to develop, explain and present a detailed, sectionalised Manufacturer's Operating Statement. You should now work through the exercises to familiarise yourself with the techniques involved before proceeding to a more detailed analysis of costs in later chapters.

Assignments

11.1 A list of items which have been extracted from the accounts of McGregor PLC is shown in Figure 11.8. This list contains both cost and financial items.

Figure 11.8

Item	Cost elements Direct and indirect			Cost		Function
	Materials	Labour	Expenses	Prime	Overhead	
Welders' basic pay						
Office stationery						
Metallurgist's salary						
Advertising						
Cutter's shift allowance						
Sheet metal						
Taxation						
Salespeople's commission						
Foreman's salary						
Factory rent						
Bad debts provision						
Welding plant hire						
Cartons for packaging						
Depreciation on directors' cars						

Required:

For each cost item only, determine the elements of cost and whether each is a prime or overhead cost by placing a tick in the appropriate column. In addition, you should describe the function for each item.

11.2 The Woolwich Engineering Company Ltd. has two factories, one a foundry producing castings which are transported to the other, where they are machined and assembled with other components purchased from outside.

	Foundry £	Machine shop £
Stock of raw materials, 1st January	2,400	
Purchases of raw materials for the year	12,400	
Stock of raw materials, 31st December	3,000	
Stock of castings and other components, 1st January		3,000
Purchases of components other than castings during the year		7,000
Stock of castings and other components, 31st December		3,400
Work-in-progress, 1st January		980
Work-in-progress, 31st December		860
Direct wages	16,000	17,000
Fuel and power	2,000	3,000
Depreciation	900	1,200
Light and heat	1,200	1,300

The warehouse figures are as follows:

1st January, 19–6, stock of finished goods	3,000
31st December, 19–6, stock of finished goods	3,500
Warehouse wages for the year	13,000
Packing and delivery expenses	700
Sales	105,000

33,000 castings were transferred to the machine shop at £1 each, the price at which they could be purchased elsewhere. 20,000 machines were delivered to the warehouse at £4 each (again the buying-in price).

Required:

(a) A Manufacturing and Trading Account for the year ended 31st December, 19–6, showing the profit and/or loss on each stage of manufacture.
(b) Give very briefly your advice to the company based on your findings.
(c) Another supplier, who has excess capacity, offers to supply the machines at £3 each. Should Woolwich accept the offer?

11.3 Mr Sellen-Goode has a pleasant job with a salary of £10,000 p.a. which is supplemented by his investment income. He has property interests as well as money in the bank earning him 10% on deposit.

Mr Sellen-Goode identifies a demand for a new product, which he calls Ganna, at 1,000 units p. a. He makes the following notes:

1. Capital required £10,000.

2. Raw materials will cost £15 per unit.
3. Factory rent need not be paid because he can use one of his own properties instead of letting it out at £1,000 p.a.
4. His wife can give up her part-time job at the local school, where she earns £1,000 p.a., to look after the office side at home.
5. Machinery can be leased for £2,000 p.a.
6. One machinist would need to be employed, costing £4,000 p.a.
7. Power and workshop expenses would work out at some £1.50 per unit.
8. Office expenses would come out at approximately £10 per week.
9. All production could be sold at £35 per unit.
10. On leaving his present company Mr Sellen-Goode would have to forego a promised promotion to Sales Director at £13,000 p.a.

Another possibility emerges for his consideration when a potential customer offers to buy his idea and employ him at £15,000 p.a. The company reckon that they can manufacture Ganna on existing plant and machinery that is currently idle and their *only* expense would be for labour and power used.

Required:

(a) Manufacturing, Trading and Profit and Loss Accounts if Sellen-Goode manufactures.
(b) Show the advantage/disadvantage of his manufacturing.
(c) Show the advantage/disadvantage of his joining his potential customer.
(d) Show the wisdom or folly from the company's point of view if they take over Sellen-Goode and his idea.

11.4 Ball and Cheyne carried on business in partnership, manufacturing metal components for plumbing and heating installations. On 1st January, 19–0, they admitted their manager, Plugg, to partnership on the following terms:

1. Interest on capital at 10% p.a.
2. Partnership salaries: Cheyne £1,800; Plugg £3,600.
3. Shares of profit: Ball 1/2; Cheyne 1/3; Plugg 1/6.

Their Trial Balance at 31st December, 1980, was:

	Debit £	Credit £
Capital accounts: Ball		60,000
Cheyne		40,000
Plugg		10,000
Current accounts: Ball		7,500
Cheyne		2,500
Plugg		—
Drawings accounts: Ball	10,000	
Cheyne	6,800	
Plugg	4,400	
Freehold premises, at cost	60,000	
Machinery, at cost	24,000	
Office equipment, at cost	4,500	
Provision for depreciation: Premises		8,400
Machinery		12,000
Office equipment		900
Sundry debtors	31,500	

Manufacturing Statements 195

	Debit £	Credit £
Sundry creditors		13,725
Stocks of raw materials 1st January, 19-0	15,000	
Stocks of finished goods 1st January, 19-0	21,000	
Purchases of materials	140,300	
Sales		262,300
Salespeople's salaries and commissions	18,000	
Distribution expenses	4,000	
Manufacturing wages	29,250	
Rates	3,000	
Machinery repairs	1,425	
Power and light (factory)	1,650	
Power and light (office)	450	
Manufacturing expenses	2,500	
Salaries	18,000	
Administration expenses	6,500	
Discounts allowed	1,100	
Cash in hand and at bank	13,950	
	£417,325	£417,325

Notes:

1. Stocks at 31st December 19-0: Raw materials, £16,500
   Finished goods, £26,500
2. Depreciation is to be provided (on cost):

	%
Premises	$2\frac{1}{2}$
Machinery	$12\frac{1}{2}$
Office equipment	20

3. Provision has to be made for doubtful debts: 1% on Sundry Debtors
4. Provision is to be made for accruals:

	£
Power and light (factory)	95
Power and light (office)	35
Manufacturing expenses	200
Distribution expenses	500

5. Four-fifths of the premises is occupied by the factory.
6. Rates of £2,500 had been paid for the year ended 31st March, 19-1.

Required:

Prepare the Manufacturing, Trading, and Profit and Loss Accounts (with Appropriation Account) for the year ended and Balance Sheet as at 31st December, 19-0.

11.5 A printer is investigating how the cost of setting up the printing of books varies with a number of factors. He believes that the principal factors are the size of the book and its degree of technical complexity. The first of these two is measured by the number of equivalent standard pages in the book. For the second the book is classified either as Novel (N), Technical (T) or Mathematical (M), which are in increasing order of printing complexity.

Details were obtained of the set-up cost of producing 22 books of varying size and complexity and these are given below:

Complexity	Number of standard pages	Set up cost £	Complexity	Number of standard pages	Set up cost £
T	362	241	M	196	143
T	264	174	T	363	234
M	420	384	T	418	246
N	437	207	N	255	133
M	374	334	N	582	247
N	242	121	M	512	412
N	339	161	T	300	161
T	285	195	M	273	256
N	362	182	M	269	277
M	183	176	N	482	199
T	451	260	T	492	296

Required:

(a) Represent the above data on a graph designed to show how the cost varies with complexity and book length, and comment on any observed features of the graph.

(b) Estimate from your graph the approximate increase in set-up cost per 100 pages for mathematical books.

(c) Estimate from your graph the set-up cost of a proposed book of length 550 pages whose complexity is mid-way between technical and mathematical.

(*JAS*)

11.6 A. B. Box Co. Ltd. manufactures metal boxes. Currently they have two different contracts to manufacture two different types of boxes, X and Y.

1. Box X was sold at the factory cost plus 25%.
2. Box Y was sold at the factory cost plus 10%.
3. During the year ended 31st March, 19–7, the following costs were incurred:

	On Box X Contract £	On Box Y Contract £
Commencing material stocks 1st April, 19–6	7,000	10,500
Direct wages cost	15,000	19,500
Depreciation: Plant and machinery	1,500	2,600
Wage costs: Plant maintenance	750	1,100
Material purchases	16,150	27,500
Factory rent and other indirect expenses	1,100	2,000
Closing material stocks 31st March, 19–7	6,500	9,200

The number of boxes produced during the year was Box X, 7,000
Box Y, 27,000

Required:

(a) Two distinct manufacturing accounts (which may be presented in columnar form) for the year ended 31st March, 19–7, one for

producing Box X and the other for Box Y, showing clearly:
1. prime cost
2. factory cost of boxes completed

There was no work in progress.

(b) The projected unit selling price for each kind of box.
(c) The gross profit for the year ended 31st March, 19–7, if 6,000 of Box X and 25,000 of Box Y had been sold and the stocks remaining were valued at factory cost.

(London)

12 Costing Systems

- When you have read this chapter you should:
- be familiar with the two main types of costing systems used by organisations
- understand the basic procedures and documents associated with these systems

12.1 Introduction

All manufacturing organisations need to maintain records of how much it has cost to produce the output of a given period since this information will be used in a number of important ways:

- to establish prices for the output produced
- to place a value on finished goods and work-in-progress and calculate the profit for the period
- to make decisions regarding future product ranges and output levels

Accurate information is therefore crucially important and this should be produced by an appropriate costing system which is efficiently maintained. The type of system used will depend on the nature of the productive process involved and there are basically two types. *Job costing systems* are used by organisations which produce, to order, a wide variety of products and therefore need to know the cost of producing each individual order or job. Examples of organisations which would use this type of system are those engaged in engineering, printing, building and vehicle repairing. *Process costing systems*, on the other hand, are used by organisations which produce large quantities of a limited range of standard products and as such do not need to cost each item of output separately. Products normally pass through one or more processes for which separate cost data is collected.

12.2 Costing procedures and documents

In order to maintain either type of costing system, it is necessary for the organisation to employ suitable procedures and documentation. In this way, costs can be recorded for particular jobs or processes and some degree of control can be exercised over the main elements of cost.

Direct materials

Normally, the procedure is that materials will only be issued from stores on the authorisation of a production supervisor or manager by means of a *materials requisition*. This document is in effect an instruction to the storekeeper to issue the materials listed and the information it contains will be used by the costing section of the accounts department. Although the detail and layout is slightly different for each organisation, Figure 12.1 illustrates the kind of information such a requisition would contain:

Figure 12.1
Materials requisition

```
MATERIALS REQUISITION

Date: _____          Requisition no: _____

Issued to job/process no: _____

Authorised by: _____

Issued by: _____
```

Description	Stock number	Number of units	Office use only	
			Price	Total £

When the required materials are issued from the stores, the materials requisition is completed by the storekeeper, with the price per unit and the total cost depending on the method of pricing stores issues used by the organisation (see Chapter 4 on stock valuation). Copies are sent to the costing section so that the appropriate charge for materials can be made to the correct job or process.

Direct labour

Cost data relating to production employees is needed for both payroll and costing purposes. When these employees spend all of their working day on a particular process, direct labour times are normally obtained from either clock cards or attendance records kept by departmental supervisors or managers. However, where employees transfer from process to process or job to job, a more detailed breakdown of how their time has been spent is needed. In these circumstances, employees are normally required to complete a *labour time record sheet*, with the details it contains verified by someone in authority. One example of such a sheet is given in Figure 12.2. The information contained on these sheets should allow the correct amount of labour costs to be charged to jobs or processes.

Figure 12.2
Labour time record sheet

			LABOUR TIME RECORD SHEET			
Employee: _____				Employee no: _____		
Grade: _____				Department/Cost centre: _____		
Week ending: _____						
				Time		Verified by:
Date	Job/process no.		From	To	Total	

Factory overheads

While the costing procedures for direct costs are reasonably straightforward, the same cannot be said for factory overheads. By their nature, overheads cannot be linked directly with a particular job or process and as a result, methods must be employed which are considered to give fair and reasonable approximations of the factory overheads incurred.

A common treatment for factory overheads follows two stages. First, the factory is divided into departments or cost centres, as they are usually known, and *all overhead costs are alloted or charged to these cost centres*. Some overheads can be identified directly with a particular cost centre and charging them is relatively easy, e.g. the department manager's salary. However, the majority of factory overheads are usually shared by all cost centres and a way must therefore be found of spreading these costs. This process of spreading costs is known as apportionment and some typical overheads and the basis for their apportionment is given in Table 12.1.

Table 12.1 *Examples of apportionment of overheads*

Overhead	Common basis for apportionment to cost centres
Rent and rates	Area occupied
Heating costs	Volume occupied
Depreciation, insurance	Capital value of plant and equipment
Canteen costs	Number of employees

Once all overheads have been charged to cost centres, the second stage in the process involves charging the overheads of each cost centre to the units of output (or cost units as they are known) which pass through them. This is known as *overhead absorption* and requires the calculation of *overhead absorption rates*. To do this, a suitable basis for absorption must be found and although opinions differ about this, it is generally thought that the overheads incurred by a particular job or process is linked to one or more of the following variables:

- direct labour hours spent on the job or process
- machine hours
- labour, materials or prime cost
- units of output produced

Example

Overhead costs of lathe department £28,000
Total machine hours 7,000

The overhead absorption rate for the lathe department could therefore be:

$$\frac{£28,000}{7,000 \text{ hours}} = £4.00 \text{ per machine hour}$$

If, therefore, a particular job required 3 hours lathe time, the charge for overheads would be

3 hours × £4.00 = £12.00

It should be noted that using different bases for apportionment and absorption would result in different charges for overheads for the same job. In this respect, costs are opinions rather than facts.

Absorbing actual overheads incurred would mean having to wait until the end of the accounting period before any costing could be completed. Since this is usually impractical, most costing systems use overhead absorption rates based on budgeted amounts for both overheads and the units of base to be used. *Budgeted overhead absorption rates* are calculated as follows:

$$\frac{\text{Budgeted cost centre overheads}}{\text{Budgeted units of base}}$$

The main difficulty with this system is that actual overheads incurred invariably differ from the overheads absorbed (charges to production) because of errors in the budgets. Any under- or overabsorption is usually accounted for at the end of the accounting period by an appropriate entry in the Profit and Loss Account. Nothing, however, can be done about customers that have been under- or overcharged. This is why it is extremely important to prepare budgets with as much care and accuracy as possible.

12.3 Job costing systems

These are systems which are used by manufacturing organisations which produce, to order, many different types of job involving different materials, processes and labour times. The costs of production of each job are normally recorded on a job cost sheet maintained by the costing section. Figure 12.3 illustrates the type of information that might be found on such a sheet.

Cost data is passed to the costing section by means of the documents considered in Section 12.2. For direct materials, for example, most of the information will be supplied on materials requisitions. However, there may also be transfers of materials from one job to another and the return of some materials to the stores. Appropriate documents would record such movements and be verified by somebody in authority. For direct labour, the information contained on labour time record sheets would be transferred to the job cost sheet.

When a job is finished, this is usually notified to the costing section by means of a *job completion ticket*. The remainder of the job cost sheet can then be completed. The charge for factory overheads will depend on the cost centres through which the job has passed and the methods and rates used. Methods for charging administration and delivery costs vary from organisation to organisation. A fixed charge for each or a percentage based on production costs are two common methods.

Figure 12.3
Job cost sheet

JOB COST SHEET		Job no:
Customer's name:		Address:
Order no:		Date commenced:
Expected date of completion:		
Actual date of completion:		
Estimate no:		Estimate: £
Passed for invoicing by:		

Direct materials	Requisition no:			Total £
Direct labour	Record sheet no:	Hours	Rate	
Factory overheads	Cost centre	Rate	Base	
Administration charge		Rate	Base	
Delivery charge		Rate	Base	
			Total cost	
			Mark-up	
			Selling price	

Example A printing organisation have prepared their overhead budgets for the next financial period and have compiled the following information:

	£000
Rent and rates	28.0
Insurance (premises)	3.6
Light and heat	11.2
Insurance (plant)	1.6
Depreciation (plant)	3.2
Power	5.5
Supervisory salaries:	
Setting	4.8

	£000
Printing	9.6
Finishing	6.2
Canteen costs	7.8
Telephone	4.5
Administrative office:	
Salaries	22.0
Stationery and miscellaneous	3.8
	111.8

There are three production departments, setting, printing and finishing, and a general office. Information relating to these departments is given in Table 12.2

Table 12.2

	Setting	Printing	Finishing	Office
Area (square metres)	400	600	300	100
Value of premises (£)	37,000	42,000	25,000	16,000
Plant values (cost) (£)	8,000	18,000	4,000	2,000
Depreciation rate (on cost)	10%	10%	10%	10%
Machinery: kilowatt rating	112	638	220	30
Staff (using canteen)	46	38	24	22
Telephones	7	4	8	31
Direct labour hours	20,000	15,000	12,000	—

From the information in Table 12.2, it is possible to calculate an overhead absorption rate for each of the three production departments. The first stage in this process is to allot all of the overheads listed to the four departments using the information given in the table. This is best achieved by an orderly cost schedule of the type shown. An explanation of how the figures are obtained is given below the schedule.

You will notice from the schedule that the figure for rent and rates, for example, is apportioned using floor area as the basis. Given that the total floor area involved is 1,400 square metres, the calculations for the apportionment are as follows:

$$\frac{\text{Units of base for cost centre}}{\text{Total units of base}} \times \text{Amount to be apportioned}$$

Setting $\quad \dfrac{400}{1,400} \times £28,000 = £8,000$

Printing $\quad \dfrac{600}{1,400} \times £28,000 = £12,000$

Finishing $\quad \dfrac{300}{1,400} \times £28,000 = £6,000$

Office $\quad \dfrac{100}{1,400} \times £28,000 = £2,000$

Cost schedule

Item	Basis	Setting	Printing	Finishing	Office	Total
Rent and rates	Floor area	8,000	12,000	6,000	2,000	28,000
Insurance premises	Value	1,110	1,260	750	480	3,600
Light and heat	Floor area	3,200	4,800	2,400	800	11,200
Insurance plant	Value	400	900	200	100	1,600
Depreciation	10% on cost	800	1,800	400	200	3,200
Power	Kilowatt rating	616	3,509	1,210	165	5,500
Supervisory salaries	Direct	4,800	9,600	6,200	—	20,600
Canteen	Staff	2,760	2,280	1,440	1,320	7,800
Telephone	Number	630	360	720	2,790	4,500
Administration						
Salaries	Direct	—	—	—	22,000	22,000
Stationery etc.	Direct	—	—	—	3,800	3,800
Total		22,316	36,509	19,320	33,655	111,800
Administration office		9,611	15,723	8,321	—	—
Total		31,927	52,232	27,641	—	111,800

When all overhead items have been apportioned or directly allocated, it is then necessary to reapportion the office costs. Office costs will be charged to units of output through the overhead absorption rates of the production departments. Since there is no one satisfactory basis for the apportionment of these costs, the usual basis is the departmental totals given at this stage:

	£
Setting	22,316
Printing	36,509
Finishing	19,320
	78,145

The reapportionment of office costs is therefore:

Setting $\quad \dfrac{£22,316}{£78,145} \times £33,655 = £9,611$

Printing $\quad \dfrac{£36,509}{£78,145} \times £33,655 = £15,723$

Finishing $\quad \dfrac{£19,320}{£78,145} \times £33,655 = £8,321$

Once the final totals for the production departments are known, it is then possible to calculate an overhead absorption rate for each of them. Since the only relevant piece of information given about them is the direct labour hours expected to be worked in each, this will be the basis for the calculation and use of the rates:

Setting $\quad \dfrac{£31,927}{20,000 \text{ hours}} = £1.60$ per direct labour hour

Printing $\quad \dfrac{£52,232}{15,000 \text{ hours}} = £3.48$ per direct labour hour

Finishing $\quad \dfrac{£27,641}{12,000 \text{ hours}} = £2.30$ per direct labour hour

The use of these rates is illustrated in the job cost sheet in Figure 12.4. The information contained on the job cost sheet is used in the first instance for pricing purposes and a copy would be passed to the office for invoicing. Any queries on detail can be checked by reference to the materials requisitions or labour time record sheets. It may also be worth investigating why the estimate was much higher than the actual selling price.

12.4 Process costing systems

These systems are used by organisations which mass produce standard products on a continuous flow basis. Since it is not

Figure 12.4

JOB COST SHEET			Job no: 248	
Customer's name: A.N.Other		Address: Anytown		
Order no: R.K. 47		Date commenced: 21st August,19-1		
Expected date of completion: 24th August,19-1				
Actual date of completion: 28th August,19-1				
Estimate no: J.M. 25		Estimate: £ 264		
Passed for invoicing by: C.L.H.				
Direct materials	Reqisition no.			Total £
	3452			29.40
	3461			75.00
	3472			5.00
Direct labour	Record sheet no.	Hours	Rate	
	R.K. 29	4	2.00	8.00
	J.B. 29	6	2.50	15.00
	H.G. 29	3	2.25	6.75
Factory overheads	Cost centre	Rate	Base	
	Setting	1.60	4 hours	6.40
	Printing	3.48	6 hours	20.88
	Finishing	2.30	3 hours	6.90
Delivery charge		Rate	Base	
		6.00	Fixed	6.00
			Total cost	179.33
			Mark-up ($33\frac{1}{3}$%)	59.72
			Selling price	239.05

necessary to record separately the cost of each unit of output, costs are recorded instead for the main production processes. Periodically, an average unit cost for these processes is calculated.

The costing procedures for direct costs and factory overheads are likely to be similar to those outlined for the job costing system. Information about direct materials issued to a particular process is obtained from materials requisitions while direct labour times are obtained from clock cards or record sheets. Factory overheads are absorbed by the main processes using an overhead absorption rate.

Cost data pertaining to a particular process obtained from these sources is recorded in a *process account*. This is an integral part of the double-entry bookkeeping system for manufacturing organisations. It is neither necessary nor practical to consider this whole system and the following example therefore shows only the process accounts without the other accounts that would be affected by the transactions listed.

Example The manufacture of a product involves two processes, A and B. Data relating to these processes for a certain period is listed below:

	Process A	Process B
Direct materials	£1,800	£2,600
Direct labour	400 hours @£2.50	700 hours @£2.50
Factory overheads	£1.20 per hour	£0.80 per hour
Units started and finished	1,000	1,000

The process accounts for this period are given in Table 12.3

Table 12.3
Process A

	Units	Per unit	£		Units	Per unit	£
Direct materials	1,000	1.80	1,800	Process B	1,000	3.28	3,280
Direct labour		1.00	1,000				
Factory overheads		0.48	480				
	1,000	3.28	3,280		1,000	3.28	3,280

Process B

	Units	Per unit	£		Units	Per unit	£
Process A	1,000	3.28	3,280	Finished goods	1,000	8.19	8,190
Direct materials		2.60	2,600				
Direct labour		1.75	1,750				
Factory overheads		0.56	560				
	1,000	8.19	8,190		1,000	8.19	8,190

The per unit figures are obtained by dividing the costs by 1,000 units. When process B is complete, the units of output are passed to the finished goods store and are recorded in the stores records.

Although the process accounts in this example are reasonably straightforward, there are many complications which can occur in practice. This makes process costing a highly technical and specialised area of accounting. Valuations of work-in-progress and the treatment of scrapped output are two common problems that would be considered in detail in a specialist costing textbook.

Summary

This chapter has shown how organisations which manufacture the products they sell employ suitable costing systems to provide them with basic cost data. Essentially, the use of either job or process costing depends on the nature of the productive process. Although there are important differences between the two types of system, it has been shown that the basic costing procedures and documents are likely to be the same for both.

Assignments

12.1 AGM Ltd. are an engineering organisation producing jobs to order. They use predetermined overhead absorption rates in charging overheads to jobs. In department A, the rate is based on direct labour hours and in department B, it is based on machine hours. The relevant budget data for the next financial year is given below:

	Department A	Department B
Direct labour cost	£60,000	£37,500
Factory overhead	£75,000	£81,000
Direct labour hours	30,000	15,000
Machine hours	—	10,000

Required:

(a) Calculate the overhead absorption rates for these two departments.

(b) The following data relates to Job Number 46:

	Department A	Department B
Direct materials	£61	£124
Direct labour hours	6	3
Machine hours	—	2

The organisation absorbs administration overheads at 20% on factory cost and uses a fixed delivery charge of £10 per job. Its profit mark-up is $33\frac{1}{3}$% on cost.

Prepare a cost statement for Job Number 46 showing the final invoice price to the customer, if VAT is 15%.

(c) If, at the end of the year, the direct labour hours worked in Department A were 34,000 and the machine hours worked in Department B were 8,500, calculate the amount of under- or overabsorption of overhead for each department if the actual overheads incurred for the year were £80,000 for Department A and £78,000 for Department B.

(d) Explain how this under- or overabsorption should be dealt with.

12.2 XYZ Ltd. is an engineering firm, whose works contain four main departments. Factory overhead recovery rates have been calculated for three of the departments as follows:

Department A: 60% on direct materials used in the department

Department B: 75% on direct labour used in the department

Department C: £2.20 per direct labour hour in the department

Administration overheads are recovered at 30% on factory cost.

It has been decided to use a full cost recovery rate for Department D, which is a machine shop, based on machine hours. The following information is available:

1. There are 10 identical machines in the department, each of which cost £5,000, and they are expected to last 9 years and then to have a scrap value of £500 each.
2. Each machine is expected to run for 7 hours per day, 5 days per week and 47 weeks per year.
3. Machine operators' wages are £125 per week, and each operator works 48 weeks and receives 4 weeks paid holiday. There are 5 operators in the department.
4. Total overhead expenses apportioned and allocated to the department are £6,400 p.a.
5. Insurance on the machinery is at the rate of 2% of the initial cost p.a.
6. Each machine uses 30 units of power per running hour, at £0.02 per unit.
7. Maintenance is £400 p.a. per machine.

Required:

(a) From the above information, calculate a machine hour rate for Department D (to the nearest penny).

(b) Prepare a statement showing the final selling price of Job Number 41, given the following information:

Department	Direct materials	Direct labour
A	40 units at £3.50 each	60 hours at £1.80 per hour
B	150 units at £1.60 each	140 hours at £1.40 per hour
C	120 units at £2.40 each	75 hours at £2.10 per hour
D	None	None

The job took 60 hours of machine time in Department D (calculations to the nearest penny).

The firm uses a profit mark-up on full cost of $33\frac{1}{3}$%, and VAT is at the rate of 15%.

(c) As well as enabling the firm to set a selling price for its jobs, how else could the information contained in such statements be useful to the firm?

12.3 Bramleys Ltd. have a factory with three workshops and a maintenance department; these are known as Departments A, B, C and D.

Investigations for costing purposes produce the following data, from which you are required to find an overhead rate per labour hour for each department A, B and C, after spreading the costs of D over the other departments.

Costing Systems 211

	A	B	C	D
General rates, areas	20%	45%	30%	5%
Insurance premiums on values at 15p per £100:				
Buildings	£32,000	£40,000	£16,000	£8,000
Plant	£24,000	£28,000	£16,000	£4,000
Light and heat, cubic basis	25%	45%	25%	5%
Plant depreciation: $7\frac{1}{2}\%$ on insurance values above				
Power: Units @ 1p per unit	43,000	54,000	24,000	6,500
The labour hours of the Maintenance Department (D) were spent in the other departments.	2,300	2,700	1,200	
The labour hours of the other departments were	22,600	16,700	10,250	

The expenses concerned were as follows. Copy out and complete the columns.

	Total	A	B	C	D
	£	£	£	£	£
General rates	2,600				
Insurance of Buildings	144				
Insurance of plant	108				
Indirect wages (as given)	4,016	1,076	2,268	672	
Light and heat	1,600				
Depreciation of plant	5,400				
Sundry expenses (as given)	450	190	100	160	
Power	1,275				
Wages, Department D only	1,900				
Materials, Department D only	607				
Sub-totals	18,100				
Department D costs spread over others per data above					
Total department cost	18,100				

12.4 Convenience Foods Ltd. produce a range of packet soups called 'Snap Soops'. The product passes through three processes before completion and being passed to the stores:

Process 1: Blending and cooking
Process 2: Dehydration
Process 3: Weighing and packaging

The cost data recorded for week 16 is given below:

Process 1
Materials: 5000 kg of meat, vegetables, flavouring etc. at £0.40 per kg
Labour: 500 hours at £2.50 per hour
Overheads: 70% of direct labour costs

Process 2
Labour: 140 hours at £3.00 per hour
Overheads: 120% of direct labour costs

Process 3
Packing materials: £500
Direct labour: 600 hours at £1.80 per hour
Overheads: 60% of direct labour costs

Assuming no opening or closing stocks of work-in-progress and negligible process losses, prepare the process accounts for week 16. The output of process 3 should be given in 100 gram packets.

12.5 International Breakfast Cereals PLC produce a variety of cereals in batches. One of their products, 'Crunchy Muesli', passes through two processes before it is passed to the stores:

Process 1: Cooking, mixing and blending
Process 2: Weighing and packaging
The output from process 2 is in 500 gram packs

Cost data relating to these two processes for week 25 is given below:

Process 1
Materials: 2000 kg of cereal, sugar and flavouring, at £0.20 per kg
Direct labour: 100 hours at £2 per hour
Overheads: £1.50 per direct labour hour

Process 2
Packing materials: £250
Direct Labour: 70 hours at £2 per hour
Overheads: £1.20 per direct labour hour

Assuming that there were no opening or closing stocks of work-in-progress and that losses in the process are negligible, draw up the process accounts for week 25. The output of process 2 should be given in 500 gram packets.

12.6 You are employed as a trainee accountant by String-Wadham Ltd., a company engaged in the sale and repair of motor vehicles. A new motor vehicle workshop has been built by the company and they are about to start using it. You have been asked to prepare the following calculations:

(a) An overhead absorption rate for the new workshop, from the following information:

 1. The buildings cost £50,000 to erect and it has been decided to depreciate them at the rate of 1% p.a. on the straight-line basis.
 2. New plant and equipment cost £70,000 and its estimated useful life is reckoned to be 10 years, when it will be disposed of for £5,000 and replaced.
 3. The new workshop doubles the existing floor area occupied by the company whose rates bill was £4,500 last year. Rates are expected to rise by 15% in the forthcoming year.

4. Electricity charges on an existing workshop amount to £1,800 and it has been estimated that the new workshop will cost 40% more than this. Charges for electricity are expected to rise by 10% in the forthcoming year.
5. As well as the fitters, the workshop will employ the following staff:

1 receptionist/typist	£5,000
1 estimator/clerical assistant	£6,200
1 workshop supervisor	£10,500

6. Insurance on the buildings and plant has been estimated at £500 p.a.
7. The general administration overheads of the company as a whole have been estimated at £40,000 and a fair apportionment to the new workshop is considered to be 30%.
8. It has been estimated that the new workshop will be used for service and repair activities for 5,000 hours during the forthcoming year.

(b) Estimate for the charge for Job Number 12 from the following information.
1. Parts and lubricants will cost £28.00.
2. The estimated completion time for the work is 3 hours.
3. The effective wage rate is £4.00 per hour.
4. The company uses a mark-up of $33\frac{1}{3}$% on cost for profit.
5. The VAT rate is 15%.

(c) Calculate the fully inclusive rate the company should charge for servicing if it is to include labour, overheads and profit.

(d) After the first two months of operation, the company finds that the new workshop is running at well below the capacity available. In order to attract more business, it is considering introducing special servicing charges at break-even prices for a trial period of a month. What is the lowest VAT inclusive charge the company could afford to offer (exclusive of parts and lubricants) if labour is paid by the hour, variable overheads amount to £1.50 per hour, and the average service takes 2 hours?

13 Break-Even Analysis: The Analysis of Cost/Volume/Profit Relationships

When you have read this chapter you should be able to:
- explain simple cost/volume/profit relationships
- use break-even analysis as a planning and control technique

13.1 Introduction

One of the most important relationships in any business is the link between sales (volume or value) and costs (fixed & variable), and an understanding of it can help managers to plan and control their budgets and to see where profit might be made. Break-even analysis is a very useful technique because it examines this link.

13.2 The break-even model

The model has two *variables*:

1. Sales, which can be expressed in volume and value terms.
2. Costs, which can be divided into fixed and variable.

The model also makes two *assumptions*, that relationships between the variables are:

1. Linear, i.e. there are straight-line proportional links.
2. Independent, i.e. if one variable changes it does not affect the other.

Drawbacks   Cost and market behaviour can be much more complicated than implied above. The model ignores:

Break-Even Analysis 215

1. Possible changes in selling price (e.g. discounts) unit variable costs (e.g. overtime premiums) and fixed costs (e.g. stepped increases).
2. Output or demand constraints.
3. The difficulties of separating fixed and variable costs in practice.

Validity

The assumptions of the model are not as restricting as they might at first appear because over a *limited range of output* they are often a reasonable approximation to reality. So when planning horizons are short, e.g. for quarterly budgets, the model is quite acceptable as non-linear changes in output or sales are unlikely in the short run. To add realism, the analysis will be restricted to short-term budgets and limited ranges of output, and the maximum potential output or sales for the time period will be defined.

Method

This will be demonstrated in the comprehensive example which now follows.

A comprehensive example
G. Taylor, a small manufacturing concern, provides the following monthly estimates:

Unit selling price	£25
Sales volume (units)	3,000
Unit variable costs	£10
Fixed costs	£30,000
Production limit (units)	4,000 maximum

Linear equations

Let X = output (in '000s of units)

C = monthly costs (in £000)

R = monthly sales revenue (in £000)

Hence, total monthly costs =

C = Fixed costs + Variable costs

$= 30 + 10X$ *Equation 1*

Each unit sells for £25 and if the organisation is selling X units the revenue is:

$R = 25X$ *Equation 2*

From Equations 1 and 2 we can derive an equation representing the monthly profit (P) by using the fact that profit is equal to revenue minus cost:

$P = R - C = 25X - (30 + 10X)$

$= 25X - 30 - 10X$

$= 15X - 30$ *Equation 3*

13.3 The break-even point (BEP)

Businesses often need to know their break-even point, where sales just equal costs, in order to establish the minimum level of output needed to avoid losses. Anywhere above this point will produce profits.

At the break-even point, profit $(P) = 0$

hence, from the example, $0 = 25X - (30 + 10X)$

$$= 15X - 30$$
$$-15X = -30$$
$$\therefore X = 2$$

i.e. the break-even level of output is 2,000 units.

In order to break even a business must cover all of its costs, both fixed and variable. Another approach to the problem is to assume that variable costs will be covered first so that any revenue remaining after these have been met can be treated as a *contribution* towards paying for the fixed costs. Any contribution remaining after this represents profit. Conversely, losses are made at any level of activity below the break-even point.

The formula for the break-even point in output terms is

$$\frac{\text{Fixed costs}}{\text{Unit contribution}} = \frac{£30,000}{£25 - £10} = 2,000 \text{ units}$$

where:

Unit contribution = Selling price − Unit variable cost
The break-even point can be expressed in sales revenue terms:

Volume × Selling Price = Revenue
2,000 × £25 = £50,000

or as a percentage of the budgeted level of output, i.e.

$$\frac{2,000}{3,000} \times 100 = 66\tfrac{2}{3}\%$$

13.4 The margin of safety (MS)

This is the difference between the planned and the break-even level of output. It shows how much sales can fall short of the budget before losses are made. The bigger the margin of safety the greater the forecast error can be before running into deficit. This measure can also be expressed in three ways:

Units of output: Budgeted output − Break-even output
= 3,000 − 2,000 = 1,000 units

Revenue: Budgeted revenue − Break-even revenue
= £75,000 − £50,000 = £25,000

Percentage: $\dfrac{\text{Margin of safety in units}}{\text{Budgeted output}} = \dfrac{1000}{3,000} = 33\frac{1}{3}\%$

13.5 Contribution/Sales (C/S) ratio

A third key measure in break-even analysis is known as the contribution/sales (C/S) ratio and is calculated as follows:

$\dfrac{\text{Unit contribution}}{\text{Unit selling price}} \times 100\%$

$= \dfrac{15}{25} \times 100 = 60\%$

C/S ratio is the percentage of selling price which contributes to fixed costs and once these have been covered it represents profit. The higher the C/S ratio the sooner fixed costs will be paid for and the faster profit will increase after the break-even point.

13.6 Calculation of estimated profit

From the example, if Taylor produces and sells 3,000 units then the profit is:

$P = 15 \times 3 - 30$ from Equation 3
$= 15$

i.e. £15,000

	£000
Check: Sales: 3,000 units × £25	75
Less: Variable costs × £10	30
Contribution	45
Less: Fixed costs	30
Profit	15

13.7 The break-even chart

An effective and useful way of presenting the model is to produce a graph of it. Relationships can then be seen at a glance and conclusions drawn. Taylor's chart is shown in Figure 13.1. Output (X) in thousand units is measured along the horizontal axis and the scale for the three monetary variables, sales, costs and profits, is marked on the vertical axis. Drawing any line which represents a linear equation involves finding any two points, preferably far apart, which satisfy the equation and then joining them with a ruler. Taking the total cost line (Figure 13.1) as an example, choose two levels of output at each end, say 0 and 4, (maximum monthly output in thousands of units).

When $X = 0$, $C = 30$ (i.e. £30,000)

Figure 13.1
Break-even analysis for G. Taylor Ltd.

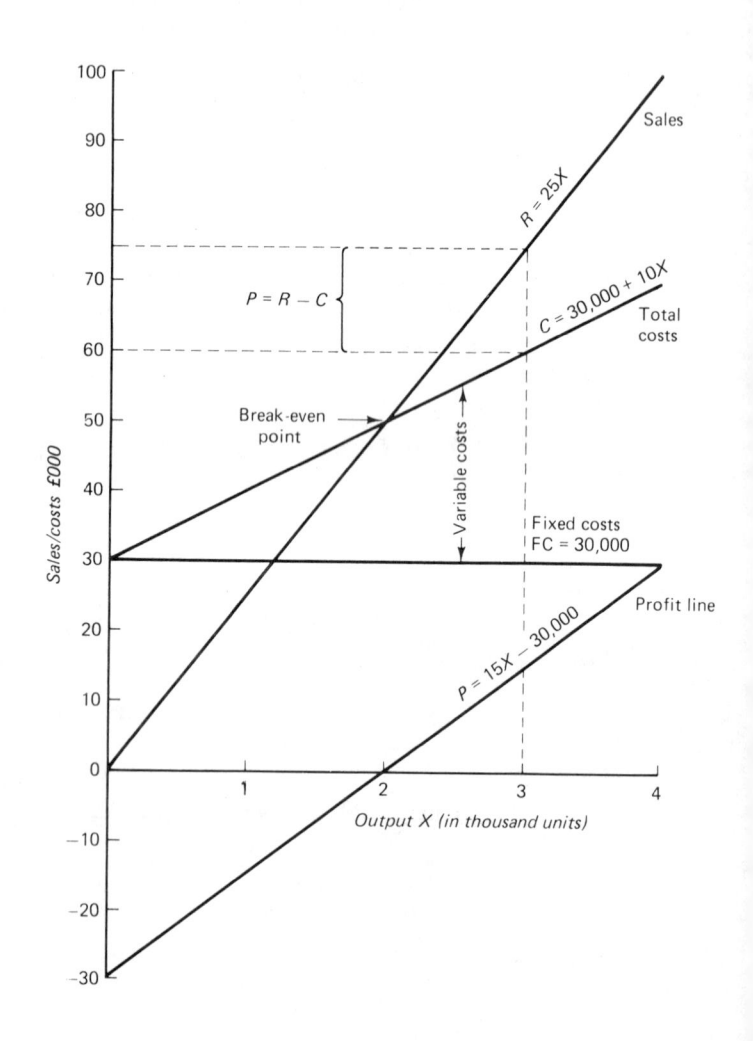

i.e. fixed costs have to be paid whether production takes place or not.

When $X = 4$, $C = 30 + (10 \times 4)$
$= 70$ (i.e. £70,000)

The two points (co-ordinates 0, 30 and 4, 70) can then be joined together. Costs at any level of output between these two extremes can then be read off from the line, e.g. when $X = 1$, $C = 40$ (£40,000).

Break-even analysis – example W. Bogart's Clothing Ltd has worked out the following profit forecast for next year, 19–5, based on full capacity production:

		£000
Sales		1,000
Direct materials	250	
Direct labour	300	550
Gross profit		450
Less: Selling expenses	100	
Depreciation	50	
Administration + finance	200	350
Net profit		100

50% of selling expenses are fixed, the remainder varying directly with sales (e.g. commission and delivery costs). All other indirect costs are fixed. At the end of 19–4 the company have a tax liability of £30,000 which will have to be paid in 19–5. Cash at the bank is presently (1st January, 19–5) £15,000.

Owing to economic uncertainties the company is now estimating that only 70% of production will be achieved during the year. Ignoring other working capital items and assuming that no further tax claims will have to be met in 19–5, we can prepare the revised profit and loss budget for 19–5 and calculate the closing balance with the bank. A break-even chart will also be shown (Figure 13.2).

Revised profit forecast, 19–5

	£000	£000	Explanatory Notes
Sales		700	
Direct materials	175		1
labour	210	385	
Gross profit		315	
Less: selling	85		2
Depreciation	50		
Administration	200	335	3
Net loss		(20)	

Fixed and variable costs must be identified.

Figure 13.2
Break-even chart for W. Bogart Clothing Ltd.

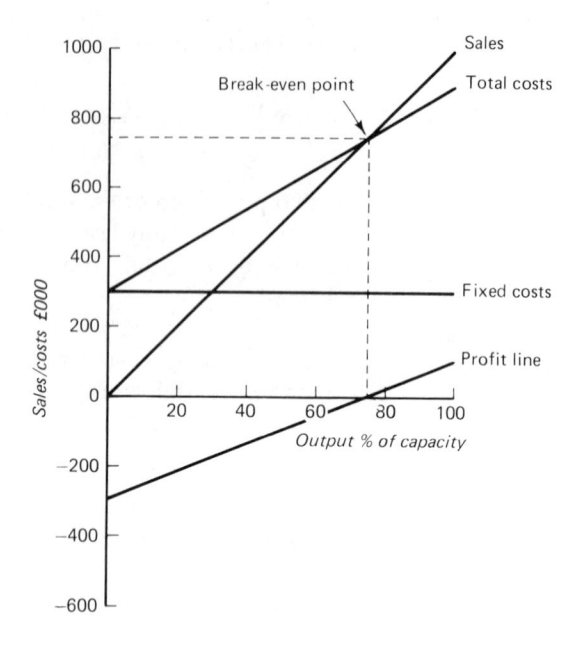

Explanatory notes

1 Direct (variable) costs are dependent on the level of sales and fall proportionately.

2 Selling costs are calculated as follows:

	£000
Fixed	50
Variable	35
Total	85

3 Other indirect costs remain constant.

Estimated bank account (£000)

			Explanatory notes
Opening balance 1st January, 19–5		15	
from trading	(20)		4
Add: Depreciation	50	30	
		45	
Less: Tax		30	
Estimated balance 31st December, 19–5		15	

4 Depreciation is added back to the results from trading (in this case the net loss of £20,000) because depreciation is a non-cash transfer in that no money changes hands.

To prepare the break-even chart we repeat the process followed in Section 13.1 except that we must consider relative proportions because we do not know how many units are produced. Hence the X axis is expressed in percentage terms.

Checks: The three key measures for Bogart's are:

$$\text{Break-even point (BEP)} = \frac{\text{Fixed costs}}{\text{Unit contribution (C/S ratio)}}$$

$$= \frac{£300,000}{1-0.6} \longrightarrow \text{Depreciation} \quad\quad 50$$

Administration	200
Half of selling expenses	50
	300

Variable costs are 60% of sales:

Direct costs	550
Half of selling expenses	50
	600

= 750,000 units

Margin of safety = Budgeted sales (revised) − Break-even sales
 = £700,000 − £750,000
 = −£50,000

i.e. Bogart needs to increase sales by £50,000 to break even.

$$\text{C/S ratio} = \frac{\text{Unit contribution}}{\text{Unit selling price}}$$

$$= \frac{0.4}{1} \times 100 = 40\%$$

3.8 Changes in the variables

So far, it has been shown that break-even analysis can be used by organisations to predict from a range of demand levels, with a set selling price and budget. However, there is no reason why possible variations in output and sales, selling price, and fixed and variable costs should not be considered.

For each of these, the organisation will want to know the effect on budgeted profit and on the three measures used in the analysis.

This consideration of alternative plans will be examined by looking at four basic ways in which the profit of a business can be increased:

(A) Increase unit selling prices.

(B) Increase volume.
(C) Decrease unit variable costs.
(D) Decrease fixed costs.

The separate effects of each of these possibilities are shown in the following calculations and in Table 13.1. Each starts from the present situation which is:

Unit selling price £2
Sales volume 1,000 units
Unit variable costs £1
Fixed costs £500

The existing profit forecast appears in the first column of Table 13.1.

Table 13.1 *Profit forecasts (£)*

	Existing profit	A	B	C	D	
Sales	2,000	2,200	2,200	2,000	2,000	Return
Less: variable costs	1,000	1,000	1,100	900	1,000	to the
Contribution	1,000	1,200	1,100	1,100	1,000	original
Less: Fixed costs	500	500	500	500	450	each
Net profit	500	700	600	600	550	time

(A) Assume that selling price can be increased by 10%. This will reduce the break-even level of output and increase the margin of safety:

$$\text{Break-even point (BEP)} = \frac{£500}{£2.20 - 1} \quad 417 \text{ units}$$

$$\text{Margin of safety (MS)} = 1000 - 417 = 583 \text{ units}$$

The unit contribution would rise by 20 p to £1.20 resulting in an increase C/S ratio of:

$$\frac{1.20}{2.20} \times 100 = 54.5\%$$

This means that higher profit is possible at the same level of output. The increase in selling price would add (1,000 × 20 p) = £200 to revenue and would therefore increase estimated profits of £500 by 40% (column A).

(B) Assume that sales volume can be increased by 10%. This has no effect on the break-even point or the C/S ratio but would increase the margin of safety from 1,000 to 1,100 units. This would add £100 (£1 contribution × 100 units) to profits which is an increase of 20% (column B).

(C) Assume that variable costs can be reduced by 10%. This would reduce the break-even point because the unit contribution increases to £2 − 90 p = £1.10 p. Hence the C/S ratio and the margin of safety increase:

$$\text{BEP} = \frac{£500}{£1.10} = 455 \text{ units}$$

$$\text{C/S ratio} = \frac{£1.10}{£2} = 55\%$$

MS = 1000 − 455 = 545 units

Overall this will increase profits by £100 (1,000 units × 10 p) which is an increase of 20% (column C).

(D) Assume that fixed costs can be reduced by 10%. There would be no change in the C/S ratio but there is a reduction in the break-even point and an increase in the margin of safety.

$$\text{BEP} = \frac{450}{1} = 450 \text{ units}$$

MS = 1,000 − 450 = 550 units

This will lead to a similar percentage increase in profits (column D). By examining some of the interrelationships it is possible to calculate, for example, that a 20% (i.e. £100) increase in fixed costs could be offset by a 5% increase in selling price, a 10% increase in volume, or a 10% decrease in variable costs. This sort of information can be very helpful for management decision making. Hence, possible alternative positions can be examined quickly.

Summary

Break-even analysis is a simple and easily prepared model which relates costs, revenues and profits, and as such is a useful aid to decision making. Based on simplifying assumptions – for clarity and ease of presentation – it provides a reasonable approximation to the real world in the short term. Of course these assumptions of cost and market behaviour can be relaxed, and more complex, and therefore more realistic models, can be developed. Such non-linear models are more time-consuming and costly but may be worthwhile doing for large ranges of output and longer planning periods. These more advanced techniques should not detract from the essential importance of the basic model; that it is easy to prepare, simple to understand and can be a useful aid to profit planning.

The assignments for this topic appear at the end of Chapter 14.

14 Costing Techniques

When you have read this chapter you should be able to:
- expand upon the concepts of cost behaviour outlined in previous chapters
- distinguish between absorption and marginal costing
- explain how the contribution concept can aid business decision making

Previous chapters have examined costs by function (production, selling administration), by element (labour, material, overhead), and by behaviour (fixed and variable).

14.1 Absorption and marginal costing: differences

The essential difference between absorption and marginal costing is that under absorption costing an attempt is made to identify all business costs with individual products or activities whereas under marginal costing only variable costs are analysed in this way and the fixed costs are treated as general costs of the organisation overall. So a marginal costing approach separates costs into fixed and variable; an absorption costing approach does not try to do this. This is why absorption costing is sometimes known as full costing.

14.2 The nature of a marginal cost

A marginal cost is the amount by which, at any given level of output, total costs change if the volume of output changes either up or down by one unit. For this reason marginal costs are also known as differential costs. For example:

Output volume (units)	100	101
Total costs (£)	4,000	4,002

In this case, the marginal cost of increasing output by 1 unit is £2 (the differential between costs at two given output levels). This does not mean that the marginal cost will be the same for different levels of output; it may well be different if output increases from 1,000 to 1,001 units, for example.

14.3 Basis of marginal costing

Marginal costing can be used over a suitable volume range providing that all costs can be classified into fixed and variable. This is sometimes quite difficult to do in practice as many cost items consist of both fixed and variable elements. If the distinction can be made, then in most cases variable costs can be treated as marginal costs.

The difference in the presentation of profit statements between the full absorption costing approach and the marginal costing approach will now be demonstrated by examples:

Toplis PLC manufactures three products, the details of which are presented in Table 14.1.

Table 14.1 *Absorption costing approach Profit Statement year ending 31st December, 19–2*

	Product A	Product B	Product C	Total
Sales	5,000	3,000	4,000	12,000
Direct material	2,000	1,300	1,200	4,500
Direct labour	1,500	400	1,000	2,900
Production overhead	500	1,250	1,000	2,750
Factory cost	4,000	2,950	3,200	10,150
Gross profit/loss	1,000	50	800	1,850
General overheads	600	300	200	1,100
Net profit/loss	400	(250)	600	750
Margin: $\dfrac{\text{Net profit}}{\text{Sales}}$ %	8	Loss	15	6.25

Assume: No stock changes

14.4 Analysis of contribution

It can be seen from Table 14.2 that the difference between sales value and marginal cost is the contribution towards the general fixed costs and the eventual net profit (if any).

Table 14.2 *Marginal costing approach Profit Statement year ending 31st December, 19–2*

	A	B	C	Total
Sales	5,000	3,000	4,000	12,000
Direct Material	2,000	1,300	1,200	4,500
Direct labour	1,500	400	1,000	2,900
Variable overheads*:				
Production	250	625	500	1,375
General	180	90	60	330
Marginal cost	3,930	2,415	2,760	9,105
Contribution	1,070	585	1,240	2,895
Fixed overheads:				
Production				1,375
General				770
Net profit				750

* The firm calculates that 50% of production overheads and 30% of general overheads are variable. The remainder will be the fixed overhead figures, of course.

The contribution can be expressed as a percentage of the sales value, and if the fixed and variable costs have been correctly separated, then this percentage will remain constant for all sales volumes within the preselected range of output. This C/S ratio was outlined in Chapter 13 and is an important feature of marginal costing because it can be used to forecast the effect of volume changes on net profit, and also to assess the relative profitability of different products or activities.

Contribution/sales relationship

Suppose that the sales of product A (in Table 14.2) increased to £6,000, then the contribution would become (21% × £6,000) = £1,260, an increase of £190 which would improve total profit by the same amount.

This type of calculation must be restricted to individual products or activities as the C/S ratio for the whole business will vary according to the product mix. The relationship between sales value and costs over a range of ouput levels can be shown on break-even charts which were explained in Chapter 13.

Relative profitability

In Table 14.1, showing absorption costing, it appears that product B, which shows a loss, is less desirable than the other products.

Limiting-factors on output

Table 14.3, however, reveals that B produces a contribution of 19.5% of sales value so there may be benefits in retaining it.

In most cases the best choice of product or activity mix is that which returns the highest C/S ratio, i.e. the highest contribution per £ of sales, but there can be exceptions to this if the business has a particular constraint.

These constraints (or key variables) might include lack of finance, skilled labour, limited market demand or restricted machine availability. In such instances, the preferred product or activity will be that which yields the highest contribution per unit of the limiting factor. Table 14.3 presents certain statistical data which can be applied to the contributions calculated in Table 14.2.

Analysis reveals that the *profitability ranking* of the various products will depend upon the limiting factor. Clearly product C is the best if there are no constraints since its contribution is 31p in every £ of sales. If, however, the products are interchangeable, and total market demand is limited, then product A will be preferable as it yields the highest contribution: £1.05 for every unit sold. Similarly there are circumstances when product B might be favoured. If demand is unlimited but there is a limit on labour availability then B should be promoted as this has the highest contribution (£1.46) per labour hour.

Table 14.3 *Contribution Statement (£) year ending 31st December, 19–2*

	A	B	C	Total
Sales quantity (units)	1,000	1,500	4,000	6,500
Price per unit (£)	5	2	1	
Sales revenue	5,000	3,000	4,000	12,000
Direct material	2,000	1,300	1,200	4,500
Labour at £1 per hour	1,500	400	1,000	2,900
Variable overheads	430	715	580	1,750
Marginal cost	3,930	2,415	2,760	9,105
Contribution	1,070	585	1,240	2,895

	A	B	C
Calculations: Contribution/Sales (C/S) ratio	$\dfrac{1,070}{5,000} = 21\%$	$\dfrac{585}{3,000} = 19.5\%$	$\dfrac{1,240}{4,000} = 31\%$
Unit Contribution (Selling price × C/S ratio)	£5 × 0.21 = £1.05	£2 × 0.195 = 39p	£1 × 0.31 = 31p
Contribution per labour hour $\left(\times \dfrac{\text{Contribution}}{\text{Sales quantity}} \div \text{Labour costs}\right)$	£1.05 × $\dfrac{1,000}{1,500}$ = 70p	39p × $\dfrac{1,500}{400}$ = £1.46	31p × $\dfrac{4,000}{1,000}$ = £1.24

Clearly it is important to identify the key constraint(s) in any situation as this can significantly affect management policy. Linear programming techniques (see Taylor & Hawkins, *Quantitative Methods in Business*) can help to identify these limiting factors.

14.5 Stock valuation

A marginal cost accounting system has implications for stock valuation which will now be examined.

The following example demonstrates how stocks are valued under absorption and marginal costs systems.

Example A newly formed company, Hooper PLC, makes microcomputers and sells them at £500 to the retail trade. It produces 100 per month at a direct cost of £200 each (printed circuits and wages). The business has monthly overheads of £10,000 which include salaries, rent, heating, lighting, insurance etc. For the first 3 months of this year they sold 250 microcomputers. The profit and value of closing stock at the end of March under both costing systems is now shown:

	Marginal cost £	Absorption (full) cost £
Production	60,000	90,000
Less: Closing stocks	10,000	15,000
Cost of sales	50,000	75,000
Overheads	30,000	
	80,000	75,000
Sales	125,000	125,000
Profit	45,000	50,000

Under absorption costing no overheads appear in the profit statement as they have been included in the cost of production. It follows that a proportion of these overheads (50/300), 1/6th, is included in the value of the 50 unsold microcomputers. Under the marginal cost method all overheads have gone into the 3-month period and hence the profit reported will be lower. There is no right way of valuing manufactured stock and compromises are often made, e.g. production overheads are often counted as part of the cost of goods produced but administrative overheads are regarded as time costs.

Stocks in published financial accounts have to be based on absorption costing according to **SSAP 9**

14.6 Marginal costing and pricing policy

A pricing strategy based on marginal costs can be a powerful and flexible tool particularly if firms have high fixed costs and irregular demand. Although prices will be based on a firm's costs (whatever the costing method), they must be set at levels that customers are willing to pay.

The reasoning behind marginal cost pricing is that fixed costs have to be paid in any case and so, in difficult times, it might be in the interest of the organisation to sell its products or services, or some of them, at prices which, whilst not recovering the full costs, nevertheless meet variable costs and make a contribution towards the unavoidable fixed costs. This may be a sensible short-term policy, although this price flexibility must be used with care and kept under control, otherwise overuse of marginal pricing could result in losses being made because *total* costs might exceed total revenues.

Case example 1 The latest Profit Statement for Horatio PLC, a manufacturer of engineering components, has just been released. It covers the year 19–4 up to September.

Horatio PLC
Profit Statement January–September 19–4

	£000	£000
Sales (7,500 units at £18.80)		141
Costs		
Materials	15	
Labour	45	
Manufacturing overheads:		
Variable	7.5	
Fixed (60,000 × 9/12ths)	45	
Administrative, selling and distribution overheads (4,000 per month)	36	
		148.5
Net loss		(7.5)

Unit cost statement	£
Direct material	2
Direct labour	6
Manufacturing overheads:	
Variable	1
Fixed (£60,000 for the year based on 15,000 units of production per annum)	4
Unit production cost	13

The sales department has just received a special order for 2,000 components at a contract price of £12 each. The managing director, Mr Osborn, is outraged.

'Business is bad enough without silly contracts like this one. Not only is the contract price less than the cost price but we'll need to spend an extra £1,000 on fixed overheads for a special design.'

Imagine you are the accountant at this firm. Can you advise Osborn?

Marginal costing approach

In deciding whether the firm should accept the order or not, disregard the fixed costs because they have to be paid for whatever is done. It is the differential costs, i.e. those which change if the order is taken, that are important in decision making.

From the unit cost statement:

Unit variable costs = £2 + £6 + £1
= £9

Hence unit contribution
= Selling price − Unit variable costs
= £12 − £9
= £3

Therefore, the special order will contribute (2,000 × £3) = £6,000 towards unavoidable fixed overheads. But note that if the order is accepted an extra £1,000 will have to be spent on design modifications. Hence the net contribution will be £5,000 and the order will improve the position of the firm by that amount.

The firm is three quarters of the way through its present trading year and has only achieved 7,500/15,000, i.e. 50% capacity, so there are idle resources with which to manufacture this special order if, *and only if*, no extra orders are likely to be won over present trends.

In the short run then it seems reasonable to accept this contract, since it keeps the men and plant working, and the company name in the public's eye. (This type of thinking also applies to 'make or buy' decisions where a company compares its own costs against bought-in prices.)

However, there are three possible drawbacks:

1. The price does not cover the production costs (never mind full costs) and this is obviously undesirable. In the long run you go out of business if full (absorption) costs are not met.
2. The price may offend other customers, who might wonder why they cannot buy the component for £12.
3. The order will tie up capacity which has an opportunity cost, i.e. it could be used in the production of more lucrative contracts if they arise.

Case example 2 Alan Wainwright runs a small hotel in Hornsea, a popular seaside resort in Yorkshire. There are 12 guest rooms (2 singles, 6 doubles and 4 for families with 3 beds in each). During the season, which is considered to be May–September inclusive, the average occupancy rate has been 16 guests per week, each guest paying £50 for 1 week's stay.

Alan's costs are as follows:

	Weekly costs in season £	Annual costs £
Food	350	
Cleaning, laundry	80	
Part-time labour	180	
Heating, lighting	30	
Maintenance		800
Depreciation		250
Rates, insurance		700
Advertising		600
Administration		150
	640	2,500

Alan wishes to know three things:

(a) Annual profits.
(b) The minimum number of guests needed each week in season to avoid making a loss (i.e. break-even).
(c) The price to charge if he opens one week out-of-season for a 'winter break'.

Calculations

Before we can answer these questions, certain assumptions have to be made:
1. Alan's own accommodation and living costs are excluded.
2. There are 22 weeks in the season.
3. All weekly in-season costs are variable.

(a) *Annual profits*   £   £
Sales revenue
(£50 per person × 16 guests per week
× 22 weeks in season)   17,600
Less: Running costs: (for 22 weeks)
  Food   7,700
  Cleaning, laundry   1,760
  Part-time labour   3,960
  Heating, lighting   660   14,080
Contribution   3,520
Less: Overheads:
  Maintenance   800
  Depreciation   250
  Rates, insurance   700
  Advertising   600
  Administration   150   2,500
Net profit   1,020

(b) The break-even point, in terms of number of guests per season, is:

$$\frac{\text{Fixed costs}}{\text{Unit contribution}} = \frac{2{,}500}{£10} = 250 \text{ guests}$$

$$\frac{3{,}520 \text{ Total contribution}}{352 \text{ Total guests per season}}$$

This is the calculation for unit contribution
= Selling price − Unit variable costs
= £50 − £40 = £10

Variable costs per week = £640
Average number of guests = 16
Unit variable costs = £640/16 = £40

The minimum number of guests needed to break even each week in season =

$$\frac{250}{22}\text{weeks} \quad 11.4 \text{ guests per week.}$$

So Alan should sensibly aim for at least 12 visitors each week in season.

(c) Alan should charge to cover his estimated running costs of £40 per person per week plus any other differential costs such as extra advertising that might be needed to attract custom off-peak. Any price above this should make a contribution towards overheads and will therefore be worthwhile trying.

Off-peak costing

Marginal cost pricing also applies to organisations with seasonal variations in demand. Public utilities (electricity, telephones) have off-peak rates to spread demand. British Rail has a fare structure designed to utilise its fixed resources seven days a week.

The price is set as a cheap-rate incentive to encourage people to use fixed resources (hotels, trains, electricity supply etc.) at times when they would usually not (winter, weekend, overnight): (see Table 14.4)

Table 14.4 *Examples of incentives to encourage people to use fixed resources*

Organisation	Price example
Hotel	Winter rates
British Rail	Weekend return
Electricity	Overnight Economy 7
Public house	'Happy hour' half-price drinks

Cheap off-peak rates are based on the premise that demand is price elastic, i.e. it is responsive to price changes. This means that total revenue (sales) should be greater if prices are reduced and hence, given that running costs are covered, contributions should be higher.

Again the basic question for the pricing decision is: Which costs change if we offer this extra product or service?

As long as the price covers the differential (marginal) costs then the policy may be worthwhile pursuing given that:

1. Full-price users do not withdraw their custom (cheap travel means a loss of exclusivity, for example).
2. There is no major switching to cheaper rates by consumers which would cause an overall drop in total revenue.

Clearly such factors depend on pricing strategy and great care should be taken when planning and controlling the pricing mix in order to get the right balance.

14.7 Advantages and disadvantages of marginal costing

Some organisations incorporate the marginal approach into their routine accounting system rather than having to undertake a special analysis whenever a particular decision has to be made. The main advantages of an integrated system are that an analysis of fixed and variable costs is ready to hand and this can be used in cost control. Actual expenditure on variable items can then be usefully compared with a budget appropriate to the actual level of activity attained rather than with a fixed budget allowance. Secondly, it is argued that managers find marginal cost statements easier to understand than those based on full costs. In particular, changes in contribution are a clear measure of the effect on profits of changes in output, whereas the inclusion of fixed overheads based on the assumption of one level of output can give quite misleading results (see Chapter 12, p. 241).

However, many accountants would say that the analysis of costs between fixed and variable is often very difficult to make and so any attempt to break down costs in this way might lead to the production of inaccurate data from which to make decisions.

In full costing each and every item of cost has to be identified with successive levels of responsibility in order that it can be allotted correctly to product costs. Under marginal costing, this need not be so and these responsibilities for cost control may be overlooked.

Under absorption costing *all* costs are accounted for and there is little danger of falling into the trap of pricing below total costs. In marginal costing, when prices are set below full costs there is always the danger that long-term losses will result.

Summary

Marginal costing is a useful decision making technique and has value in special contract, make or buy, product mix and pricing decisions. If it is part of an integrated accounting system it can improve cost control and the analysis of results. Its limitations must be recognised and these will depend on the nature and type of business operation as well as the planning, control and review procedures which are present.

Assignments

14.1 The budgeted costs and revenues of product X for the next financial year are as follows:

	Costs per unit £
Direct materials	6.00
Direct labour	8.00
Variable factory overhead	1.00
Variable selling overhead	2.00

In addition, fixed overheads for this year are as follows:

	£
Factory overheads	40,000
Administration	20,000
Selling	40,000

Budgeted sales are 10,000 units and £33 per unit.

(a) Calculate and explain the significance of:
 1. The break-even point in both units and sales (£).
 2. The margin of safety in both units and sales (£).
 3. The contribution/sales ratio.

(b) Show the effect on profit, by means of a statement, of the business taking either of the following courses of action:
 1. Reducing the selling price to £25 per unit and increasing output to 14,000 units.
 2. Raising the selling price to £40 and reducing output to 7,000 units.

(c) What are the main weakness of this type of analysis?

14.2 The normal output of Interchange Ltd., a manufacturing company, is 10,000 units p.a. of a uniform product. The following information is available:

Price/costs per unit (£)	
Direct material	10.00
Direct labour	14.00
Selling price	64.00

In addition to the above costs, the behaviour of overheads in relation to output has been analysed and the following data provided.

		Output (units)	
Overhead	8,000	Normal output 10,000	12,000
Total factory (£)	96,000	100,000	104,000
Total administration (£)	40,000	40,000	40,000
Total selling and distribution (£)	108,000	120,000	132,000

From the above information:

(a) Determine the nature and elements of the above overhead costs.
(b) Calculate the break-even point in terms of:
   1. units; 2. sales (£).
(c) Calculate the effect that the following would have on the break-even point and profits:
   1. If the selling price was reduced to £60 and the quantity produced and sold increased to 12,000 units.
   2. If the selling price was increased to £70 and the quantity sold and produced reduced to 8,000 units.
(d) What are the drawbacks of this type of analysis?

14.3 HWLC management are justifiably proud of their new college which provides splendid amenities for their students. When they are approached by the Students' Union they happily give permission for a weekly discotheque to be held in the main hall. The only proviso they make is that the enterprise must be self sufficient and must not look to the College for any subsidies. The youngsters are happy to agree to this proviso and agree to pay a notional charge of £100 per week, for use of the hall, lighting, heating, cleaning etc. They sign a contract for a disco to appear each week for £50 and are reasonably successful from the outset. Whereas they are not losing money they are unhappy about the numbers at their dances. They would like to see numbers increase, and eventually plan to fill the hall which has a capacity of 1,000.

To this end they decide to have each month a 'Group Night' when they will pay £500 to employ a well known pop group to supplement their disco. They decide also that they will spend £50 per month in promoting and advertising this event and that, for these evenings only, they will double the normal entrance fee to £1 per head.

After the first such 'Group Night' the student committee are advised that the hall was only half full and, even allowing for the fact that they made their usual 30p per head average profit on bar receipts and parking, the evening was loss making.

The committee argued furiously; one half wanted to drop the groups and revert to the ordinary disco as before, whilst the other claimed that more people would have come had the price not been increased. This faction claimed that the hall would be full if the normal admittance charge was levied. It was pointed out that, if the numbers were to be increased substantially in this manner, extra staff would be required and that would mean spending an extra £50.

(a) Approximately how many come to the ordinary disco?
(b) What was the profit/loss on the first 'Group Night'?
(c) Is it feasible to have the groups without raising the original admission price?

14.4 (a) A statistician working in your business has established the following relationship between costs, production and sales revenues for a particular product:

Total cost, $TC = 7.5 + \dfrac{X}{5}$

Total revenue, $TR = R = \dfrac{X}{4}$

where TC and TR are (monetary amounts) in £000 and X is the production in thousands of units.

Required:

Produce a graph of these relationships and find:
1. The break-even level of production.
2. The unit selling price.
3. The unit contribution.
4. Profits if 230,000 units are sold.
5. The extra production required to maintain profits if fixed costs rose to £10,000.
6. The change in the break-even production level [as in (1)] if the price is raised by 20%.

(b) The sales manager of Appleturnover Ltd. maintains he could increase the sales volume (in units) of any of the company's products by 50% if he was authorised to give a 10% price discount and commission appropriate additional advertising. The Board wish to know the maximum additional advertising expense they can incur without the Manager's proposal resulting in a smaller profit.

Required:

Draw up a model in the form of an equation for this problem and comment on what it shows.

14.5 The budget committee of Peter Foster Ltd. have prepared preliminary forecasts for the forthcoming financial year. The sales forecast is 80,000 units at £15 each and a target profit of 5% of sales is envisaged. The variable cost of one unit is estimated at £10. The managing director, after studying these figures, expressed disappointment and called for suggestions aimed at a higher profit margin. In due course, the following alternatives were suggested for consideration:

1. Spend £80,000 on television advertising (expected to increase turnover by 25%).
2. Increase the selling price by 10% (expected to reduce the number of units sold by 5%).
3. Reduce the selling price by 5% (expected to increase the number of units sold by 20%).
4. Centralise the accounting function and so reduce the fixed costs by £30,000 p.a.
5. Spend £20,000 on a cost reduction exercise (expected to cut the variable cost by 10%).

As management accountant, you are asked to calculate (for each suggestion separately):

(a) The revised net profit.

(b) The percentage on sales value represented by the revised net profit.

Also

(c) What assumptions are made about price elasticity in 1. and 2.?

14.6 A hotel has accommodation for 200 guests and is open 350 days p.a. The capital employed in the total amounts to £350,000.

The present position is that the business is making an annual loss, as follows:

	£	£
Income (at £13.50 per guest per day)		630,000
Variable costs: Restaurant, cleaning etc.	105,000	
Fixed cost: Staff, building etc.	630,000	735,000
Net loss for the year		105,000

£525,000 of the fixed expenses are unavoidable even if the hotel is closed; the remaining £105,000 p.a. (i.e. £300 per day) may be reduced by employing less staff over short periods of closure.

Required:

(a) Calculate, the minimum number of guests per day at which the hotel becomes profitable. You may assume that all guests pay a standard charge of £13.50 per day.

(b) Calculate the percentage utilisation of capacity that has to be achieved if a return on capital of 15% is required.

(c) If the maximum annual utilisation of capacity that may be achieved is 65%, what should the price charged per guest per day be if a 15% return on capital is to be realised?

(d) What is the minimum number of guests per day that it is worthwhile admitting to the hotel in the short run before it is considered that the hotel should be closed down for a short period, e.g. seasonally? You should assume a price per guest as calculated in (c) above

(e) What other considerations, outside the financial implications, would have to be taken into account before the hotel was closed for a short period?

14.7 The Redken Bus Company has recently received a licence to operate a bus service and is considering its pricing policy. Market research indicates that passenger demand is particularly sensitive to the fares charged and estimated statistics have been prepared for two alternative pricing policies, namely:

	Policy A	Policy B
1. Fare charge per mile	4p	5p
2. Number of buses required	10	7
3. Estimated annual mileage of each bus	60,000	60,000
4. Estimated average number of passengers carried per bus	25	20
5. Estimated passenger miles [(2) × (3) × (4)]	15,000,000	8,400,000

The following financial statistics are estimated for each bus in operation:

Initial capital cost	£100,000
Estimated disposal value (after 200,000 miles)	£20,000
Licence and insurance p.a.	£400
Repairs and maintenance per mile	10p
Fuel per mile	20p
Driver/conductor wages p.a.	£10,000

Required:

(a) Compute the expected profit contribution of the alternative policies.

(b) Compute the minimum average number of passengers required to break even under each policy.

(c) Indicate any other factors which might influence the decision.

(*ICA*)

14.8 Dave Sheargold is the manager of the Boothferry Park Stadium which has a capacity of 10,000 seats. He is considering whether to promote a one day pop concert featuring a famous group known as 'The Terminal Stupids'. From enquiries he has been able to assmble the following data about the venture:

	£
Allocated share of rent, overheads etc.	11,500
Hire of security force, cleaning and ushering	9,200
Advertising	6,900
Ticket printing	2,300
Miscellaneous expenses (additional lighting etc.)	4,600
The Group's fee	23,000
	57,500

Whatever the price of the ticket, value added tax of 15% must be added to it. For example, a ticket with a basic price of £5.00 must be sold for £5.75. All prices shown include VAT.

(a) Assuming three quarters of the seats are sold; what price should the average ticket be to allow one performance *break even*?

(b) Suppose that Dave believes that he can secure the best return by pricing as follows:

Number of seats	1,000	1,000	2,000	5,000	1,000
Price (£)	12.65	10.35	9.20	5.75	3.45

How much *surplus* would be produced for the Stadium if the concert is a sell-out?

(c) Gizzard Puke, the manager of 'The Terminal Stupids', contacted Dave to suggest an *alternative arrangment* of a fee of £11,500 plus £1.40 per ticket sold, whatever the price. If you were Dave would you accept this offer? Explain the reason(s) for your answer. Can you suggest other arrangements which might appeal to both parties?

14.9 A new product has successfully passed through research and development and test marketing and a national launch is now planned. Forecasts suggest three possible sales levels, depending on the price charged:

Sales policy	1	2	3
Unit selling prices (£)	30	28.50	27
Unit material cost (£)	15	15	15
Unit labour cost (£)	6	6	6
Sales estimate (units)	3,000	7,500	12,000

Notes

- these sales policies are mutually exclusive
- production fixed costs are £20,000 up to 6,000 units but, if production levels increase above this, costs will rise to £40,000. Maximum production capacity is 12,000 units for the forecast period
- royalties have to be paid as follows:

Units sold	Total royalties (£)
0–6,000	1,500
6,001–9,750	10,000
9,751–12,000	24,500

- ignore stocks

Required:

(a) Draw a graph to show how the results of the three different levels of activity compare.
(b) 1. Use the graph to estimate the relevant break-even points.
    2. Calculate the level of activity you would recommend to give maximum profit. Check your answer with the graph.
(c) Comment on your results and the validity of the methods used.

14.10 The following details are available for three similar products which use the same type of material and labour:

Product	Standard £	Premium £	Extra £
Selling price	120	180	240
Direct materials (£2.40 per kilogram)	12	79.20	54
Direct wages (£4.80 per hour)	48	26.40	72
Variable overheads	24	13.20	36

Variable overheads are recovered at the rate of £2 per direct labour hour. Total fixed overheads are estimated at £72,000.

Required:

(a) Prepare a budget and calculate priority rankings for these products given the following constraints:
   1. When the market for sales is limited by volume.
   2. When the market for sales is limited by value.
   3. When the supply of labour and/or materials is limited.
(b) Can you give examples of industries or products where such constraints exist at the moment?
(c) Calculate the maximum profit and the unit sales when the total raw material available is 36,000 kg and the maximum sales potential is: Standard, 960 units; Premium, 840 units; Extra, 1,080 units.

14.11 Garnett Ltd. makes a personal microcomputer which it sells for £96. It is selling well and Ray Garnett, the chief executive, had told his production manager to increase output at the end of the second quarter in anticipation of higher sales in quarter 3. The latest operating statement showed that the sales volume had increased during quarter 3, but the profit shown was less than reported profits in the previous quarter (see statement below). Ray was mystified; he had always understood that if more products were sold, more profit could be earned.

Garnett Ltd: Operating statement

	Quarter 2	Quarter 3
Sales of microcomputers (units)	2,500	3,000
	£000	£000
Sales value	240	288
Cost of sales:		
Opening Stock	18	48
Cost of production	180	156
Total	198	204
Less: Closing stock	48	24
	150	180
Underabsorbed fixed overhead		
Total manufacturing cost	150	195.84
Operating profit	90	92.16

Operating statement (continued)

	Quarter 2	Quarter 3
Less: Administrative and selling expenses:		
Variable	12	14.4
Fixed	65.28	65.28
	77.28	79.68
Net profit	12.72	12.48

Ray fired off a memo to his accountant, Ken barlow.

Internal memorandum

From: Ray Garnett
To: Ken Barlow
Subject: Quarterly operating statements

I'm not too happy with the type of profit statement you issued. It strikes me that when sales increase by 20% we should show more, not less, profit.

How can I tell how much profit we are going to make in the future with these kinds of figures?

Furthermore you told me the monthly break-even point was 2,600 units. How can this be so when our quarter 2 sales of 2,500 microcomputers earned £12,720? Can you check this please?

Last month you metntioned something about marginal cost accounting. I'm not sure that I understood what you were muttering about but I do remember your comment about a 'sensible treatment of fixed costs'. Can you prepare something for me to look at?

It's probably best if you use the last 2 quarters' figures as an illustration, then we could decide whether to carry this marginal costing business further. Love to the kids, Ray.

Ken Barlow smiled as he read the memo. He had tried on several occasions to interest Ray in marginal costing but had failed to get his ideas across. Ray seemed to get confused about the treatment of fixed manufacturing overhead and its effect on stock valuation. Now was Ken's chance to make a good presentation of the case for marginal costing.

First of all he summarised the unit costs of production used to complete the quarterly statement:

	Quarter 2	Quarter 3
Production units	3,000	2,600
Manufacturing costs:	£	
Unit variable costs	20.40	
Unit fixed costs*	39.60	
	60.00	

*The fixed overhead per unit is based on quarterly fixed expenses of £118,800 dividend by normal production of 3,000 units per quarter.

Required:

(a) Prepare Ken Barlow's answer to Ray Garnett's memo including the accounting statements to back his argument for marginal costing. Your reply should include an attempt to give a valid explanation for the £240 profit difference.

(b) Recommend, with reasons, whether Garnett Ltd. should keep to its present cost accounting system or convert to marginal costing.

15 Budgeting

When you have read this chapter you should:
- understand the importance of planning through budgets
- understand how the main types of budget are prepared and the relationships between them
- understand how budgets are used for reviewing and controlling performance

15.1 Introduction

All business organisations, regardless of their size or type, will have some kind of plan for their future operations, ranging from a few calculations on the back of an envelope to an elaborate budgetary control system maintained by computer. Business plans have two broad objectives:

1. They give organisations some idea of the direction in which they are headed.
2. They provide a yardstick against which actual results can be compared.

Both of these are extremely important because without a plan, the organisation has no means of judging whether or not it is moving in the right direction and achieving satisfactory results. The purpose of this chapter is to show how budgeting works in principal and to consider the main stages involved:

- planning
- control
- review

15.2 Planning by means of budgets

A budget is a technical term for a plan expressed in quantitative terms. Bearing in mind that budgets are used for both planning and control purposes, they can be prepared in two different ways:

1. By *function* and *nature*. For example, the production cost budget could be subdivided between direct labour, direct materials and production overheads. This budget could then slot easily into a budgeted Profit and Loss Account for the business as a whole which would be used to assess the viability of the overall plan.

2. By *departments* or *areas of responsibility*. These are most frequently referred to as *cost centres* or *budget centres* and provide the basis for detailed analysis and review of performance. In the first instance, the most difficult decision with this type of budgeting concerns the appropriate number of cost centres. It is necessary for the organisation to strike a balance between too few cost centres, where the depth of analysis is restricted, and too many cost centres, where the system is unwieldy and expensive to administer.

In order to clarify this picture, Figures 15.1 and 15.2 show a production budget prepared in these two ways. Similar budgets will be prepared for all the main headings of revenue and expense, and from these the Final Accounts, or Master Budgets as they are often called, will be made up. In preparing budgets, the organisation must recognise the key budget or limiting factors, i.e. constraints on the activities or resources of the organisation which will provide a boundary to its likely achievements. Some typical

Figure 15.1
Production cost budget for planning purposes

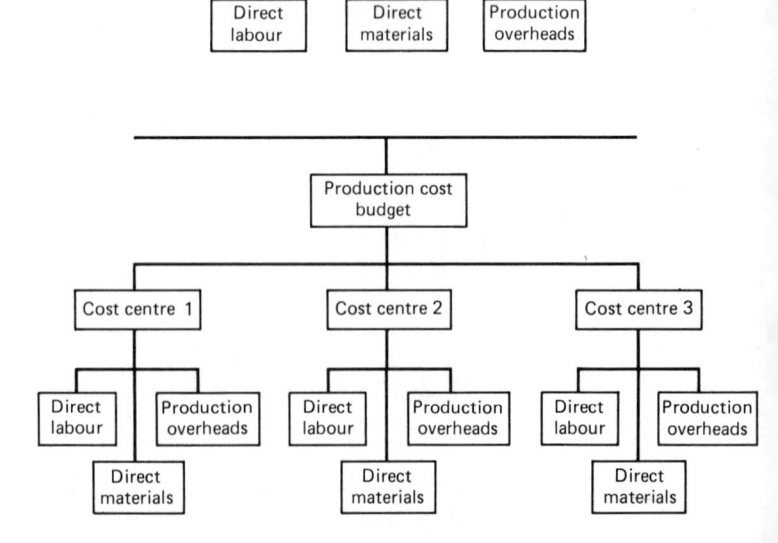

Figure 15.2
Production cost budget for control purposes

examples of limiting factors are productive capacity, the supply of skilled labour, the availability of natural resources and the size of the potential market. There is no point, for example, producing 5,000 units per week if the market will only buy 500, unless stocks are being built-up for sale later in the year.

15.3 Preparing a set of budgets

Sales budgets

These are the first and most important budgets that the organisation needs to prepare since the information they contain will have an impact on all the other budgets which should follow. Many factors will need to be considered and assessed and the final budget should culminate from a co-operative effort between sales managers and sales team. Factors taken into account should include:

- the level of demand in previous periods
- costs of production and prices
- competitors' products and prices
- market research findings
- size and quality of the sales force
- expenditure on advertising and promotion

Selling, distribution and administrative cost budgets

Budgeted sales volume and revenue will have a direct bearing on the costs associated with selling and distributing the product and the administration costs involved in processing orders, maintaining records, paying employees etc. Some elements of cost are easier to budget than others. Many of the costs associated with offices and retail outlets, for example, tend to be fixed. Rent and rates, light and heat, insurance, depreciation and staff salaries are included in this category and are relatively easy to establish. Other costs, however, are determined by a combination of factors like the number of customers and the size and frequency of orders, and as such are more difficult to budget. Order processing costs and distribution costs would fall into this category.

Production budgets

These budgets follow directly from the sales budgets and, in the first instance, the nature of the product and available storage space will be the key factors considered in relation to sales volume. If, for example, the products are perishable, they will tend to be manufactured just prior to sale. If, on the other hand, the product is non-perishable, the organisation can choose between two extreme solutions:

1. It can plan for an even production rate throughout the year so that seasonal variations in sales volume will be reflected in stock changes. Therefore, in periods when sales are below average, stocks will be built up to be run down when sales are above average.
2. It can plan to vary the production rate with the sales volume so that stocks will tend to remain at a constant level throughout the planning period.

In theory, it is possible for the organisation to achieve an optimum solution to this problem whereby the costs associated with stockholding are minimised. Unfortunately, the complications of the real world mean that in practice optimum solutions are a little harder to come by.

Direct materials budgets

These budgets follow directly from the production budgets and take account of the quantities of materials that will be needed to meet production requirements and the prices that will be paid for the materials. This involves the careful assessment of a number of important factors, including:

- the quality of materials to be used
- the amount of waste and scrapped production expected
- the age and condition of the machinery being used with the materials
- the skill of the machine operators
- past movements of materials' prices
- suppliers' price lists

Direct labour budgets

As with the materials budgets, these follow directly from the production budgets since there is a direct link between production levels and workforce requirements. In preparing these budgets, a number of important factors will need to be taken into account:

- past records of productive efficiency
- production methods and machinery and the likely effects of any changes
- union agreements on manning levels and working practices
- the likely effects of incentive schemes

Budgeting for rates of pay is relatively easy since these are normally established by negotiations between employers and unions. However, difficulties can arise when these rates are renegotiated part-way through the planning period and planners must try to anticipate the settlement. Many organisations review their budgets at this point and revise them in the light of the new agreement.

Factory overhead budgets

Preparing these budgets involves the same procedures as given for

Cash budgets

the direct costs since each item which comprises factory overheads must be considered separately. However, as previous chapters have pointed out, the added problem with factory overheads is that many are shared by a number of cost centres (e.g. rent and rates) and fair bases for their apportionment must be found. Chapter 12 has already shown that this is not as easy as it may sound.

All the budgets considered so far have a direct bearing on the cash balance of the organisation since all business transactions eventually involve cash flowing into or out of the organisation. The cash budget is therefore crucially important and central to the budgeting process. Cash is the life-blood of all business organisations and cash management is a major part of the day-to-day work of many accountants. There are two main components to all cash budgets.

Cash receipts Receipts are normally generated from sales and a distinction is necessary between cash and credit, since the timing of the inflows will be different. Apart from sales, other sources of cash might include dividends and interest received, the issue of shares and debentures, and the disposal of fixed assets.

Cash payments A major element under this heading will be the payments made for the expense budgets considered earlier. However, it is important to recognise here that it is not the purpose of a cash budget to measure profit and, therefore, prepayments will be included while accrued expenses will be excluded. Other payments might include amounts for fixed assets, redemption of shares and debentures, taxes and dividends.

A budgeting example Brian and Steve have decided to open a motor spares shop and have formed a limited company, BS Motor Spares Ltd, to commence trading on 1st January, 19–1. Since leaving school, both have worked in this trade and feel that they now have enough experience and financial backing to make a success of this venture. Having carefully considered the first six months of trading, they have put together the following information:

1. The share capital of the company will be made up of 10,000 £1 ordinary shares, divided equally between the two owners. This cash will be paid into a business bank account on 1st January, 19–1.

2. The lease on suitable premises will cost £5,500 and this will be paid in January. The lease is for 5 years with a monthly rent of £300 for the first two years. The rent is payable in advance.

3. Fixtures and fittings costing £1,500 and a motor van costing £2,000 will be acquired during January for cash. They expect to use

the fixtures and fittings for 10 years before changing them while the motor van will be used for 4 years. The van should fetch £400 when sold while the fixtures and fittings should realise another £200.

4. An opening stock of £1,800 will be acquired for cash on 1st January and will be maintained at this level for the remainder of the year. Suppliers have agreed that subsequently one month's credit will be allowed on all other purchases.

5. A mark-up of 100% on cost will be used to establish selling prices initially, and this will be modified later if necessary in the light of prices charged by their main competition.

6. Cash sales for the first six months of trading have been estimated as follows:

January: £3,100   February: £3,800   March: £3,200
April: £4,100   May: £4,500   June: £5,000

In addition, credit sales to local dealers and garages should be as follows:

January: £400   February: £500   March: £600
April: £500   May: £400   June: £500

They have decided to allow one month's credit.

7. Each partner has agreed to take a salary of £400 per month and review this in the light of the trading results.
8. Rates for the first six months of £600 will be paid in May.
9. General running expenses have been estimated at £240 per month.
10. Staff salaries will amount to £400 per month.

Brian and Steve require a financial plan for the first six months of trading and, in the first instance, this will include:

- a cash budget
- a Profit and Loss Account
- a Balance Sheet

Solution

The required statements are now given with explanatory notes. These should be referred to as they arise.

Cash budget for the six months ended 30th June, 19–1

	January £	February £	March £	April £	May £	June £	Explanatory notes
Receipts							
Share capital	10,000						
Cash sales	3,100	3,800	3,200	4,100	4,500	5,000	

	£	£	£	£	£	£	Explanatory notes
Credit sales		400	500	600	500	400	1
	13,100	4,200	3,700	4,700	5,000	5,400	
Payments							
Lease	5,500						
Fixtures and fittings	1,500						
Van	2,000						
Stock	1,800						
Purchases		1,750	2,150	1,900	2,300	2,450	2
Rent	300	300	300	300	300	300	
Rates					600		
Running expenses	240	240	240	240	240	240	
Directors' salaries	800	800	800	800	800	800	
Staff salaries	400	400	400	400	400	400	
	12,540	3,490	3,890	3,640	4,640	4,190	
Summary							
Opening balance	—	560	1,270	1,080	2,140	2,500	
Receipts	13,100	4,200	3,700	4,700	5,000	5,400	
	13,100	4,760	4,970	5,780	7,140	7,900	
Payments	12,540	3,490	3,890	3,640	4,640	4,190	
Closing Balance	560	1,270	1,080	2,140	2,500	3,710	

Budgeted Profit and Loss Account for the six months ended 30th June, 19–1

	£	£	Explanatory notes
Cash sales		23,700	3
Credit sales		2,900	
		26,600	
Cost of goods sold		13,300	4
Gross profit		13,300	
Rent	1,800		
Rates	600		
Running expenses	1,440		
Directors' salaries	4,800		
Staff salaries	2,400		
Depreciation:			
Lease	550		
Fixtures and fittings	65		
Motor van	200		
		11,855	
Net profit		1,445	

Budgeted Balance Sheet as at 30th June, 19–1

	Cost £	Accumulated depreciation £	Net £	Explanatory notes
Fixed assets				
Leasehold premises	5,500	550	4,950	
Fixtures and fittings	1,500	65	1,435	
Motor van	2,000	200	1,800	
	9,000	1,015	8,185	

Budgeted Balance sheet (continued)

	£	£	£	Explanatory notes
Current assets				
Stocks, at cost		1,800		6
Trade debtors		500		7
Bank		3,710		
		6,010		
Current liabilities				
Trade creditors		2,750		8
Working capital			3,260	
Capital employed			11,445	
Financed by				
Ordinary share capital			10,000	
Profit and loss balance			1,445	
			11,445	

Explanatory notes

1 The company offers one month's credit so these figures assume that January's sales are paid for in February, February's are paid for in March, etc.

2 Suppliers have granted one month's credit so there will be a delay of one month in payments to suppliers. Sales in January are budgeted at £3,500 (i.e. £3,100 cash and £400 credit). Since the company uses a mark-up of 100% on cost, the equivalent gross margin on sales is 50%. Therefore, sales of £3,500 would require purchases of:

£3,500 × 50/100 = £1,750

These purchases are paid for in February. February's sales are £4,300 i.e. £3,800 cash and £500 credit. Purchases in February are therefore £2,150, paid for in March.

3 Sales figures for the six months are obtained by simply adding monthly figures provided in the information.

4 Since the company uses a uniform mark-up of 100%, the cost of goods sold is half the sales figure.

5 The Profit and Loss Account provides for depreciation for half a year.
(a) Since the lease is for 5 years, annual depreciation should be £5,500/5 = £1,100. Therefore, depreciation for six months is £550.
(b) The fixtures and fittings will cost £1,500 but should realise £200 after 10 years. The net cost is therefore £1,300, giving an annual depreciation of £130 and half a year's depreciation at £65.
(c) The motor van will cost £2,000 and should realise £400 after 4 years. The net cost is therefore £1,600, giving an annual depreciation of £400, and a half a year's at £200.

6 The opening stock is to be £1,800 and it will be maintained at this level throughout the year. The closing stock is therefore the same.

7 By the end of June, credit sales in June will not have been paid for, giving trade debtors of £500.

8 Purchases in June will not be paid for until July. Sales in June are estimated to be £5,500 (£5,000 cash and £500 credit), giving purchases of £2,750. This is the amount outstanding to suppliers.

The information contained in these statements should give the prospective partners a much clearer picture of their financial position after six months trading than was the case previously. They now have a sounder basis for a decision as to whether or not they should pursue this venture. Although on the face of it the venture appears to be viable, at least over the first six months, success hinges on the ability of the partners to generate a sufficient level of sales. If the sales budgets are over-generous, then the financial picture would be quite different. There is therefore an element of risk that could be investigated further if more information about potential sales was provided. However, only the partners themselves can decide whether or not the expected return is sufficient to compensate for the risks and effort involved.

15.4 Control and review

Assuming that a decision was made to proceed with this venture, performance should be carefully monitored to ensure that the organisation is progressing in the right direction and that any problem areas are identified as soon as possible. This can be done by regular comparisons of actual results with budgets so that significant differences or variances can be investigated and the appropriate corrective action taken. The important point about variance analysis is that the people running the organisation should be able to learn from past experience so that future performance can be improved or budgets modified to take account of prevailing conditions.

In order to illustrate these points more fully, assume that actual results for the first six months of trading are available for BS Motor Spares. In order to highlight significant variances in the Profit and Loss Account, a statement like the following one could be used:

Profit and Loss Account for the six months ended 30th June, 19-1

	Budget	Actual	Variance
	£	£	£
Cash sales	23,700	19,400	4,300(A)
Credit sales	2,900	2,400	500(A)
	26,600	21,800	4,800(A)
Cost of sales	13,300	10,900	2,400(F)
Gross profit	13,300	10,900	2,400(A)

Profit and Loss Account (continued)

	Budget £	Actual £	Variance £
Rent	1,800	1,800	—
Rates	600	700	100(A)
Running expenses	1,440	1,220	220(F)
Directors' salaries	4,800	4,200	600(F)
Staff salaries	2,400	2,200	200(F)
Depreciation	815	815	—
Net profit (loss)	1,445	(35)	1,480(A)

Obviously, performance has not lived up to expectations, with the organisation showing a loss for the first six months of trading as against a budgeted profit. The variances in the right-hand column show how this has come about, with adverse variances (A) reducing profits and favourable variances (F) increasing profits. The analysis of performance could centre on two main areas of interest: sales and costs.

Sales

Sales revenue was not as high as expected and this was one of the major contributory factors to the organisation's making a loss instead of a profit. Isolating the causes for this could be made easier by a monthly breakdown of the sales figures, if possible, subdivided into product groups. If particular months have been poor, it could be that there is a seasonal pattern to demand which should be allowed for in future budgeting exercises. Alternatively, the first few months of trading could have been harder than expected with new customers difficult to attract. The breakdown into product groups could reveal particular problem areas which could be due to a lack of competitiveness. This could suggest that the marketing side of the business needs to be strengthened, with a budget allowed for promotion and advertising and some modification to the pricing policy.

Costs

Generally, costs are lower than expected and this has partly compensated for the fall in sales revenue. Running expenses could be lower due to the lower sales revenue, although pinpointing the reasons for this requires a detailed breakdown of the main items comprising this group. The partners have decided to take a lower salary in response to the shortfall in sales, and staff salaries are down for the same reason. In general, therefore, satisfactory control has been exercised over costs, with some timely and significant reductions in response to the weaker sales performance.

Reviews of this kind should help managers to learn from their experience and to identify a range of options open to the business which could improve future performance.

Summary

Budgeting can be seen as the process of establishing financial plans for organisations and then controlling and reviewing performance through variance analysis. Variance analysis involves a comparison of budgeted with actual results and the investigation of the causes for the significant differences (variances). For example, sales and cost variances which are considered exceptional will be the focus of management attention, and management will seek to put into practice appropriate corrective measures to avoid falling below planned levels in the future. Similar comparisons will be made between budgeted and actual receipts and payments, debtors and creditors etc. Although nothing can be done about the past, it is possible to learn from mistakes so that future decisions may be improved. The process of establishing budgets will also improve with experience.

Assignments

15.1 Slidetab and Company Ltd. are about to start in business and have prepared budgets for the first months of trading. The following information is available:

(a) 100,000 £1 ordinary shares are to be issued at par (face value) and these will be paid for in instalments:

£0.50 per share on application in March;
£0.25 per share on allotment in April;
£0.25 per share on first and final call in May.

(b) Rent is £18,000 p.a., payable on the 1st of each month.

(c) Purchases have been budgeted as follows:

March: £15,000   April: £15,000   May: £22,000
June: £25,000   July: £27,000   August: £50,000

All purchases are on credit and the terms are that they will be paid for as follows:
50% in the following month, thereby obtaining a 2% cash discount;
50% one month after (without a discount).

(d) Wages and salaries will be:

March: £10,000   April: £11,000   May: £15,000
June: £20,000   July: £21,000   August: £25,000

These will be paid during the month in which they are incurred.

(e) Overhead expenses will be 5% on sales, paid in each month.

(f) Fixtures and fittings costing £25,000 will be acquired in March and paid for immediately. Equipment costing £30,000 will be acquired in

March and paid for in April. (Depreciation is to be provided at 20% on cost p.a.)

(g) Sales have been budgeted as follows:

| March: £25,000 | April: £26,000 | May: £46,000 |
| June: £56,000 | July: £64,000 | August: £71,000 |

50% are cash sales and 50% credit sales. The average delay in the receipt of cash from debtors is estimated at 2 months. The organisation expects to use a uniform mark-up of 100% on the purchase price of stock to obtain their selling prices.

Required:

From the budget data:

(a) Prepare a monthly cash budget for the first six months of trading.

(b) Prepare a budget Profit and Loss Account for the first six months and a budgeted Balance Sheet as at 31st August.

(c) Draft a report to the Managing Director of Slidetab and Company highlighting the main features for these budgets.

15.2 BS Ltd. manufacture various products from single plant. Department 4 produces a product which has a selling price of £2.50 per unit. Monthly budgets for the next financial year have been prepared and show that expected production and sales are 40,000 units per month, representing 50% of the department's capacity. Budgeted costs per month are shown below.

Direct labour	£24,300
Direct materials	£27,800
Factory overhead costs	£48,700
Distribution costs	£ 4,000
Sales people's commission	£10,000
	£114,800

The following additional information is available regarding the budgets:

(a) The organisation operates a group premium bonus scheme whereby production workers in Department 4 are paid a basic day rate plus £0.10 per unit produced.

(b) Factory overhead costs include amounts apportioned for costs shared with other departments (e.g. rent and rates, light and heat, insurance etc.) totalling £16,400. £13,200 of these are fixed costs. Of the remainder, £2,800 are considered to be variable costs.

(c) Direct materials and selling distribution costs are considered to be completely variable.

At a recent meeting of the organisation's budget committee, the Sales Director suggested that production and sales of the department could be increased by 50% if the selling price was reduced to £2.25 per unit. The Chairman responded by saying that this was not viable and would only serve to increase the losses incurred by the department. His recommendation was immediate closure of the department.

Required:

(a) On the basis of this information, prepare departmental budgets for the

committee showing the organisation's position if:
1. the department was closed.
2. the reduction in selling price was adopted.

(b) Explain any other factors that should be considered by the organisation before a decision is made.

15.3 John Blunt plans to start a business on the 1st July, 19–1, by introducing capital of £10,000 which will be paid into a business bank account. He will make an immediate payment of £11,800 for equipment. In addition, he will buy stock costing £6,800 on credit. Suppliers have agreed to give him two months' credit on all purchases. He will maintain his stock at this level throughout the year and has offered customers a credit period of one month.

John has made some preliminary calculations and expects to earn a gross profit of 25% on sales and incur the following expenses for the first year of trading:

Rent	£8,000
Sundry expenses	£6,000
Depreciation	£2,000

These costs will remain fixed whatever the level of sales achieved. Rent is paid quarterly in advance and sundry expenses are expected to be incurred at an even rate throughout the year and paid as they are incurred.

John intends to withdraw £400 per month for his personal use and expects that his sales will be between £8,000 and £10,000 per month for the first year, (all sales on credit). As he will need to secure overdraft facilities from his bank during the first year of trading, he has asked you to prepare the necessary financial statements to support his application:

(a) A monthly cash budget, and a Profit and Loss Account and Balance Sheet for the first year of trading, assuming sales of £8,000 per month.

(b) The Final Accounts for the same period but assuming sales of £10,000 per month.

(c) A report on the financial implications of his proposed plans.

15.4 The sales budget for EM Ltd. is £516,000 for the year ended 30th June. The sales break-down for this budget is given below

Product	Quantity	£
A	25,000	50,000
B	75,000	165,000
C	40,000	70,000
D	110,000	231,000
	250,000	516,000

The actual results for the year are as follows:

Product	Quantity	£
A	30,000	58,000
B	70,000	154,000
C	40,000	60,000
D	70,000	147,000
E	40,000	80,000

Required:

(a) Prepare a statement showing budget and actual results for the period, showing the variances that have occurred.

(b) Analyse the cause of the variances in sales income for the period.

15.5 The summarised Balance Sheet at 31 October, 19–7, of Keensuppliers Ltd. is as follows:

	£		£	£
Ordinary share capital	30,000			20,000
Share premium account	4,700	Freehold premises at cost		
	34,700	Fixtures and fittings		
Less: Profit and loss account	5,700	At cost	6,000	
	29,000	*Less:* Depreciation to date	1,800	4,200
Bank overdraft	5,000	Trading stock	7,800	
Trade creditors	5,200	Trade debtors	7,200	15,000
	£39,200			£39,200

The company is now reviewing its activities with a view to improving performance as far as profit is concerned.

The following budgeted information relates to the forthcoming financial year ending 31st October, 19–8:

(a) The cost of goods sold will be 80% of sales revenue throughout the year.

(b) Fixed overheads will be:

Rates, heat and hight   £4,000
Basic salaries   £10,000
General administration   £6,100

(c) Staff bonuses will be 50% of gross profit.

(d) Cash sales will be £50,000, the remainder be paid at the end of the month following the month of sale.

(e) Depreciation policies:
Freehold premises—nil
Fixtures and fittings—10% on cost of assets held at the accounting year end.

(f) It is considered it will be necessary to obtain some additional shelving (fixtures and fittings) in January, 19–8, at an estimated cost of £2,000.

(g) Trade suppliers give two months' credit; it can be assumed that all overheads, staff bonuses and the additional shelving will be the subject of cash transactions.

(h) All trading transactions will take place at even rate throughout the year.

(i) Trading stock at 31st October, 19–8, will be 5% of cost of goods sold during the year. It is assumed that all trade debtors and trade creditors at 31st October, 19–7, will be settled in November, 19–7.

It is not planned to declare any dividends for the forthcoming year. Ignore bank overdraft interest and taxation.

The Directors, who still see very difficult times ahead, are considering two alternative plans for the year to 31st October, 19–8:

    Plan A – To increase sales so that after taking all costs and expenses into account, they will just break-even (i.e. the net profit will be nil).

Plan B – To increase sales so that, after taking all costs and expenses into account, they will make enough profit to extinguish the present debit balance on the Profit and Loss Account.

Note: Assume the financial year consists of twelve months of equal duration.

Required:

(a) The estimated Trading and Profit and Loss Account for the year ending 31st October, 19-8, and the estimated Balance Sheet at that date if Plan A is followed.
(b) A computation of the sales for the year ending 31st October, 19-8, and trade creditors at that date if Plan B is followed.

(AEB 'A' Level)

16 Standard Costing

When you have read this chapter you should:
- understand the basic principles involved in preparing standard costs
- understand how the main variances are calculated and analysed
- understand how standard costing can be used to promote effective organisational control

16.1 Introduction

The preparation of standard costs

Standard costing can be seen as a logical extension of budgetary control and is best applied in situations where standard products or processes are the norm. The use of standard costing as a control technique involves a number of stages:

Since the standard costs are the yardstick against which actual performance will be matched, it is crucial that they are set with extreme caution, having regard to a number of factors:

(a) The market conditions in which the organisation will operate over the planning period. This will affect the price of the resources used by the organisation and should be taken into account when establishing standards for material prices, labour rates and overhead costs.

(b) The expected level of operating efficiency. Standards should be based on a review of past performance and any changes in working methods or replacement of plant and machinery should be reflected in the standard operating times.

(c) Expected activity levels. Forecast demand for the organisation's output will affect production requirements and this will have a bearing on the standards set, particularly for overhead costs.

The analysis of variances

You should know that a variance is the difference between budgeted (standard) and actual results. A major benefit of standard costing is that it allows a detailed analysis of variances and this should facilitate the discovery of underlying causes. This is

Standard Costing

normally achieved by means of regular variance reports directed at responsible individuals.

Taking appropriate action

The accurate preparation of variance reports is obviously important but they do not of themselves control the activities of organisations. An investigation of a variance which is considered significant should prompt action by people in the organisation. This may be the modification of future activities or the amendment of the standards against which future comparisons will be made. What constitutes appropriate action is of course, to a large extent, a matter of opinion. This is why some ventures succeed while others fail.

It is worth noting here that standard costing has little prospect of succeeding as a control technique unless standards are *attainable* and *controllable* by the individuals who are asked to account for them. Standards which are considered to be unattainable and outside control provide no incentive for improved future performance and are therefore of limited value.

Example The calculation and interpretation of a comprehensive set of variances is now explained by reference to the following example for Becnat Ltd.

Becnat Ltd. manufactures and sells a product, the standard production costs of which are as follows:

	Cost per unit £
Direct labour: 2 hours @ £2.50 per hour	5.00
Direct materials:	
A 5 units @ £0.20 per unit	1.00
B 2 kg @ £0.80 per kg.	1.60
Production overheads:	
Fixed: £0.60 per direct labour hour	1.20
Variable: £0.50 per direct labour hour	1.00

The fixed overhead recovery rate is based on a budgeted production volume of 3,000 units per month.

During April 19–1, 3,200 units of output were completed and actual costs incurred for this month are given in the following operating statement:

Operating Statement for April, 19–1

Direct labour (6,200 hours)	17,400
Direct materials:	
A (19,200 units)	3,450
B (6,300 kg)	4,980
Fixed overheads	3,740
Variable overheads	3,650
	33,220

16.2 Labour variances

Any variance between standard and actual labour costs can be attributed to differences in wage rates paid (wage rate variance) and/or differences in hours used to produce the output (labour efficiency variance). With all variance analysis it is important to use the correct standards for the output actually achieved. There is no value, for example, in comparing standards for 3,000 units with the actual results for 3,200 units. So, in the first instance, it is important to *establish standard costs for the output actually achieved*. From this, the overall labour cost variance is calculated for Becnat Ltd. as follows:

	£
Actual costs	17,400
Standard costs	
3,200 units × 2 hours × £2.50	16,000
Cost variance	1,400(A)

Since the actual cost is higher than standard, the variance of £1,400 is adverse and means that actual profit will be £1,400 lower than was budgeted. This is shown by the letter A in brackets after the amount. If the actual cost had been less than standard, then the variance would have been favourable and shown by F in brackets.

It is possible to subdivide the cost variance into two:

A labour rate variance

This can be calculated in a number of ways, one of which is:

(Standard rate − Actual rate) × Actual hours

By removing the bracket, the formula becomes:

Standard rate × Actual hours − Actual rate × Actual hours
= £2.50 × 6,200 hours − £17,400
= £15,500 − £17,400 = £1,900(A)

Therefore, as a result of paying higher wage rates, labour costs were £1,900 higher than standard. This could be caused by a number of factors but the most probable is that the wage rate was negotiated at a higher level than was anticipated when the standard was set. Alternatively, machine breakdowns or poor production scheduling may have resulted in more overtime working than was anticipated and hence the payment of higher rates.

A labour efficiency variance

(Standard hours − Actual hours) × Standard rate

(6,400 hours − 6,200 hours) × £2.50 = £500(F)

Standard hours are calculated as:

Actual output × Standard hours per unit
= 3,200 × 2 hours = 6,400 hours

The actual hours used to produce the output were less than standard and as a result, there was a saving of £500 in labour costs. There could be many reasons for this variance. Improvements in working methods, tools or machinery, or better production scheduling are two possible explanations. However, an individual's efficiency can also be affected by a multitude of personal factors that are more or less obvious, depending on the nature of the productive process.

A useful check with labour variances is that the rate and efficiency variances should tally back to the cost variance, as the following statement shows:

	£
Rate variance	1,900(A)
Efficiency variance	500(F)
Cost variance	1,400(A)

16.3 Materials variances

Variances between standard and actual materials costs can be attributed either to the price paid for the materials (materials price variance) and/or the quantity of materials used (materials usage variance). The cost variances for Becnat Ltd. are calculated as follows:

	£
Material A	
Standard costs:	
5 units of material × 3,200 units of output × £0.20	= 3,200
Actual costs	3,450
Cost variance	250(A)
Material B	
Standard costs:	
2 kg × 3,200 units of output × £0.80	5,120
Actual costs	4,980
	140(F)

The costs variances can be subdivided into two:

Materials price variances

(Standard price − Actual price) × Actual quantity

= (Standard price × Actual quantity) − (Actual price × Actual quantity)

Material A

($£0.20 \times 19,200$ units) $- £3,450$
$= £3,840 - £3,450 = £390(F)$

Material B

($£0.80 \times 6,300$ kg) $- £4,980$
$£5,040 - £4,980 = £60(F)$

Because the prices paid for both materials were lower than standard, this has resulted in a cost saving on both. There are a number of reasons why these variances could have occurred. For instance, predicting future price movements is a difficult task at the best of times and it could be that the organisation predicted a higher price than was necessary. Alternatively, a lower grade of material could have been used. A more commendable explanation is of course that a supplier charging a lower price for the same quality has been located by the organisation.

Materials usage variances

(Standard quantity $-$ Actual quantity) $\times$ Standard price

Material A

(16,000 units $-$ 19,200 units) $\times £0.20 = £640(A)$

Standard quantity $= 5$ units of material $\times 3,200$ units of output $= 16,000$ units

Material B

(6,400 kg $-$ 6,300 kg) $\times £0.80 = £80(F)$

Standard quantity $= 2$ kg $\times 3,200$ units of output $= 6,400$ kg.

The adverse variance for material A could be due to a machine breakdown, resulting in scrapped material, theft or a poor quality of material. The favourable variance for material B could be due to the reverse of these or an overgenerous standard.

In a similar manner to labour variances, it is possible to tally the price and usage variances with the cost variance, as Table 16.1 shows:

Table 16.1

	Material A	Material B
Price variances	390(F)	60(F)
Usage variances	640(A)	80(F)
	250(A)	140(F)

16.4 Variable overhead variances

As before, the cost variance is determined by comparing actual cost with the standard cost for the output achieved (for Becnat Ltd.).

	£
Standard cost	
3,200 units of output × 2 hours × £0.50	3,200
Actual cost	3,650
Cost variance	450(A)

The variance is adverse, which means that variable costs were higher than they should have been for the output achieved. The reasons for this can be explained by two further variances:

An expenditure variance

This is the difference between the actual costs incurred and the standard costs expected for the number of hours actually used to produce the output, i.e.

Actual costs − Standard costs for the hours actually used

£3,650 − 6,200 hours × £0.50

= £3,650 − £3,100 = £550(A)

Therefore, the organisation spent more than they should have done on items comprising variable overheads and the causes for this overspending can only be isolated by investigating each item in detail.

An efficiency variance

There is a parallel between this variance and the efficiency variance for labour except that here attention is focused on the effect of using more or less hours than standard on overhead costs. The variance can be calculated as follows:

(Standard hours − Actual hours) × Standard overhead rate

(6,400 hours − 6,200 hours) × £0.50 = £100(F)

Because it took less time than expected to complete the output, there was a saving in variable overheads. The possible causes are the same as those for the labour efficiency variance, e.g. improvements in working methods or tools etc.

The expenditure and efficiency variances tally back to the cost variance as follows:

	£
Expenditure variance	550(A)
Efficiency variance	100(F)
Cost variance	450(A)

16.5 Fixed overhead variances

As with all the other variances, the first stage in the analysis of fixed overhead variances is the calculation of the cost variance (for Becnat Ltd.):

	£
Standard costs	
3,200 units × 2 hours × £0.60	3,840
Actual costs	3,740
Cost variance	100(F)

This can be subdivided into two further variances:

An expenditure variance

The standard for fixed overheads was established on the basis of a production volume of 3,000 units per month. The budget for fixed overheads was therefore established as follows:

3,000 units × 2 hours × £0.60 = £3,600

The difference between this amount and actual cost is the expenditure variance, i.e.

Budgeted fixed overheads − Actual fixed overheads
= £3,600 − £3,740 = £140(A)

There was, therefore, overspending on items comprising fixed overheads and the reasons for this should be analysed by considering the main items individually.

A volume variance

This variance arises because the level of activity actually achieved is always likely to differ from the level of activity on which the standard overhead rate is based. Technically, the figure given for standard fixed overheads of £3,840 is wrong because it is based on 3,200 units of output. The fact that the organisation produced 200 units more than expected should not affect the standard because the costs are fixed by definition. Any errors in establishing a standard for fixed overheads due to differences in volume of output is corrected by this variance. It can be calculated as follows:

(Budgeted activity − Actual activity) × Standard overhead rate
[(3,000 units × 2 hours) − (3,200 × 2 hours)] × £0.60.
(6,000 hours − 6,400 hours) × £0.60 = 240(F)

The implication of this variance is that the organisation made better use of productive facilities than expected and, as a result, made a gain of £240 by spreading fixed overheads over a larger output. As with all the other variances, the reasons for this one should be investigated but volume variances are almost inevitable when fixed overheads are built into the standard costing system. Accurate forecasting of activity levels is almost impossible and many organisations base the standard overhead rate on an average for a year so that favourable variances in some months are counterbalanced by adverse variances in others. Alternatively, the increase in production volume may be in response to an upward shift in demand and if this expected to continue, the possibility of amending the standard should be given careful consideration.

16.6 Variance report

For a standard costing system to be effective, variances should be reported to responsible individuals on a regular basis by means of variance reports. The structure and layout of these reports will vary from organisation to organisation and the following is one possibility for reporting the variances for Becnat Ltd. Many variations on this would be equally acceptable.

Variance Report for April, 19-1

Variance	Adverse £	Favourable £
1. Labour		
Rate	1,900	
Efficiency		500
Cost	1,400	
2. Material A		
Price		390
Usage	640	
Cost	250	
3. Material B		
Price		60
Usage		80
Cost		140
4. Variable overheads		
Expenditure	550	
Efficiency		100
Cost	450	
5. Fixed overheads		
Expenditure	140	
Volume		240
Cost		100
Overall cost variance	1,860	

It is important to stress that this report will provide the starting point for an investigation into the causes of the variances, and eventually decisions regarding appropriate future action should be taken. To avoid wasting time investigating trival variances, many organisations establish limits beyond which a variance is considered to be significant and should therefore be the subject of further analysis, e.g. any variance exceeding £100 or 5% of the standard should be investigated. Alternatively, some organisations use a statistical approach and investigate those variances which are shown to be statistically significant. This requires a sound understanding of sampling theory with which you may or may not be familiar.

Summary

This chapter has shown that standard costing is a logical extension of budgetary control and involves three main stages: the preparation of standard costs, the analysis of variances, and the taking of appropriate action. By means of a comprehensive example, the calculation of the main cost variances has been illustrated together with some suggestions for the possible causes for these variances. The importance of promoting appropriate action by individuals within the organisation has been stressed. Accurate reporting of variances is only the springboard for effective organisational control.

Assignments

16.1 The standard costs of producing one unit of output are as follows:

100 metres of direct materials at £1.10 per metre
60 hours of direct labour at £2.10 per hour
Factory overheads are absorbed at a standard rate of 40% of direct labour costs
The standard selling price is £310 per unit

During May, actual costs incurred were as follows:

For an output of 80 units
    7,600 metres at £1.10 per metre   3,800 hours at £2.10 per hour
      600 metres at £1.00 per metre   800 hours at £2.40 per hour
Factory overheads: £4,850
Sales 60 units at £310 each
      20 units at £295 each

Required:

(a) Prepare an operating statement showing clearly the variances that occurred during May.

(b) Analyse in detail the cause of the variances.

16.2 The standard costs of processing 100 tonnes of chemicals is as follows:

320 tonnes of raw materials at £10 per tonne
240 direct labour hours at £1.90 per hour
Factory overheads of £2.50 per direct labour hour
Standard selling price £55 per tonne.

During May, 800 tonnes were produced and sold and actual results were as follows:
2,480 tonnes of raw materials were used at a cost of £29,760
1975 direct labour hours at a cost of £3,456
Factory overheads £4,620

Sales: 720 tonnes at the standard price
80 tonnes at £58 per tonne

Required:

Prepare a management report which will include:
(a) A statement showing the variances for the month.

(b) An analysis of the variances, indicating their possible causes.

16.3 DRC Ltd manufactures two products, 'super' and 'deluxe', the standard conversion costs of which are as follows:

Super 8 hours per unit
Deluxe 12 hours per unit
Direct wages £2.20 per hour
Variable overheads £0.30 per hour
Fixed overheads £0.60 per hour

Budgeted and actual output for one month were as follows:

	Super	Deluxe
Budget	420	250
Actual	450	195

The actual costs for the month were as follows:

Direct wages (for 5800 hours)	£13,920
Variable overheads	£ 3,450
Fixed overheads	£ 6,940

Variable overheads vary directly with the number of hours worked.

Required:

Prepare a statement showing an analysis of the variances that occurred during this month.

16.4 The table below shows the summarised trading results of PP Ltd for two years.

	19–1	19–2
Sales	72,000	90,000
Less:		
Direct wages	12,000	13,800
Direct materials	24,000	36,000
Overheads	24,000	29,000
	12,000	11,200

The company manufactures a single product. During 19–1 the selling price was £9.00 per unit and at the beginning of 19–2 this was increased to £10.00. A quarter of the overheads are variable in relation to the number of units produced. At the beginning of 19–2, direct materials prices increased by 20%, and direct wage rates by 15%. Expenditure of fixed overheads also increased by £4,000.

268 Accounting: A Practical Approach

Required:

From this information, prepare a statement analysing the reasons for the decrease in profit in 19–2. (*Note*: Assume that stock levels remained unchanged throughout this period.)

16.5 GMT Ltd. produce and sell one product, Zappo, and have recently installed a full standard costing system. The following operating statement, prepared in standard costing format, has been passed to the managing director for perusal. Since the Managing Director is not fully conversant with standard costing techniques, you have been to explain each of the items in the statement, thereby analysing the difference between budget and actual profit.

Opening statement for March, 19–0

	£	£	£
Budgeted profit			45,000
Add: Favourable variances			
Sales volume margin	2,500		
Materials price	1,600		
Wage efficiency	750		
Fixed overhead volume	450		
		5,300	
Less: Adverse variances			
Sales price	1,500		
Material usage	950		
Wage rate	1,050		
Fixed overhead expenditure	540		
		4,040	
			1,260
Actual profit			46,260

16.6 Bromtech Fertilisers Ltd. use a standard costing system and the details relating to one of their products, 'compound Q', are given below:

Budgeted production/sales: 10,000 units at £20.00 per unit

Standard direct costs per unit:
Materials: 3 kg at £2.20/kg
Labour: 2 hours at £3.00/hour

Actual results for the first quarter of 19–6 are given below:

Sales/production: 12,000 units at £18.00 per unit
Direct materials consumed: 40,000 kg costing £90,000
Direct labour: 25,000 hours at £3.20 per hour

Required:

Prepare a financial statement which reconciles actual results with those budgeted for the quarter.

Case Studies

Assignment 1

THE DOG AND FIRKIN

The Dog and Firkin is a small, out-of-the-way pub in the Suffolk countryside. It is a tied house of Grotneys Ltd, a national brewery, for some years has been somewhat neglected, and is marking time in terms of performance.

Grotneys are concerned about results shown in Tables 1 and 2, and the area manager has warned you that a visit from the brewery is due within a week or so, in order to review operations.

Assume that you are the tenant of the pub, and run it with your spouse and assistance from part-time employees.

(1) Comment on the sales performance over the last 5 years shown in Table 3.

    (a) Suggest ways in which turnover could be improved.

    (b) What kind of accounting and statistical information would you use to answer (a)?

    (c) In case you are challenged, calculate your annual earnings for the year ended 11th March, 19–1. (Be prepared to defend this against hostile brewery officials.)

    (d) What sort of perks come with the tenancy of a pub?

After the visit from the brewery, you receive the following letter:

GROTNEYS LTD
Eastern Area Office
44 The Strand
IPSWICH

Tel (0473) 00902/6

Ref AJL/ag
5th April, 19–1.

Mr and Mrs J King
The Dog and Firkin
Ridgewell
Near Halston
SUFFOLK

Dear Mr and Mrs King

Following my visit to you last week, I have given careful consideration to the existing arrangements under which you manage the Dog and Firkin, and to the suggestions you then made which might lead to a continuation of these arrangements on a mutually more profitable basis.

I have come to the conclusion that your proposals – although imaginative and enterprising – cannot be relied upon to arrest, let alone reverse, the decline in takings in real terms (i.e. after taking into account indirect taxes and inflation) from which the public house is suffering. With distribution costs as high as they now are, I can justify supplying an outlet as remote from our nearest brewery as the Dog only if each delivery is really large – and yours, obviously, are not. Since there is no real prospect of achieving a satisfactory level of profits, I must confirm what I mentioned earlier – that, with effect from 1st July, 19–1, I shall no longer supply you and, as far as Grotneys are concerned, the pub will be closed.

However, I am very much aware of your family's long association with the premises, and it is certainly no part of Grotney's policy to cause unnecessary domestic upset on these occasions. Accordingly, I offer you the first chance to buy the freehold, before the house goes onto the open market for sale by auction. I am advised that, taking into account the existing earning capacity, the size of the grounds, the scope for building development, and the general amenity of the area, £60,000 is a fair price. On payment of this sum, you would be entitled to treat the place as your own – to run as a 'free house', expand, change, develop, or resell, as you wish.

I am sorry that our connection must come to an end, but I am sure that you, as business people, understand why. Thank you again for your excellent hospitality; if there were only the customers . . . !

I look forward to hearing from you soon.

Yours sincerely

A. J. L. Lindsay
Area Manager

You and your spouse have a total of £40,000, largely money you have recently inherited.

(2) In view of the performance of the Dog and Firkin to date, would it be a wise commercial move to purchase it, considering:

    (a) ways in which the turnover might be improved given the new status of the pub as a free house, in addition to the proposals you have made under 1 (a)

    (b) the likely effect of economic trends on the sales of beer, wine, bar snacks and possible restaurant food

(3) If you decide to go ahead with the purchase explain which is the best form of business organisation for you to adopt, giving reasons.

(4) What extra administrative problems do you think you would take on, and how would you propose dealing with them?

Table 1
Dog and Firkin Public House
Revenue Account for the year ended 11th March, 19–1

	£	£	£
Takings			28,645
Cost of goods sold:			
Stock at 12th March, 19–0	428		
Purchases	18,530		
	18,958		
Less stock at 11th March, 19–0	410		18,548
			10,097
Gross profit			
Interest on brewery deposit (net)			63
			10,160
Expenses			
General:			
Rent	1,924		
Rates	839		
Insurance	85		
Laundering, cleaning & gardening	288		
Fuel	861		
Repairs	75	4,072	
Bar:			
Wages: general	1,045		
wife	985		
Flowers and papers	66		
Glasses	11		
Sundries	38	2,145	
Miscellaneous:			
Use of car	300		
Bank charges	18		
Gratuities	289		
Telephone	102		
Dog (proportion of upkeep)	75		
Fittings (written off)	100		
Accountancy fee	30		
Licence fee	7		
Performing rights	22	943	7,160
Net profit			3,000

Table 2
Statement of financial position as at 11th March, 19–1

	£	£	£
Capital employed			
Capital at 12th March, 19–0		2,070	
Profit for year to 11th March, 19–1		3,000	
		5,070	
Deduct drawings for year		3,710	
Worth of business at 11th March, 19–0			1,360
Represented by			
Fittings value at 12th March, 19–0 plus additions	573		
Less: Written off	100	473	
Car Park		115	
Security with Brewery		1,213	

Table 2 (continued)

	£	£
Stock	410	
Cash at bank	—	
Cash in hand	129	
		2,340
Less:		
Bank Overdraft	447	
Trade creditors	31	
Fees accrued due	30	
VAT accrued due	472	980
		1,360

Note: Most of the fixtures and fittings were installed 10 years ago.

Table 3
Sales over the last five years:

	£
19–1	28,645
19–0	25,653
19–9	24,224
19–8	23,114
19–7	21,843

Assignment 2

SOCCER FINANCES

The 92 clubs of the Football league are limited liability companies run largely by rich local business men as a 'hobby'. At the last count (January 1983) only 20 clubs had chartered accountants at board level. No wonder finances are in such dire straits.

Top soccer players are now well paid. The Professional Footballers' Association (PFA) reckons that the following figures are fairly typical:

Division	Annual income £000s
1	15 – 30
2	9 – 16
3	7 – 12
4	4 – 11

Of course, there are considerable bonuses to be made, but this depends on good results, and there are a few superstars who can earn more by appearing in advertisements.

Gates

So many Football League clubs are in financial trouble nowadays that the causes of this decline need to be examined. Football attendance has been gently declining since World War 2 (except for a brief pause after England won the World Cup in 1966), but it has nose-dived over the last two years (see Figure 1).

Case Studies 273

Figure 1
Soccer's vanishing supporters

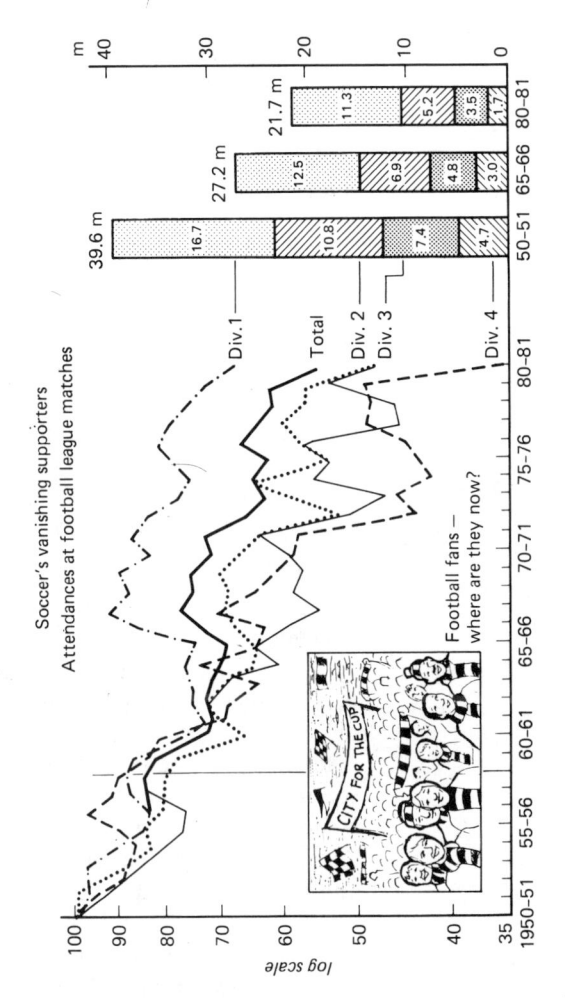

Soccer's vanishing supporters — Attendances at football league matches (log scale)

Period	Div. 1	Total	Div. 2	Div. 3	Div. 4
50-51	16.7	10.8	—	7.4	4.7	(39.6 m)
65-66	12.5	—	6.9	4.8	3.0	(27.2 m)
80-81	11.3	—	5.2	3.5	1.7	(21.7 m)

Football fans — where are they now?

Reasons? Those most commonly cited include the recession ('the worst since the 1930s'); the price of football (add the cost of travel, programme and refreshment to the £1.50 – £3 for a standing ticket and the thrifty spectator is not left much change out of £5); the menacing presence of louts and hooligans; and the wayward performance of the England team. Right at the top of the list is affluence. With the spread of ownership of a car, home and garden, people have many other ways to spend their Saturday afternoons.

Required:

Suggest ways that the clubs could cope with a reduced demand for their 'product'. Your report should include details of:

- cost-cutting exercises
- sources of outside income
- 'product' improvements to the game and the ground

Some research will be necessary. Try and back up your views with some facts and figures.

Assignment 3

TAYLOR'S TOYS LTD

Taylor's Toys Ltd (TT) is based in a town on the south coast of England, and manufactures train sets for the UK market and overseas. It casts, assembles and packages the trains in its own factory. TT has a world-wide reputation for modelling, but has recently been losing market share (down from 80% in the early 1970s to 50%) to foreign companies. One in particular, the German firm Ziescher which imports the Lynx range from Italy in both continental and British styles, now has 20% of the market.

Douglas Taylor, TT's owner and managing director, is very concerned about the future of the company, and calls a board meeting.

Douglas Taylor:
'Our profits have been declining for three years now, and our performance for the first half of this financial year has been quite disgraceful. It seems to me that the toy industry is like a working scale model of the rest of Britain's economy; outdated products, soaring sterling, unfavourable demographics and a foreign stranglehold on vital new technology. All this, plus the caprices of the average nine-year-old customer, and a nation of hard-up mums and dads – no wonder we're going bust!

As you know, several toy makers have announced recent losses and made closures with the inevitable forced redundancies which I'm concerned to avoid. Now, you've all studied the reports (Table 1–4) which were circulated last week, and we must agree upon a strategy to see us through this economic recession.'

Jim Osgerby (sales director):
'On current projections, our sales will only be £21m for this year. The order levels for July–September, the crucial period for us ahead of the Christmas toy-buying spree, have dropped and, for the year as a whole, it looks as though we'll be $12\frac{1}{2}$% down in volume terms on last year. However, I think that there are marketing opportunities which, if acted upon, will help to improve turnover.

Private research indicates that the toy market is price elastic and, with mums and dads looking for bargains this Christmas, I reckon we could slash prices to last year's levels and sell 900,000 sets annually. If we back this up with easier credit and give our retailers more time to pay, I think we're on to a winner. Obviously it would be timely to boost both trade and consumer advertising to promote these schemes.

In the longer term, we must start to rethink our product policy. Three of our ten products account for 70% of sales value, and furthermore, we haven't had a new product for three years. Ziescher, on the other hand, are about to launch two new models for the Christmas campaign.'

Peter Hopkins (finance director):
'But hang on, Jim, you're making some alarming assumptions here. It's not as though we have a premium-pricing policy at the moment, so I don't see the benefit of cutting our margins. As far as exports are concerned, adverse exchange rates will all but erode the price-reduction you recommend. Secondly, I can't see the bank financing extended-credit schemes. In any case, the interest would be prohibitive. If anything, we need to tighten up on credit and get some real cash in.

The short-term solution to our problems surely lies in cost-saving exercises. What we need is an internal economy drive–concentrate on the successful products and run down our loss-leaders. I reckon with this rationalisation, we could cut fixed costs by up to one quarter and we can offload 10% of our production workers.'

Amanda Knox-Johnson (personnel director):
'I must protest, Peter. TT has a loyal workforce with a marvellous strike-free record. We owe it to them to keep jobs here. Mark my words, we'll need their skills when things pick up again. If anything, I'd prefer to introduce short-term working as a temporary solution, and there is goverment assistance available for such schemes.'

David Sheargold (production manager):
'TT strength has always been its good quality and varied product range. We need more products, not less. We've a good team here, and I want to keep them together'.

Jim Osgerby:
'And why just train sets? Electronic toys, clumsy novelties a few years ago, took a noticeable share of the British toy market last year. Most of them are imported from Hong Kong, South Korea or America. The popular models were amazingly successful, but British electronic rivals suffered. Worthington's lost a lot of money trying to get into the electronic games business. But I'm sure that this is an area we should get into and, if we plan carefully, electronic games could be our life-line.'

Table 2

	19-7	19-8	19-9
	£m	£m	£m
Sales	16.5	18.67	20
Profits (before tax)	1.8	1.5	1.2
Net assets	7.5	7.5	8.0

	Actual 19-0		Budget 19-0	Actual* 19-0
Average price of train set	£25		£30	£30
Number of sets sold	800,000		740,000	290,000

	£m		£m	£m
Total revenue	20		22.2	8.7
Direct costs per set (£):				
Materials	2.80		3.36	3.35
Labour	3.40		3.90	4.10
Other	0.70		0.84	0.85
Total direct costs	5.5		6.0	2.4
Contribution	14.5		16.2	6.3
Fixed costs	13.3		14.6	7.5
Pre-tax profits	1.2		1.6	(1.2)

* ½ year to June 30th, 19-0

David Sheargold:
'Well, I'm not sure about that idea, Jim. It's a high-risk specialist area, and we haven't got the in-house expertise. We'd have to buy in with a subsequent loss of some control or change our production methods – and that takes time and money.'

Peter Hopkins:
'Yes, that scheme is not on unless we get extra backing or go into a joint-venture deal. And that will be difficult to swing in the present circumstances.'

Douglas Taylor:
'Before we break for coffee, can I round up by making the following observations. It strikes me that in a declining market we must do any or all of four things: rationalise, raise value-added, export more, or pick a winning product.

I'd like your considered views on these matters before our next meeting. But let's not confuse our short- and long-term objectives. I would like agreement on some rapid measures to reverse our worsening profit and liquidity position. Only then can we consider our longer-term strategy.'

Table 1
Sales value index (January 19–8 = 100)

	19–8 Budget	actual	19–9 Budget	actual	19–0 Budget	actual
January–March	100	98	120	120	130	120
April–June	90	93	100	96	110	100
July–September	160	170	190	184	200	—
October–December	100	110	110	105	120	—

Table 3
Percentage sales by area

	19–5 TT	Total	19–9 TT	Total
UK	70	10	60	8
USA	10	35	12	36
Europe	15	25	20	25
Other	5	30	8	31

Table 4
Balance Sheets

	19–9 £m	Budget 19–0 £m	To date* 19–0 £m
Fixed Assets			
Buildings (cost)	1.5	1.5	1.5
Plant and equipment	1.5	1.5	1.5
Depreciation	1.0	1.25	1.375
	2	1.75	1.625
Current Assets			
Stock + work in progress	6.0	6.5	7.5

Table 4 (continued)

	19–9 £m	Budget 19–0 £m	To date* 19–0 £m
Debtors	4.3	4.7	5.0
Cash	0.1	0.1	0.075
	10.4	11.3	12.575
Less: Current Liabilities			
Creditors	3.0	3.6	4.8
Tax provision	0.6	0.8	—
Proposed dividends	0.3	0.4	—
Bank overdraft	0.5	0.5	1.2
	4.4	5.3	6.0
Net working capital		6.0	6.0	6.575
Net Assets employed		8.0	7.75	8.2
Financed by:			
Share capital	5.0	5.0	5.0
Reserves	0.7	0.7	0.7
Retained profit	0.3	0.8	—
Long-term borrowing	2.0	1.25	2.5
	8.0	7.75	8.2

* ½ year to 30th June, 19–0

Required:

(1) What, in your opinion, went wrong in the first 6 months of 19–0? Compare budget with actual figures in your analysis.

(2) Estimate the year end results for 19–0. Carefully state your assumptions.

(3) What do you understand by the terms 'rationalise' and 'raise value-added' which Douglas Taylor mentioned? Give examples.

(4) Suggest recommended courses of action that the company should pursue. Be sure to distinguish between your short-term and long-term solutions.

(5) If workers must be sacked, how would you advise the company to communicate this to them?

(6) Using the available accounts:
   (a) comment on the company's performance and prospects from the shareholders' point of view
   (b) as manager of the company's bank, comment on the banks involvement with Taylor's Toys

Assignment 4 NORTHBOROUGH MOTORS LTD

Northborough Motors Ltd is a motor trading company selling new and used cars. Over the last two years it has suffered from a declining demand for cars which has led to its failure to repay the balance of a bank loan taken out four years ago to expand premises and working capital. This amount was due on 31st December, 19–2. The latest set of accounts are attached.

Northborough's bankers, Westnat, have now written to them expressing concern about the loan and have requested a meeting with the directors to discuss their plans for dealing with the repayment.

In preparation for this meeting, it has been decided to prepare a financial budget for the next six months for which you have been given responsibility. The following are considered to be reasonable assumptions from which to work:

(a) Last year, sales volumes fell by 15%. Next year, a 5% increase in volume is expected. In the six months to 30th September, 19-3, selling prices are expected to be 5% higher on average. A similar rise in manufacturers' prices means that the gross margin should be maintained at 15%.

(b) In the six months to 30th September, 19-3, salaries will rise by 3% and loan and overdraft interest is estimated at £15,200. General expenses will rise by 6%.

(c) Stocks, debtors and creditors will rise by 5% in value terms.

(d) Depreciation will be provided at the normal rate for the company.

Northborough Motors Ltd
Profit and Loss Account for year ended 31st March, 19-3

	£	£
Sales		1,468,470
Cost of sales		1,250,500
Gross margin		217,970
Salaries	150,530	
General expenses	25,450	
Interest payments	20,700	
Depreciation	6,300	
		202,980
Net profit		14,990

Northborough Motors Ltd
Balance Sheet as at 31st March 19-3

Share capital and reserves	£	£	Fixed assets	£	£
Called up capital* 200,000 £1 shares fully paid		200,000	Freehold premises at cost of valuation		185,000
General reserve		24,650	Equipment at cost	42,000	
Net profit		14,990	Less depreciation	11,550	
					30,450
Net worth		239,640			215,450
Current liabilities			Current assets		
Creditors	64,800		Stock	140,760	
Bank loan	100,000				
Overdraft	10,270		Debtors	58,500	
		175,070			199,260
		£414,710			£414,710

* The authorised share capital is 250,000 × £1 ordinary shares

Northborough operates on two premises 1½ miles apart. The smaller premises concentrates on sales. Its estimated market value is £30,000. The large premises deals with sales, general administration, preparation of cars for sale and guarantee work. Its estimated market value is £155,000.

Details of staff employed at end of March 19–3.
The staffing level has remained at its current level for the past 2 years.

Numbers	Job title/description	Age	Length of service (years)	Cost to firm £
1	Managing director	52	6	18,000
1	Administration manager	42	10	12,000
1	Sales manager	40	10	9,530
3	Sales staff	25	3	7,500
	(2 employed on larger premises)	35	15	7,500
		29	1	7,500
1	Secretary to managing director	26	5	4,500
1	Secretary/clerical assistant	20	1	3,000
	Some secretarial work, general assistance to management, filing			
1	Accounts clerk	50	15	5,500
	Deals with invoices, bills, assembling financial data, wage payments			
2	Receptionists	21	6 months	3,450
	Both employed on larger premises	38	6	3,450
2	Stores	62	4	4,500
	Maintaining stock levels, dealing with inquiries, providing spare parts	23	4	4,500
1	Chief Mechanic	45	10	8,500
10	Mechanics	62	12	5,400
	Ensure cars to be sold in	56	20	5,400
	working order, carry out	52	4	5,400
	finishing processes, repair	45	6	5,400
	work under terms of guarantee	36	2	5,400
	1 attached to smaller sales	34	15	5,400
	premises on a rota system	31	1	5,400
	1 apprentice (paid £2,500)	24	2	5,400
		21	5	5,400
		17	6 months	2,500

Total staff costs: £150,530

N.B. All of the mechanics and store room staff are members of the TGWU.

Only 70% of existing workshop capacity is utilised for after sales and guarantee work.

(1) Prepare a Profit and Loss Account, Balance Sheet and Cash

Flow Statement for the six months ended 30th September, 19–3. These statements should be attached to a memorandum to the managing director. He has specifically asked you to calculate how much the company could afford to repay without extending its overdraft beyond that shown in the balance sheet as at 31st March, 19–3.

At the above mentioned meeting, Westnat agrees to extend the loan period for a further two years on two conditions:

(a) £25,000 will be payable on each of the following dates, together with interest accrued at 15% p.a.:
   30th September, 19–3
   31st March, 19–4
   30th September, 19–4
   31st March, 19–5

(b) The bank overdraft must be extinguished by September 19–3. One important effect of this will be to reduce loan and overdraft interests to £10,000.

(2) During the meeting, the bank manager makes the following comment: 'I cannot understand why you are budgeting for only 5% increase in volume next year. I know the figures for new car registrations were fairly desperate in 19–1 but there were promising signs, particularly towards the end of 19–2, that demand was beginning to pick up. This should surely continue during 19–3.

With reference to appropriate data, is the manager correct in his assertion? If so, how can you explain why Northborough is forecasting only a 5% increase in volume in the coming year? Is there more reliable data to which reference should be made to confirm the trends from Northborough's point of view?

You should draft a letter to the bank manager giving a suitable reply to each of these questions.

(3) In veiw of the conditions attached to the loan by the bank, the managing director has asked you to explain whether the company will be in a position to make the first repayment on 30th September, 19–3. Draft your reply in the form of a memorandum.

(4) Write a report, addressed to the managing director, explaining the measures the company could take to cover the first instalment. A full discussion of each of the measures, its financial effects and the problems or difficulties associated with it, is expected.

Answers

This section contains answers to the first three assignments from each chapter, and to all four CMAs. The teacher's guide which accompanies this book covers the remainder of the assignments.

1.1 (a) *Objectives*

Taxman	to get sufficient information from business to calculate Income or Corporation Tax and Value Added Tax.
Bank manager	looking for adequate income and the recovery of money rather than large profits, preferring security to speculation. He/she will need to see forecasts including cash budgets before granting credit, e.g. an overdraft.
Building society	(c.f. bank manager) looking at the riskiness of the business and the likelihood of being able to keep up the mortage repayments on the house.
Potential partner	will be viewing the business in terms of security and potential growth of earnings, whether retained or withdrawn. He/she may also have a 'competitor's eye' on them, so perhaps only a limited exchange of information would be beneficial initially until the real motives are known.

Business accounts are essential for effective decision making. They show the financial position of an organisation, its cash and profit, and can help managers to plan and control activities. Similarly other interested parties can examine the accounts to see how successful the organisation has been. They may look at certain parts of the accounts for confirmation that their own particular interests are being looked after (e.g. a sound liquidity position and 'safe' investments will keep the bank manager happy).

1.2 *Information*

Organis-ation	Strategic	Tactical	Operational
British Rail	Line Closures (e.g. Serpell Report, Beeching Plan)	Pricing of inter-city	Staff rosters
Super-market	Store openings + locations	Stocks carried	Merchandising + display arrangements
College/ school	Number of student places	Courses offered	Lecture plans

Strategic information concerns the broad nature of the organisation and has long-term implications for the whole organisation.

Tactical information is needed by middle and senior managers and is more detailed. It might be an action plan or budget, usually for less than 1 year.

Operational information includes the straightforward day to day facts and figures which are needed to run any organisation.

1.3 Although some companies have made genuine attempts to produce readable and informative reports many annual accounts are not as helpful as they should be because:

- managers are reluctant to volunteer information other than the minimum demanded by law
- they are often expressed in technical terms which only the analyst can fully understand
- they are designed primarily as a promotional vehicle for shareholders and businesses have been slow to adapt them for other purposes, e.g. employee and public relations

Employees' version
Workers will be predominantly interested in job prospects, pay and security. Thus it will be useful to know the organisation's long-term plans – its proposals for diversification and growth (or rationalisation and contraction) and its profitability. From the company viewpoint it may be useful to show certain labour performance criteria, e.g. sales per employee to indicate the trends in labour productivity.

The exercises for chapter 2 are intended for revision purposes and should be a formality for those students who have picked up the basic book keeping principles covered in Core 2, Numeracy and Accounting, and other foundation courses. It is anticipated that students could undertake these assignments very early on to refresh/remind themselves of Year 1 work.

2.1 (a)

Sales invoice
is the document on which a customer is sent details of purchases (or services provided) and the amount owing. The invoice will include VAT details and any discount terms (cash or trade).

Supplier invoice
is as above, but this time the organisation is paying (i.e. you are the customer).

Wage analysis printout
is a listing of employee wages
- by component (e.g. national insurance contribution)
- by department
- by job

Bank statement
is an itemised account of net indebtedness to the bank.
N.B. dr   your withdrawal
       cr   your gain (the bank owes you money)

Credit note
is issued to a customer usually after the acknowledgement of a faulty or an incorrect supply of goods. The credit note makes up for the shortfall and allows the customers to 'spend' up to the amount shown.

(b) There is no one answer to this question but students should attempt to include:
- cash book (cash + bank)
- wages
- creditors
- debtors (a small retailer might have credit customers)
- sales (by category? e.g. sweets, cigarettes etc.)

284 Accounting: A Practical Approach

- expenses (probably broken down into:
    - rates
    - rent
    - heating and lighting
    - depreciation of fixtures + fittings)
- capital   owner's account
- drawings
- fixed assets – shop (kind and buildings)
    - delivery van?
    - fixtures and fittings

2.2

Double-entry book keeping system used by a small retailer

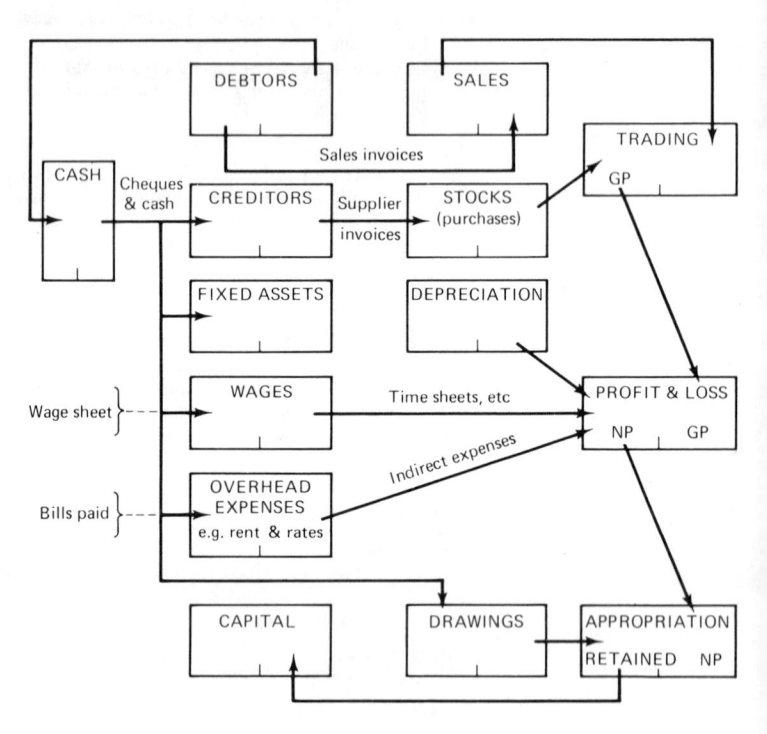

```
                 ┌──────────┐       ┌──────────┐
                 │ DEBTORS  │       │  SALES   │
                 └──────────┘       └──────────┘
                              Sales invoices          ┌──────────┐
                                                      │ TRADING  │
  ┌──────┐  Cheques                                   │   GP     │
  │ CASH │  & cash  ┌──────────┐ Supplier ┌──────────┐└──────────┘
  │      │────────→ │CREDITORS │ invoices │  STOCKS  │
  └──────┘          └──────────┘          │(purchases)│
                                          └──────────┘
                    ┌──────────────┐      ┌──────────────┐
                    │ FIXED ASSETS │      │ DEPRECIATION │
                    └──────────────┘      └──────────────┘

                    ┌──────────┐                        ┌──────────────┐
  Wage sheet }---→  │  WAGES   │  Time sheets, etc →    │PROFIT & LOSS │
                    └──────────┘                        │  NP    GP    │
                                       Indirect expenses└──────────────┘
                    ┌──────────┐
  Bills paid }---→  │ OVERHEAD │
                    │ EXPENSES │
                    │e.g. rent │
                    │ & rates  │
                    └──────────┘

                    ┌──────────┐   ┌──────────┐   ┌──────────────┐
                    │ CAPITAL  │   │ DRAWINGS │   │APPROPRIATION │
                    └──────────┘   └──────────┘   │RETAINED   NP │
                                                  └──────────────┘
```

2.3

Rupert Digger

Sales		45,147
Cost of goods sold to customers		25,320
		19,827
Wages	4,000	
Salary	10,000	
Sundries	2,750	
Depreciation	200	
		16,950
Profit		2,877
Assets		
Shop		90,000
Van (net)		1,800
Cash		1,350
Less owing		(1,600)
Net assets		91,550

Rupert will need to keep a:
> Profit and Loss Account – to show his true profit or loss and if he has succeeded in increasing funds or capital during the year. (The return on capital employed is 3%.)
> Balance Sheet – to show what he owes and what he owns at the end of the year.
> Cash book – to show how much cash he has to pay his bills.

Together the accounts should provide him with information to help run his business as well as meeting the legal requirements of other interest groups like government (the taxman).

3.1 **(a)** Advantages might include:
- speedier and more accurate production of monthly statements leading to:
- more useful information for management
- better financial control
- potential savings in staff and associated overhead costs
- more detailed financial analyses and exception reports on request

(b) *Assumed*: Computer configuration is keyboards/VDUs and magnetic disc storage. This is the most common at present for accounting systems.

Sources: files held on magnetic media (usually disc) updated by keyboard entry

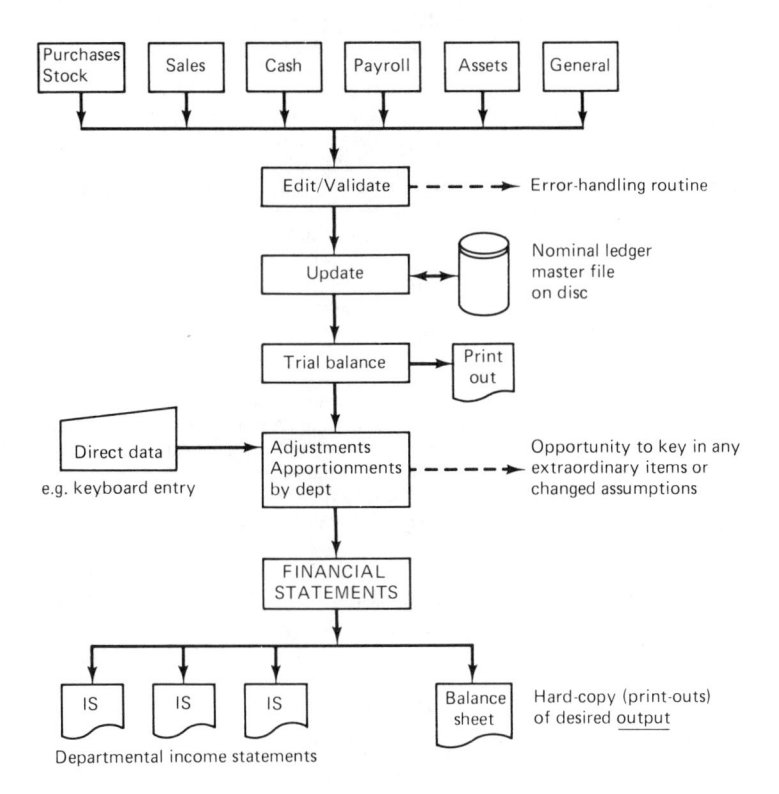

Sources boxes: Purchases/Stock, Sales, Cash, Payroll, Assets, General

→ Edit/Validate – – – → Error-handling routine

→ Update ←→ Nominal ledger master file on disc

→ Trial balance → Print out

Direct data e.g. keyboard entry → Adjustments Apportionments by dept – – – → Opportunity to key in any extraordinary items or changed assumptions

→ FINANCIAL STATEMENTS

→ IS IS IS Balance sheet — Hard-copy (print-outs) of desired <u>output</u>

Departmental income statements

3.2 *Which one do I buy?*
There is a wide choice of systems available and the decision isn't made any easier by the knowledge that there are probably cheaper and better versions being developed. Remember that you are buying a system – not just a computer. This will probably include a disk drive and printer which can both be costly. The hardware, in turn, is no good without the software to run it. A good analogy is with video tape recorders (VTRs). It is generally accepted that the V2000 system is more advanced but pre-recorded tapes are virtually unobtainable for it. Hence the success of the market

leader, the VHS system, which has more 'software', i.e. tapes to run with it. VCRs, at least in principle, run any sort of software, but micros are usually limited, so it is vital to check the software available.

10 Commandments

1. Set your budget, giving maximum/minimum prices.
2. Find out which systems fall into that range and forget the rest.
3. Ponder a while on why you are buying a micro.
4. Write out a list of reasons.
5. Find out which software will be most likely to satisfy your requirements (close + constant reference to your written list of reasons).
6. Find out which machines offer the facilities, in terms of hardware and software, that will meet your requirements.
7. You should now have a shortlist of machines + the software you want to run on them. If not, write one.
8. Find out how you will be able to get the shortlisted machines. Ideally buy from a locally based friendly micro dealer. Next best, a shop; worst, mail order.
9. Test drive the machine and read the manual. Contact local user groups, local store – 'no hands-on; no hands in pocket'.
10. Choose and be confident.

Match your requirements up to the software you can get.
Be imaginative.
For word-processing and filing large amounts of information:
- almost certainly need floppy disks
- or the facility for connecting them up when you can afford them
- a CP/M to control disk drives
  (helpful if machine can run this)
- a decent keyboard/documentation/display
- port to connect up to decent printer
- function or programmable keys – asset

N.B. Manufacturer of hardware is rarely sole supplier of software.
Supplier – delivery/reliability
– after-care service
– guarantees

3.3 This answer is based around a standard procedure in any organisation, payroll processing. Assume that workers can be either weekly-paid, based on timesheets issued and collected each week, or monthly-paid salaried staff. Assume also that any changes, e.g. new recruits, promotions, retirements, people leaving, are recorded on change notes.

The system can be depicted as follows:

Inputs	*Processes*
	Update runs
Timesheets	Main payroll runs
Change notes	Error checking/validation

Files	*Outputs*
Master File	
Weekly paid	Summary reports
Monthly paid	– for management
(old + new)	Cheques
Transaction File (T/F) – valid	Timesheets (new)
timesheets	Payslips
T/F – updates (monthly)	
T/F – changes (weekly/monthly)	Update listing – to show changes
Print File(s) – straightway	
or later (spooling)	Error reports
Reference File e.g. for national insurance codes and corresponding deductions	

Clearly it is important that the payroll is accurate and secure. Hence the system should include sophisticated data vet and validation techniques to guard against fraud and abuse.

4.1 (a) This is the dictum of SSAP 9 and can be achieved using a number of different approaches i.e. aggregate, category and article. 'Cost' can also be interpreted in a number of different ways.

In a period of changing prices, the method of stock valuation will affect both gross and net profit and the net worth of the organisation, e.g. during a period when prices have been rising FIFO will give a higher value of closing stock than LIFO with consequent effects on net worth.

	FIFO	NRV
(b) (i)		
A	70 at £2.85 = £199.50	70 at £3.20 = £224
B	80 at £3.75 = £300.00	80 at £3.85 = £292
C	560 at £1.05 = £588.00	580 at £1.25 = £700
	£1,087.50	£1,216.00

Closing stock value

Aggregate method £1087.50

Article method £
A 198.50
B 292.00
C 588.00
 £1079.50

(ii) LIFO
A 45 at £2.30
 25 at £2.85 = £174.75
B 80 at £3.40 = £272.00
C 580 at £0.85 = £476.00
 £922.75

Aggregate method = £922.75

Article method
A £174.75
B £272.00
C £476.00
 £922.75

4.2 (a)
Plant Account

19–5		19–6	
Sept 30 Cash (A)	2,400	June 30 Balance cd	6,000
19–6			
Jan 31 Cash (B)	3,600		
	6,000		6,000
19–6		19–6	
July 1 Balance bd	6,000	June 30 Balance cd	13,200
Nov 1 Cash (C)	6,000		
19–7			
Feb 28 Cash (0)	1,200		
	13,200		13,200
19–7		19–7	
July 1 Balance bd	13,200	July Disposals (B)	3,600

4.2 (a) (continued)

19–8			19–8		
May 1 Supplier (E)		3,000	May 1 Disposals (A)		2,400
			June 30 Balance cd		10,200
		16,200			16,200
19–8			19–8		
July 1 Balance bd		10,200	Disposals		6,000
19–9			19–9		
May 30 Cash		7,200	June 30 Balance cd		11,400
		17,400			17,400
19–9					
July 1 Balance bd		11,400			

(b)
Provision for depreciation Account

19–7			19–6		
June 30 Balance cd		1,370	June 30 Profit and loss		330
			19–7		
			June 30 Profit and loss		1,040
		1,370			1,370
19–8			19–7		
June 30 Disposals		930	July 1 Balance bd		1,370
June 30 Balance cd		1,210	19–8		
			June 30 Profit and loss		770
		2,140			2,140
19–9			19–8		
June 30 Disposals		1,000	July 1 Balance bd		1,210
June 30 Balance cd		890	19–8		
			June 30 Profit and loss		480
		1,690			1,690
			19–8		
			July 1 Balance bd		690

(c)
Disposals Account

19–7			19–8		
July Plant		3,600	June 30 Provisions for:		
19–8			Depreciation		830
May 1 Plant		2,400	Cash		560
			Supplier		1,800
			Profit and loss		2,910
		6,000			6,000
19–9			19–9		
Plant		6,000	Provisions for		
			Depreciation		1,000
			Insurance		850
			Profit and loss		4,200
		6,000			6,000

Workings
Y/E 30th June, 19–8
Provisions for depreciation = £
Machine A = $12,400 \times 10\% \times \frac{3}{4}$ = 180

$$B = 13{,}800 \times 10\% \times \frac{5}{12} = \underline{150}$$
$$\underline{\underline{330}}$$

Y/E 30th June, 19–7
Provisions for depreciation
			£
M/C A & B	£8,000 × 10%	=	600
M/C C	£6,000 × 10% × $\frac{8}{12}$	=	400
M/C D	£1,200 × 10% × $\frac{4}{12}$	=	40
			£1,040

Y/E 30th June, 18–8
Provisions for depreciation
			£
M/C C	£8,000 × 10%	=	800
M/C D	£1,200 × 10%	=	120
M/C E	£3,000 × 10% × $\frac{2}{12}$	=	50
			770

Provisions for depreciation on machines disposed of
M/C A – £180 + £240	=	£420
M/C B – £150 + £360	=	£510
		£930

Y/E 30th June, 19–0
			£
M/C D	£1,200 × 10%		120
M/C E	£3,000 × 10%		300
M/C F	£7,200 × 10% × $\frac{1}{12}$		60
			480

Depreciation provided on press disposed of:

$$£400 + £600 = £1{,}000$$

4.3 (a) *Provision for depreciation*

Machine £000

	A	B	C
Cost	40	60	80
31 Dec 19–6 depreciation	10		
Net book value	30		
31 Dec 19–7 depreciation	7.5	7.5 (½ year)	
Net book value	22.5	52.5	
31 Dec 19–8 depreciation	5.625	13.125	20
Net book value	16.875	39.375	60

(b) *Fixed assets* – Machinery

1 Jan 19–6	Bank (A)	40,000	30 June 19–9		
30 June 19–7	" (B)	60,000	disposal	40,000
30 June 19–9	New engine*	5,000	c/d 31 Dec 19–9	245,000
1 Jan 19–8	(C)	80,000		
1 July 19–9	(D)	100,000		
		285,000		285,000

* It is assumed that this adds to the cost of the machine.

4.3 (b) (continued)

Provision for depreciation – Machine A

Disposal	27,625	1 Jan 19–9 Depreciation to date	23,125
		Depreciation to 30 Jun	4,500[1]
	27,625		27,625

Provision for depreciation – Machine B

1 Jan 19–9 depreciation to date	20,625
31 Dec 19–9 annual depreciation	13,500[2]
	34,125

Disposal (Machine A)

Trade in allowance	15,000	Cost	40,000
Accumulated depreciation	27,625	Profit on sale	2,625
	42,625		42,625

Provision for depreciation (Machine C)

1 Jan 19–9 depreciation to date	20,000
31 Dec 19–9 annual depreciation	18,000[3]
	38,000

Provision for depreciation (Machine D)

1 July 19–9 ½ year's depreciation   11,250[4]

Calculations

Note 1, Machine A   annual depreciation $= \dfrac{\text{Cost} - \text{residual value}}{\text{No. of years of useful life}}$

$= \dfrac{£40,000 - 4,000}{4}$

$= £9,000$ per annum.

∴ ½ year depreciation $= £4,500$

Note 2, Machine B   annual depreciation $= \dfrac{£60,000 - 6,000}{4}$

$= £13,500$

Note 3, Machine C   annual depreciation $= \dfrac{80,000 - 8,000}{4}$

$= £18,000$

Note 4, Machine D   annual depreciation $= \dfrac{100,000 - 10,000}{4}$

$= £22,500$

∴ ½ year's depreciation $= £11,250$

(c) Depreciation does not automatically provide funds for replacement nor does it affect cash flow. Funds could be set aside and invested in the hope that the realisable sum will be enough to buy new assets, but this is not usually done in isolation; rather businesses co-ordinate their budgets to include cash and working capital needs as well. Kim and Don should forecast their liquidity needs more carefully to avoid unexpected bank overdrafts.

(d) Depreciation is charged to the Profit and Loss Account on an annual basis as an expense and is designed to give the fairest 'spread' of costs over the appropriate time period.

The annual depreciation charge is a book entry which represents a fraction of the estimated overall loss on the asset (i.e. the difference between buying and selling price).

The matching principle tries to ensure that costs and revenue belong to the correct accounting period and that the method and rate for depreciation presents a 'true and fair view' of the organisation. Clearly there are many problems with the accuracy of the information on cost, useful life and residual value, and all of these can affect the choice of both method and rate of depreciation.

5.1 The letter should point out that verbal agreements are difficult to enforce. Agreements of this kind are normally called into question when there is a fundamental dispute between the partners.

A written agreement is therefore much easier to verify and should cover the following points:-

- The responsibilities to be assumed by each partner
- the initial capital of each partner
- the profit/loss sharing ratio
- interest on capital and drawings
- salaries
- drawing rights

Finally, the letter should point out that without a partnership agreement, the provisions of the Partnership Acts will apply. This may, of course, be grossly unfair.

5.2
B. Bright and S. Smart
Profit and Loss Account for the year ended 31st December, 19−1

	£	£		£	£
			Sales	21,050	
Stock, 1st Jan 19-1	1,250		Less: Returns	172	
Add: Purchases	7,686				20,878
	8,936				
Less: Returns out	248				
	8,688				
Less: Stock, 31st Dec. 19-1.	1,540				
Cost of goods sold		7,148			
Gross profit		13,730			
		20,878			20,878
Provisions for			Gross profit		13,730
Depreciation			Discounts received		68
Equipment		560			
Motor van		600			
Carriage out		243			
Discounts allowed		242			
Salaries		1,260			
Bad debts		100			
Provision for doubt-					
ful debts		140			
Rent & rates		600			

5.2 (continued)

	£		£
Wages	3,827		
Light & heat	400		
General expenses	472		
Postage & stationery	300		
Net profit	5,054		
	13,798		13,798
Salaries:		Net profit	5,054
Smart	1,000		
Interest on Capital:			
Smart	150		
Bright	150		
Share of Profits:			
Smart	1,251		
Bright	2,503		
	5,054		5,054

B. Bright and S. Smart
Balance Sheet as at 31st December, 19-1

	Cost	Accumulated depreciation	Net
	£	£	£
Fixed assets			
Equipment	2,800	560	2,240
Motor van	1,800	600	1,200
	4,600	1,160	3,440
Current assets			
Stock		1,540	
Debtors	1,374		
Less: Provision for bad debts	140		
		1,234	
Bank payments		40	
Bank		1,490	
		4,304	
Current liabilities			
Creditors	1,230		
Accruals	60		
		1,290	
Working capital			3,014
Capital employed			6,454

Financed by:	Capital	Current	Total
	£	£	£
Smart	2,500	651	3,151
Bright	2,500	803	3,303
	5,000	1,454	6,454

Current Accounts

	Smart	Bright		Smart	Bright
Drawings	1,750	1,850	Salaries	1,000	—
			Interest on Capital	150	150

	Smart	Bright		Smart	Bright
Balance b/d	651	803	Share of Profit	1,251	2,503
	2,401	2,653		2,401	2,653
			Balance b/d	651	803

5.3
Mustoe, Rafferty & Morgan
Profit & Loss Account for the year ended 30th September, 19–2

	£	£
Sales		95,246
Less: Returns		641
		94,605
Stock 1 Oct, 19–1	7,280	
Add: Purchases	37,654	
	44,934	
Less: Returns	423	
	44,511	
Less: Stock 30 Sept, 19–2	8,245	
Cost of sales		36,266
Gross profit:		58,339
Discounts		247
		58,586
Discounts	43	
Motor expenses	2,436	
Wages & salaries	18,400	
Printing & stationery	240	
Rent & rates (8430 – 420)	8,010	
Light & heat (1584 + 147)	1,731	
General expenses	241	
Provisions for depreciation:		
Motor vehicles	1,880	
Equipment	520	
Fixtures & Fittings	905	34,406
Net profit		24,180
Add: Interest on drawings:		
Mustoe	657	
Rafferty	766	
Morgan	719	2,142
Profit available for appropriation		26,322
Salaries		
Morgan		3,000
Interest on capital:		
Mustoe	1,000	
Rafferty	500	
Morgan	500	2,000
Share of profit:		
Mustoe	10,661	
Rafferty	5,331	
Morgan	5,330	21,322
		26,322

5.3 (continued)
Partners' current accounts

	Mustoe	Rafferty	Morgan		Mustoe	Rafferty	Morgan
Balances b/d	6,574			Balances b/d	1,564	562	
Drawings		7,658	2,418	Salaries			3,000
			7,188	Interest on			
Interest on drawings	657	766	719	capital	1,000	500	500
				Shares of profit	10,661	5,331	5,330
Balances c/d	5,994			Balances c/d		2,031	1,495
	13,225	8,424	10,325		13,225	8,424	10,325
Balances b/d		2,031	1,495	Balances b/d	5,994		

Mustoe, Rafferty & Morgan
Balance Sheet as at 30th September, 19-2

	Cost	Accumulated Depreciation	Net
Fixed assets	£	£	£
Motor vehicles	9,400	6,580	2,820
Equipment	5,200	2,020	3,180
Fixtures & fittings	18,100	4,505	13,595
	32,700	13,105	19,595

Current assets			
Stocks		8,245	
Debtors		1,540	
Rates prepaid		420	
		10,205	

Current liabilities			
Creditors	4,821		
Light & heat owing	147		
Bank overdraft	2,364		
		7,332	
Net current assets			2,873
Total assets less current liabilities			22,468

Partners' interests	Capital Accounts	Current Accounts	Total
Mustoe	10,000	5,994	15,994
Rafferty	5,000	(2,031)	2,969
Morgan	5,000	(1,495)	3,505
			22,468

6.1
Cream Cakes Ltd.

Cash Book (£000)

Receipts		Payments	
Opening capital	60	Shops	80
Loan	40	Fixtures	10
Sales	143.6	Purchases	109
		Wages	12.2
		Interest	2
		Overheads	2
		c/d	28.4
	243.6		243.6

b/d £28,400

Income statement (£000)

Sales		143.6
Stock	2	
Purchases	110	
Cost of sales		112
Gross profit		31.6
Less:		
Interest	2	
Overheads	2	

6.1 (continued)

Depreciation		2
Wages	12.2	18.2
Net profit		13.4

Balance Sheet (£000)

Fixed assets			
Shops		80	
Fixtures	10		
Less depreciation	2	8	
Van		3	
			91
Current assets			
Cash		28.4	
Less: Current liabilities			
Creditors		6	
Net working capital			22.4
Net assets employed			113.4
Authorised share capital		100	
Issued share capital		60	
Retained		13.4	
Loan		40	
			113.4

6.2 In raising £40,000 in new capital, the company must basically consider three options:

1. The issue of ordinary shares
2. The issue of preference shares
3. Obtaining a long term loan

These options are not of course mutually exclusive, which means that the company may well decide to opt for a mix of financing as the best way ahead. The main considerations for each of the choices are as follows:

1. *Ordinary shares*
If the past performance of the company has been to the satisfaction of the existing shareholders, it may be that they will be prepared to risk a further investment in the form of more shares. However, they may not be too happy to see new investors brought in from outside, thereby diluting their interest in the company. The main advantage from the company's point of view is that a dividend does not have to be paid on ordinary shares if circumstances do not justify one.

2. *Preference shares*
These shares are more attractive than ordinary shares in that they have a fixed rate of dividend associated with them and therefore offer more security of income to the investor. The company on the other hand loses flexibility in that it has a commitment to find the fixed dividend. However, if the shares are the cumulative type, dividends can be deferred until a later date if conditions are not conducive to paying them.

3. *Long term loans*
From the point of view of existing shareholders, borrowing is an attractive proposition if the return expected on the investment exceeds the cost of borrowing. Then the shareholders are gaining by using other people's money. The main disadvantage is that if the plans go wrong, the company is faced with the problem of paying fixed interest charges when it may be difficult to do so.

6.3 (a) Appropriation account for the year ended 30th June, 19-1

	£000s	£000s
Net profit for 19-1		300
Add: Balance b/f		1,200
		1,500
Less: *Appropriations*:		
Preference dividend	45	
Ordinary dividend	300	
Ordinary share capital (scrip issue)	1,000	
		1,345
Balance c/f		155

Balance Sheet as at 30th June, 19-1

Fixed assets	Cost £000s	Depreciation £000s	Net £000s
Premises	1,500	–	1,500
Equipment	150	60	90
Motor vehicles	60	12	48
	1,710	72	1,638

Current assets			
Stocks		2,410	
Debtors & prepayments		840	
Bank		962	
		4,212	
Current liabilities			
Creditors & Accruals	650		
Preference dividends	45		
Ordinary dividends	300		
		995	
Net current assets			3,217
Total assets less current liabilities			4,855

Financed by:
Capital & Reserves

Called up share capital	
3,000,000 £1 ordinary shares	3,000
500,000 £1 9% preference shares	500
Undistributed profits	155
General reserve	800
10% debentures	400
	4,855

(b) 1. The amount of profit for the year/in previous years.
2. The amount of cash available.
3. The profit required for reinvestment.
4. The amount of dividend paid in previous years/by other similar companies.

(c) Debenture interest is an expense which goes in the profit & loss section, and not an appropriation of profits about which the directors have veto.

(d) The scrip issue makes no difference, in the sense that the proportion of the company owned by an individual investor is the same before and after the issue. There is an important difference in that investors will have shares which have a lower value than previously and this may make it easier to liquidate part of their investment in smaller denominations.

7.1 Cash Flow Statement for the year ended 31st December, 19-2

	£	£
Sources of cash		
Net profit		18,900
Add: Depreciation		4,600
		23,500
Add: Loss on disposal of fixed assets		600
Continuation from trading		24,100
Sales of equipment		1,800
		25,900
Applications of cash		
Purchase of fixed assets	3,000	
Drawings	12,300	
Investments	2,600	
Loan repayment	6,000	
Increase in stocks	4,000	
Reduction in creditors	800	
		28,700
Reduction in cash		2,800

7.2 Sources and Applications of Funds Statement for the year ended 31st December, 19-2

	£000	£000
Sources of Funds		
Net profit before tax	2,123	
Add: Depreciation	520	
Loss on disposal of fixed assets	12	
	2,655	
Less: Profit on disposal of investments	40	
Funds generated from operations		2,615
Sale of fixed assets		24
Issue of shares		750
Sales of investments		200
		3,589
Applications of Funds		
Tax paid	475	
Dividends paid	600	
Fixed assets purchased	1,256	
Redemption of debentures	300	
		2,631
Increase in working capital		958
Increases/(decreases) in working capital		
Increase in stocks		195
Increase in debtors		280
Increase in bank		638
Increase in creditors		(155)
		958

7.3 Balance Sheet as at 30th June, 19-2

	£	£	£
Fixed assets			
At cost or valuation		114,100	
Less: Depreciation		16,700	
			97,400
Current assets			
Stocks		31,200	
Debtors		12,100	

	£	£	£
Bank		5,600	
		48,900	
Current liabilities			
Creditors	11,400		
Taxation	9,200		
		20,600	
Working capital			28,300
Capital employed			125,700
Financed by:			
Ordinary shares			40,000
Undistributed profits			29,700
Revaluation reserve			24,000
10% debentures			32,000
			125,700

Reservations about this balance sheet include:
(a) Separate figures for machinery, equipment and motor vehicles cannot be given.
(b) The calculation of the net profit figure cannot be verified.
(c) The dividends paid on the ordinary shares are not given.

8.1 and 8.5

Interpretation of annual reports
General
Reports are designed at the company's discretion and are as yet non-standardised. They should be used as reference documents. Before any analysis ask yourself:
- What do I already know about the company?
- Are its products useful, reliable and updated?
- What is the reputation of the company?
- Is the company in the news?
- Are there any significant market trends related to the company?
- Will the current economic situation affect the company?

Check in *Who Owns Whom* and the relative performance section of the *'Times' 1000*. Quality newspapers and trade magazines, publications like the *Stock Exchange Official Yearbook* and the *Investors Chronicle* can all give background information to make the report and monitored movements of share price more meaningful.

Basic information from reports about past activities can be used to help predict future activities. Information falls into 3 areas:
1. earnings, income, profit and losses
2. financial resources, assets and liabilities
3. future plans for the year ahead

This information relates to one's perspective, i.e. are you an investor, market analyst, prospective employee, customer?

Layout
Because of the non-standardisation of reports there is no simple method of analysis, but by checking the contents page and 'skim' reading, try to identify:
1. The *auditors' report* will tell you if the accounts are prepared correctly and are a true and fair record.
2. Look out for *notes* to accounts. These might be extensive but will detail depreciation and inflation policies, etc.
3. *5 to 10 year summary statement*, if it exists, will be a helpful review of trends (although take care that apparent impressive sales growth is not just due to inflation).
4. *Charman's statement and directors' report* might identify future prospects and hint at present problems.
5. *Miscellaneous*: each report is different. Some give well designed visual presentation of market shares, etc. Be extra careful when looking through a report for an international group as often subsidiary home and overseas comparison are also presented.

Ratios

Ratios just 'take a view'. By themselves they are meaningless unless compared to previous years and, if possible (though very problematic), to similar firms in the same industry.

1. *Investment decisions*
   'Should I buy shares in the company?'
   (the potential investor)
   (a) Earnings per share

   $$\frac{\text{Profits to ordinary shareholder (after tax, interest and preference dividend)}}{\text{Number of ordinary shares}}$$

   expressed in pence.
   (b) Return on equity

   $$\frac{\text{Profits to ordinary shareholder}}{\text{Ordinary shareholder equity}}$$

   expressed as a percentage.
   (c) Dividend cover

   $$\frac{\text{Earnings per share}}{\text{Dividend per share}}$$

   expressed as X number of times.
   (Many companies retain 50% of profit, so a good yardstick is over 2X.)
   (d) Price earnings (P/E) ratio
   Shows the number of years needed to earn the price paid for the shares out of profits at the current rate. If prospects are good and investors expect higher future earnings, P/E ratio will be high.
   (e) Value-added statement
   If it exists it can highlight productivity.
   (f) Gearing

   $$\frac{\text{Long-term debt (including preference shares)}}{\text{Equity}}$$

   Highly geared companies, those with disproportionately large long-term (LT) debts, need high profits to give ordinary shareholders (equity) some return.
   Expressed as a ratio, e.g. 70:30.

2. *Performance measures*
   'Is it an efficient company?'
   (all interest groups but particularly the managers)
   (a) Return on Capital Employed (ROCE)

   $$\frac{\text{Operating profit (before interest, tax dividend)}}{\text{Capital employed}}$$

   Similar to return on equity but expressed as a percentage of capital. A key ratio which influences investment decisions and is used as an inter-decision internal appraiser.

   (b) • Asset Turnover   • Margin

   $$\frac{\text{Sales (turnover)}}{\text{Net assets (working capital)}} \qquad\qquad \frac{\text{Net profits}}{\text{Sales}}$$

   This expresses management's efficiency. In fast moving consumer goods markets a low profit margin is usual.
   Expressed as a ratio, e.g. 1:1.

3. *Trade analysis*
   'Should I do business with the company?' (the potential supplier, the bank manager)

(a) Current ratio

$$\frac{\text{Current assets}}{\text{Current liabilities}}$$

This will indicate the company's payment policy; 1 : 1 is a guideline. Look out for any trends such as increased bank overdrafts.

(b) Acid test

$$\frac{\text{Liquid assets (current less stock)}}{\text{Current liabilities}}$$

This, the 'guide ratio', shows to what extent short-term (ST) assets are available to meet ST liabilities. It should be greater than 1.

5. *Employment analysis*
'Should I work for the company?'
(the job applicant)
Check the report narrative for growth potential, e.g. by looking at research and development (R&D) expenditure, opening of new branches, new product launches.
Look for details concerning pensions, facilities, profit sharing and acknowledgement of social responsibilities.

Conclusion
When writing up the assignment do not copy straight out from the report. Only do quantitative analysis if it is meaningful to you. Put cuttings in an appendix, or indeed paraphrase or summarise the main points, which is far better. Do not be worried if the shares have not moved much or if there has been little press reportage on the company; this would be usual.

8.2 (a) The return on capital employed for 19–2 is 14.2% compared to 15.7% in 19–1 after adding back loan interest. This is for the most part due to an increase in the net assets (or net capital employed) of the business, which have not generated significantly higher profits.

A closer examination of the Balance Sheets shows that the net increase of £210 in net assets is due to increased fixed assets of £330 less a reduction in net current assets of £120. The increased investment has apparently failed to generate additional profits in 19–2. The reasons for this could be that the fixed assets were purchased late in 19–2 and will generate increased sales and profits in 19–3. Alternatively it could be that the additional fixed assets have led to higher sales in 19–2 but these sales have not resulted in more profits.

(b) Turning to the company's liquidity, we can calculate that the current ratio has decreased from 2.25 in 19–1 to 1.25 in 19–2, a significant and worrying drop. The liquid ratio has dropped from 1.0 to 0.5, which is again an alarming decrease. The significance of these figures is that very soon (if not already) the company will be unable to pay its debts as they become due, with the result that creditors may refuse to supply further goods and/or put the company into liquidation.

(c) The importance of adequate working capital in the financial management of a business can best be explained by an examination of the working capital cycle. A company purchases goods from its suppliers who will usually grant a limited period of credit (one month is usual). These goods are held for resale or turned into products for resale. In order to keep the working capital requirement as low as possible, stocks should be kept as low as possible. However, stocks must always be sufficient to satisfy the optimum sales level. Stocks are turned into sales, often credit sales which result in debtors. A company should make every effort to keep these as low as possible in order to prevent capital being tied up in debtors, and/or debtors turning into bad debts. The working capital cycle is then completed with the turning of debtors into cash.

Working capital must therefore be sufficient to bridge the gap from the time the company pays its creditors to the time it is paid by its debtors, i.e. the time the working capital cycle takes to complete. Lack of sufficient working capital hinders the functioning of this process and thus the operation of the business and its ability to make profits.

Workings		19–1	19–2
1	Return on Capital Employed	$\dfrac{63{,}500 + 18{,}000}{520{,}000} \times 100 = 15.7\%$	$\dfrac{66{,}000 + 38{,}000}{730{,}000} \times 100 = 14.2\%$
2	Current ratio	$\dfrac{360}{160} = 2.25$	$\dfrac{400}{320} = 1.25$
3	Liquid ratio	$\dfrac{160}{160} = 1.00$	$\dfrac{160}{320} = 0.5$

8.3 (a)

	Eastwood PLC	Industry average
1. ROCE: $\dfrac{\text{Net profit before tax} + \text{interest}}{\text{Net assets}} = \dfrac{340}{3{,}400}$	10%	16%
2. *Current Ratio*: Current assets : current liabilities 1,600 : 800	2 times	2.2 times
3. *Debtors collection period*: $\dfrac{\text{Debtors}}{\text{Sales}} \times 365 \quad \dfrac{900}{6{,}000}$	55 days	50 days
4. *Acid test*: Liquid assets : current liabilities 1,000 : 800	1.25 times	1.0 times
5. $\dfrac{\text{Net profit}}{\text{Sales}}$: Margin $\dfrac{340}{6{,}000}$	5.7%	7%
6. *Sales to net assets* $\dfrac{6{,}000}{3{,}400}$	1.8 times	4.5 times

Assuming that the figures are prepared on a comparable basis and that we are therefore comparing like with like, the following comments can be made about Eastwood PLC's performance compared with the industry average.

The primary ratio (ROCE) (1.) is 6 percentage points below the average and seems poor for this industry. An examination of the margin (5.) and asset turnover (6.) reveals that the problem may be mainly due to an inefficient use of assets, which are only generating 1.8 times more sales compared to 4.5 times for the industry overall. This should prompt management to examine the asset structure in much more detail to discover inefficiencies, possible cost cuttings or productivity improvements.

On the liquidity side the current ratio (2.) is slightly below the industrial one, but this should give no cause for concern, particularly when the acid test (5.) is strong. If anything debtors and cash may be too high and this should be looked into, although the average debtors collection period of 55 days (3.) is only 5 days worse than the norm.

8.3 (b) *Gearing*

If an organisation uses outside funds (loans) to buy assets it incurs an unavoidable fixed cost in terms of interest payments. This means a greater degree of risk if expansion fails to live up to expectations. The proportion of debt:equity finance gives an idea of the degree of risk the organisation is running.

Formula

$$\text{Gearing} = \frac{\text{Long-term borrowing}}{\text{net capital employed}}$$

Calculations

	£000	Gearing
Myers	$\dfrac{500}{4,525}$	11%
Longson	$\dfrac{4,000}{6,300}$	63.5%

Myers PLC is low-geared in that the bulk of its finance is equity, and it therefore runs little risk because it can vary the dividend payout to shareholders according to profits, i.e. ordinary shares have a variable interest rate. In good years shareholders may be rewarded well but in bad years (loss-making or start-up periods) the directors may decide to pay out little or nothing, keeping back profits to finance operations. Longson PLC is high-geared, however, as most of its funds have been raised externally through debentures. Management are therefore faced with fixed interest payments of (£4m × 15%) = £600,000 each year, irrespective of performance, which means Longson PLC is a higher-risk company. This can be demonstrated by looking at the hypothetical profit figures for the two companies at the extremes of the business cycle. (Profits are expected to fluctuate up to 50% below[a] or above[b] the present level.)

Business cycle:

	'Bad' year[a]		'Good' year[b]	
	Myers	Longson	Myers	Longson
Profit before loan interest	300	450	900	1,350
Interest	75	600	75	600
Profit after interest	225	(150)	825	750

Hence Longson PLC is high-risk in the sense that, in bad years, it might incur a loss because of the high interest payments. A high-geared company represents a risk to shareholders because dividends can be extremely volatile, and also to debenture holders because of the lower interest cover.

9.1 19–1

Depreciation based on historic cost = £40,000 × $\dfrac{10}{100}$ = £4,000

Assume that the average replacement cost for 19–1 is given by:

£40,000 × $\dfrac{110}{100}$ = £44,000

The depreciation based on this value is:

£44,000 × $\dfrac{10}{100}$ = £4,400

Therefore the depreciation adjustment is:

£4,400 − £4,000 = £400

Balance Sheet as at 31st December, 19–1

	£
Plant & machinery at replacement value*	48,000
Depreciation to date	4,800
	43,200

* $£40,000 \times \dfrac{120}{100} = £48,000$

19–2
Assume that the average replacement value for 19–2 is given by:

$$£40,000 \times \dfrac{135}{100} = £54,000$$

Depreciation based on this value is:

$$£54,000 \times \dfrac{10}{100} = £5,400$$

Therefore the depreciation adjustment is:

$$£5,400 - £4,000 = £1,400$$

Balance Sheet as at 31st December, 19–2

	£	£
Plant and machinery at replacement value*	60,000	
Depreciation to date	12,000	
		48,000

* $£40,000 \times \dfrac{150}{100} = £60,000$

9.2
The overall purpose of current cost accounting as set down in SSAP 16 is to maintain the real value of a company's net worth during inflationary periods. This is achieved by making a number of adjustments to net profit as calculated using historic costs principles. Without going into the technical details of each adjustments the following paragraphs indicate their fundamental purpose.

(a) *Cost of sales adjustment*
The purpose of this adjustment is to allow for the fact that stock sold during an accounting period will need to be replaced if the business is to continue to operate. The replacement cost of the stock will probably be higher than the historic cost and some of the 'apparent' profit made on the sale should be retained for the purpose of stock replacement at higher prices. A simple method for calculating the adjustment involves the use of appropriate index numbers which reflect the change in the cost of stock over the accounting period.

(b) *Depreciation adjustment*
This is designed to reflect the increased cost of replacing fixed assets during periods of inflation. Provisions for depreciation based on replacement cost are compared with the provisions based on historic cost, and the difference between the two gives the adjustment. This adjustment is sometimes complicated by backlog depreciation, i.e. the need to provide depreciation based on current replacement cost for previous years as well as the current year.

(c) *Monetary working capital adjustment*
Holding monetary working capital during periods of inflation will also involve the company in a loss of value. Monetary working capital in simple terms is the difference between debtors and creditors, and this adjustment attempts to maintain the real value of any change in this over the accounting period. Obviously, if the company's creditors exceed debtors, then the company benefits from this and the adjustment will reflect this.

(d) *Gearing adjustment*
If a company is financed by people other than shareholders (and this is normally

the case), then some of the burden of inflation will be borne by them. The gearing adjustment therefore reduces the adjustments shown above, depending on the proportion of assets financed by the other providers of finance.

9.3 (a)
Cost of sales adjustment in £000

Opening stock	$400 \times \dfrac{125}{120}$	=	500
Purchases			4,200
			4,700
Closing stock	$800 \times \dfrac{125}{127}$		787
Current cost of sales			3,913

Therefore, cost of sales adjustment =
£3,913 − £3,800 = **£113**

Depreciation adjustment in £000
Average replacement value of fixed assets:

$$£1,500 \times \dfrac{190}{150} = £1,900$$

∴ Depreciation based on this value is

$$£1,900 \times \dfrac{10}{100} = £190$$

∴ Depreciation adjustment
= £190 − £150 = **£40**

Current cost Profit & Loss Account for the year ended 31st December, 19–4

	£000	£000
Net profit as per historic accounts		660
Less: Current cost adjustments		
Cost of sales	113	
Depreciation	40	
		153
Current cost operating profit		507

9.3 (b)
Current cost balance sheet as at 31st December, 19–4

	£000	£000
Fixed assets		
At replacement value	2,000	
Depreciation to date	800	
		1,200
Current assets		
Stocks, at replacement value	819	
Bank	420	
Working capital		1,239
Capital employed		2,439
Financed by:		
Ordinary shares		860
Profit & loss balance		1,107
Current cost reserve		472
		2,439

10.2 (a)
Profit and Loss Account for the Year ending 31st December, 19-6

Receipts		11,750	(Note 1)
Less: Materials		7,630	(Note 2)
		4,120	
Less: Direct wages		350	(Note 3)
Gross margin		3,770	
Less: Expenses			
Petrol	253		
Stationery	24 (Note 4)		
Audit	25 (Note 5)		
Depreciation:	(Note 6)		
Motor van	150		
Loose tools	75		
Sundries	90		
Total expenses		617	
Net profit		3,153	

Note 1
Receipts include:

	£
Cash receipts for work done for householders	950
Cash receipts for work done for building contractors	9,050
Amounts owing to Stornaway at 31st December, 19-6	1,750
Total income	11,750

Although the owner has not as yet received £1,750, this sum belongs to the 19-6 trading year because this was when he earned the money.

Note 2
Materials include:

Amounts paid to creditors for materials used	6,890
Creditors for materials at 31st December, 19-6	740
Total material costs	7,630

Once again materials worth £7,630 have been used up in this period. Whether they have been paid for or not is not the concern of the Profit and Loss account.

Note 3
Wages paid to casual labour have been treated as a direct cost in this case. Presumably if Stornaway had had less work he would have employed fewer people.

Note 4
Stationery and postage payments were £35 but £11 of this was left over and will therefore not be used up until next year. Hence the £11 must be charged as an expense when that stationery etc. is used up, i.e. some time in 19-7. This pre-payment will appear on the Balance Sheet under current assets.

Note 5
The audit fees belong to the year in question and are charged to the Profit and Loss Account accordingly.

Note 6
An estimate of loss of value of certain fixed assets must be made and charged as an expense. In this example we are given the rates of depreciation (see Chapter 4 for choice of method and rate).

10.2 (b) The Balance Sheet can now be illustrated along with explanatory notes.

Before we can complete the Balance Sheet, however, we need to know Stornaway's cash position at the year end. As all receipts and payments were in cash the calculation will follow thus:

Cash Flow Statement year ending 31st December, 19-6

Receipts
1st January initial capital	5,800	
Cash from households	950	
Cash from contractors	9,050	
Total receipts		15,800

Payments
Cash taken for private use	3,000	
Van	750	
Petrol	253	
Creditors (supplies)	6,890	
Wages	350	
Stationery	35	
Tools	300	
Gate	90	
		11,668
Cash on 31st December		4,132

Notice that the cash book is not concerned with what receipts or payments are for, simply that the cash transactions have taken place. Consequently items appear in the cash book, e.g.

1. payments for fixed assets and
2. other time periods (£11) which are not included in the Profit and Loss Account.

Balance Sheet on 31st December, 19-6

	Cost £	Depreciation £	Net £
Fixed assets (Note 1)			
Motor van	750	150	600
Loose tools	300	75	225
			825
Current assets (Note 2)			
Debtors	1,750		
Prepaid	11		
Cash	4,132		
		5,893	
Less: *Current liabilities* (Note 3)			
Creditors	740		
Owing	25		
		765	
Net working capital (Note 4)			5,128
Net assets employed (Note 5)			5,953
Financed by: (Note 6)			
Capital	5,800		
Add Net profit	3,153		
Less Drawings	3,000		5,953

Notes to Balance Sheet

Note 1 Fixed assets are entered at cost (original purchase price) less depreciation to date to give the net book value.

Note 2 Current assets include outstanding amounts owing (£1,750), plus £11 paid in advance for future benefits (in this case use of stationery and postage), and any cash at the year end. There is no end-stock in this particular business because the owner is a jobbing builder and has used up materials on the individual jobs at the year end.

Note 3 Current liabilities (short-term debts) are the suppliers (£740) and auditors (£25) who are still owed money.

Note 4 The outstanding debts are deducted from current assets to give net working capital

current assets − current liabilities = net working capital
£5,893   −   £7,65   =   £5,128

This is a test of liquidity and shows that the organisation has surplus funds in that Stornaway has £5,893 of 'near-money' to pay off any immediate commitments (£765).

The working capital ratio is   5893:765
                                7.7:1

i.e. for every £1 owing, there is £7.70 of near moeny available (see Chapter 8).

Note 5 Net assets employed = fixed assets + net working capital i.e. £825 + 5128 = £5983. This is sometimes referred to as the net worth of the business.

Note 6 This part of the Balance Sheet shows where the funds have come from. In this case they have been provided exclusively by the owner, Stornaway. He introduced £5,800 into the business and to this is added the net profit made in the year (calculated in the Profit and Loss Account). On the other hand, if there had been a net loss this would have reduced the capital. Finally, drawings are deducted because Stornaway has taken out £3,000 for his own spending. The net result of £5,953 is the capital employed which, of course, is equal to the net worth figure. So the Balance Sheet balances.

(C) *Analysis*

1. Factory wages £100 × 52   5,200
   Bank interest 10% of £5,800   580
   Annual income   5,780

2. Net Profit   3,153

Stornaway has already taken £3,000 of this. Hence it appears that, in financial terms, Stornaway should not have gone into the building trade. Other advantages and disadvantages are as follows:

Advantages
Presumably being your own boss is preferable to a factory job. You reap all the profits and it may be possible to offset certain private expenses against tax (euphemistically known as tax-minimisation).

Disadvantages
However, the building trade is a high risk business susceptible to seasonal and cyclical economic factors and there are a large number of bankruptcies in this field. Additionally, Stornaway, has unlimited liability (he can lose everything) and, being self employed, cannot draw holiday or sick pay.

10.3
Profit and Loss Account for the period July-December, 19-6

	£	£
Sales		15,000
Opening stock	—	
Purchases	14,050	
	14,050	
Closing stock	2,800	
Cost of sales		11,250
Gross profit		3,750
General expenses	2,760	
Depreciation	300	
Insurance	250	
Advertising	475	
		3,785
Net loss		(35)

Balance Sheet as at 31st December, 19-6

	£	£	£
Fixed assets			
Furniture and equipment		3,500	
Depreciation to date		300	
			3,200
Current assets			
Stocks		2,800	
Debtors		6,000	
Prepayments		725	
		9,525	
Current liabilities			
Creditors	2,250		
Bank overdraft	2,510		
		4,760	
Working capital			4,765
Capital employed			7,965
Financed by:			
Share capital			8,000
Profit and loss balance			(35)
			7,965

310 Accounting: A Practical Approach

11.1

There is no set solution to this exercise as the answer is dependent upon how you envisage the structure of Mcgregor PLC.

Item	Cost elements Direct and Indirect			Cost		Function
	Materials	Labour	Expenses	Prime	Overhead	
Welders' basic pay		✓		✓		Production
Office stationery	✓				✓	Administration
Metallurgist's salary		✓			✓	Research and development
Advertising			✓		✓	Marketing
Cutter's shift allowance		✓		✓		Production
Sheet metal	✓			✓		Production
Taxation	Not applicable – tax is not a 'cost'					
Salespeople's commission			✓		✓	Selling
Foreman's salary		✓		✓		Production
Factory rent			✓		✓	Administration
Bad debts provision			Not applicable			
Welding plant hire			✓	✓		Production
Cartons for packaging	✓				✓	Distribution
Depreciation on directors' car			✓		✓	Administration

11.2 (a)

Woolwich Engineers Manufacturing and Trading Account year ending 31st December 19-6

	Foundry £	£	Machine Shop £ Components	£			Warehouse £ Finished goods	£
Stocks:			3,000					
Raw materials								
Opening	2,400		(Outside) 7,000					
Purchases	12,400		(Transfer) 33,000			(Transfer)	80,000	79,500
	14,800		43,000				83,000	13,000
Less: Closing	3,000		3,400				3,500	700
Materials used		11,800	Components used	39,600		Cost of sales		93,200
Direct wages		16,000		17,000		Wages		105,000
Prime cost		27,800		56,600		Packing		11,800
Overheads								
Fuel and power	2,000		3,000			Sales		
Depreciation	900		1,200			Profit		
Light and heat	1,200		1,300					
		4,100		5,500				
Work-in-progress								
At start								
31st January				980				
At end 31st								
December—				860		120		
Total		31,900				62,220		
Notional profit		1,100				17,780		
Transfered to								
machine shop		33,000	Transfered to warehouse			80,000		

11.2 (a) (continued)

(b) Measured against the external prices given, the company appears to be performing well although foundry costs are much the same as elsewhere.

Unit costs in the: foundry   97p
: machine shop   £3.11

(c) This kind of comparative information can be used in make/buy decisions. The manufacturer is offering to supply the machines for £60,000 – £62,220, i.e. £2,220 less. Profits would therefore rise by this amount and capital at present tied up in the business could be released for other purposes. But the saving is not significant and factors such as undesirable unemployment and loss of manufacturing status must be considered. Additionally there is no guarantee that the arrangement is permanent. If the supplier finds alternative uses for his capacity he may switch supplies, or raise prices, in the future.

11.3 (a) Manufacturer's Operating Statement Sellen Goode (proposed)

	£	£
Sales		35,000
Raw materials	15,000	
Power etc.	1,500	
Total direct		16,500
Less:		
Labour	4,000	
Office	520	
Machinery	2,000	6,520
Net Profit		11,980

Assumptions
- 52 week year
- no drawings (salaries to wife or himself)
- produces and sells 1,000 units
- he has £10,000 capital

(b) *Sellen Goode* (present position)

	£
Salary	13,000[1]
Investments (property)	1,000[2]
Bank interest	1,000[3]
Wife's income	1,000
	16,000

Assumptions
[1] Promotion granted
[2] Property (Note 3 in the question)
[3] 10% on £10,000 deposit account

(c) Same as (b) except his salary will be £2,000 more, plus one-off payment if he sells the idea. Looks the best proposition.

(d) Company's Profit and Loss Account (proposed)

Direct costs (same as S-G)	16,500
Admin expenses (salary)	7,500
	24,000

∴ advantageous for company to produce for themselves (cost £35,000 from S-G)

Assumptions
- spare capacity
- no other overheads absorbed
* • ½ S-Gs salary charged to Ganna

12.1

(a) Department A – £2.50/labour hour
Department B – £8.10/machine hour

(b) Cost statement Job Number 46

		£	£
Department A			
Direct materials		61.00	
Direct labour	6 × £2	12.00	
Overheads	6 × £2.50	15.00	
			88.00
Department B			
Direct materials		124.00	
Direct labour	3 × £2.50	7.50	
Overheads	2 × £8.10	16.20	
			147.70
Factory cost:			235.70
Mark up for Admin cost −20%			47.14
			282.84
Delivery charge			10.00
			292.84
Mark up for profit −33⅓%			97.61
			390.45
VAT 15%			58.57
Selling price			449.02

(c)

	£
Department A	
Actual overhead incurred	80,000
Less Overhead absorbed.	
34,000 × £2.50	85,000
Over absorption	5,000

	£
Department B	
Actual overhead incurred	78,000
Less Overhead absorbed	
8,500 × £8.10	68,850
Under absorption	9,150

(d) To ensure that the matching concept is observed, overhead under or over-absorbed during the accounting period should be taken to the Profit and Loss Account. Over-absorption would be shown as an addition to profit while under-absorption is shown as a deduction.

12.2

Annual costs incurred by Department D

	£
Depreciation	5,000
Operators' wages	32,500
Overhead expenses charged	6,400
Insurance	1,000
Maintenance	4,000
Total (excluding power)	48,900

12.2 (continued)

Estimated machine hours
10 × 7 × 5 × 47   16,450
Therefore full cost recovery rate is:

$$\frac{£48,900}{16,450} = 2.97$$

Plus Power costs = 0.60

3.57 per machine hour

(b) Computation of selling price for Job Number 41

	£	£
Department A		
Direct materials	140	
Direct labour	108	
Overheads	84	
		332
Department B		
Direct materials	240	
Direct labour	196	
Overheads	147	
		583
Department C		
Direct materials	288	
Direct labour	157.5	
Overheads	165	
		610.50
Department D (60 hours × 3.57)		214.20
Factory cost		1739.70
Plus administrative overheads (30%)		521.91
		2261.61
Plus Profit mark-up (33⅓%)		753.87
		3015.48
P.us VAT (15%)		452.32
		3467.80

(c) • To value jobs in progress and finished jobs.
• To compare actual cost with pre-determined standards for control purposes.

12.3

Overhead analysis

	Departments			
	A	B	C	D
	£	£	£	£
General rates	520	1,170	780	130
Insurance (buildings)	48	60	24	12
Insurance (plant)	36	42	24	6
Indirect wages	1,076	2,268	672	—
Light and heat	400	720	400	80
Depreciation (plant)	1,800	2,100	1,200	300
Sundry expenses	190	100	160	—
Power	430	540	240	65
Wages	—	—	—	1,900
Materials	—	—	—	607
	4,500	7,000	3,500	3,100

	£	£	£	£
Reapportionment of Department D	1,150	1,350	600	(3,100)
Total	5,650	8,350	4,100	—

Overhead absorption rates:-
Department A: £0.25, Department B: £0.50, Department C: £0.40

14.1 (a) *Contribution per unit*

	£	£
Selling price		33.00
Less Variable costs		
Direct materials	6.00	
Direct labour	8.00	
Factory overhead	1.00	
Selling overhead	2.00	17.00
Contribution		£16.00

1. Break-even point:

$$= \frac{\text{Fixed costs}}{\text{Contribution per unit}} = \frac{£100{,}000}{£16}$$

= 6,250 units

= £206,250 in sales

2. Margin of safety:

= 10,000 units − 6,250 units

= 3,750 units

= £123,750 in sales

3. Contribution sales ratio:

$$= \frac{£16}{£33} \times 100 = 48.5\%$$

(b)

Item	Original		Alternative 1		Alternative 2	
	£	£	£	£	£	£
Sales		330,000		350,000		280,000
Variable costs						
Direct materials	60,000		84,000		42,000	
Direct labour	80,000		112,000		56,000	
Factory overheads	10,000		14,000		7,000	
Selling overheads	20,000		28,000		14,000	
		170,000		238,000		119,000
Contribution		160,000		112,000		161,000
Fixed costs		100,000		100,000		100,000
Net profit		60,000		12,000		61,000

(c)
- Many semi-variable costs are difficult to analyse into fixed and variable elements.
- Straight-line functions are assumed for costs and revenues.
- Difficult to apply with a multi-product firm.

316 Accounting: A Practical Approach

14.2 (a) For the purpose of break-even analysis, costs must be segregated into fixed and variable elements.

With semi-variable costs, these elements can be determined graphically or by calculation, using 'high-low' technique.

Factory overheads

$$£104,000 - £96,000 = \frac{£8,000}{4,000}$$

Variable element = £2.00 per unit
Fixed element = £80,000

Administration
Fixed overheads = £40,000

Selling and distribution

$$£132,000 - £108,000 = \frac{£24,000}{4,000}$$

Variable element = £6 per unit
Fixed element = £60,000

The assumption is that the variable overheads follow a linear function.

(b) 1.
Break-even points:

$$= \frac{\text{Fixed costs}}{\text{Contribution per unit}}$$

$$= \frac{£180,000}{£32}$$

$$= 5,625 \text{ units}$$

Check: sales	£360,000
Less: Variable cost	180,000
Contribution	180,000
Less: Fixed cost	180,000
Profits	—

2. $\dfrac{\text{Fixed costs}}{\text{Contribution/sales ratio}}$

$$= \frac{£180,000}{50\%}$$

$$= £360,000$$

Check: 5,625 × £64 = £360,000

Alternative methods of calculation are also acceptable.

14.2 (c) 1.
The break-even point:
contribution per unit falls to £28

Thus $\dfrac{£180,000}{£28}$

= 6429 units

Effect on profits
Output (units)   12,000   10,000

	£	£
Sales	720,000	640,000
Variable costs	384,000	320,000
Contribution	336,000	320,000
Fixed costs	180,000	180,000
Profits	156,000	140,000

2. The break-even point:
   contribution per unit rises to £38

   Thus $\dfrac{£180,000}{£38}$

   = 4737 units

Effect on profits

Output (units)	8,000	10,000
	£	£
Sales	560,000	640,000
Variable cost	256,000	320,000
Contribution	304,000	320,000
Fixed costs	180,000	180,000
	124,000	140,000

(d) The analysis normally assumes linear functions for costs and revenues, and that fixed costs do not change for all levels of capacity.

It assumes production and sales changes will always coincide. This may not be the case, particularly with increases in output.

The actual product mix may not coincide with the budgeted data; significant differences can arise.

Changes in critical cost factors, e.g. labour, material and overhead costs, may arise and the analysis require adjustment.

14.3

(a)
	£
Use of hall	100
Disco	50
Fixed costs	150

Each person (x) contributes 50p admission + 30p profit on bar + parking.

Each person (x) contributes 80p to cover these overheads. This is made up of 50p admission fee and 30p average profit per head on bar receipts + parking.

Hence $.8x = 150$ to break even

∴ $x = 187.5$

∴ Roughly 190 people attended the ordinary disco as the students' union were not losing money.

(b)
Group night	£
Use of hall	100
Disco	50
Group	500
Advertising	50
	700

The hall was $\frac{1}{2}$ full, i.e. 500 people.

∴ Revenue = 500 × £1.30 = £650

∴ Loss on group night = £700 − £650 = £50

(c) Total costs (including extra staff £50) = £750

∴ Number of people required to break even $\frac{750}{0.8} = 937.5$

(d) The arguments obviously depend on whether the entertainment is price-elastic or not. Many factors may influence this, particularly the choice of group.

15.1 (a) Cash Budget for March to August

	March £	April £	May £	June £	July £	August £
Inflows						
Share issue	50,000	25,000	25,000	—	—	—
Cash sales	12,500	13,000	23,000	28,000	32,000	35,500
Credit sales	—	—	12,500	13,000	23,000	28,000
	62,500	38,000	60,500	41,000	55,000	63,500
Overflows						
Rent	1,500	1,500	1,500	1,500	1,500	1,500
Purchases (1 month)	—	7,350	7,350	10,780	12,250	13,230
Purchases (2 months)	—	—	7,500	7,500	11,000	12,500
Wages/salaries	10,000	11,000	15,000	20,000	21,000	25,000
Overhead expenses	1,250	1,300	2,300	2,800	3,200	3,550
Fixtures and fittings	25,000	30,000	—	—	—	—
	37,750	51,150	33,650	42,580	48,950	55,780
Summary						
Opening balance	0	24,750	11,600	38,450	36,870	42,920
Net inflow(outflow)	24,750	(13,150)	26,850	(1,580)	6,050	7,720
Closing balance	24,750	11,600	38,450	36,870	42,920	50,640

(b) Profit and Loss Account for six months ending 31st August

	£	£
Sales		288,000
Less Cost of sales (50%)		144,000
Gross margin		144,000
Plus: Discounts received		1,040
Less:		
Rent	9,000	
Wages and salaries	102,000	
Overhead expenses	14,400	
Depreciation:		
Fixtures and fittings	2,500	
Equipment	3,000	
		130,900
Net profit		14,140

Balance Sheet as at 31st August

	£	£	£
Fixed assets			
Fixtures and fittings, at cost		25,000	
Less: Depreciation to data		2,500	
			22,500
Equipment, at cost		30,000	
Less: Depreciation to date		3,000	
			27,000
			49,500
Current assets			
Stock	10,000		
Debtors	67,500		
Bank	50,640		
		128,140	
Current liabilities			
Creditors		63,500	
			64,640
			114,140
Financed by:			
Issued share capital			
100,000 × £1 ordinary shares			100,000
Reserves			
Retained earnings			14,140
			114,140

(C)

Report to the Managing Director should consider the following:

1. Substantial cash balances throughout the period which must be monitored and controlled. Cash is a non-earning asset and as such should be minimised by:

(a) reducing the share issue, leaving funds to call on at a later date

(b) investing more in stocks, thereby hedging against inflation

(c) reducing creditors, thereby gaining additional discounts

(d) placing cash on short-term deposit thereby earning interest

2. Long credit period granted to customers so that by the end of the period, over 23% of sales are outstanding debts. This should be reviewed with an eye to reduction, although this may be a deliberate policy to stimulate demand for the products of a new company.
However, in the longer term, this should be reviewed fully.

3. Net margin has been substantially reduced by high wage and salary costs which are therefore worthy of further investigation.

15.2 (a) 1.
Profit Statement for Department 4

	£	£
Sales		100,000
Less: Variable costs		
Direct labour	24,300	
Direct materials	27,800	
Factory overheads	32,700	
Distribution	4,000	
Commission	10,000	
		98,800
Contribution		1,200

Therefore closure of the department would involve a loss of the contribution from Department 4, which would reduce overall profit of B.S. Ltd.

2
Profit Statement for Department 4

	£	£
Sales		135,000
Less: Variable costs		
Direct labour	26,300	
Direct materials	41,700	
Factory overheads	49,050	
Distribution	6,000	
Commission	15,000	
		138,050
Contribution		(3,050)

Thus, because of the substantial variable costs involved with the product, the company will incur a loss if it pursues the sales director's policy

(b) There are many factors worth considering in relation to their decision:
- the relationship between this product and others produced by the company (i.e. it could be a loss-leader)
- the possibilities of increasing the selling price or reducing production costs
- the alternatives to this product and the costs involved in establishing it
- the possibility of using the capacity to produce more of the company's others products

15.3 (a)
Cash budget for year ending 30th June, 19–2

	July	August	September	October	November	December	January	February	March	April	May	June
Inflows												
Capital	10,000	—	—	—	—	—	—	—	—	—	—	—
Sales	—	8,000	8,000	8,000	8,000	8,000	8,000	8,000	8,000	8,000	8,000	8,000
Outflows												
Purchases	—	—	12,800	6,000	6,000	6,000	6,000	6,000	6,000	6,000	6,000	6,000
Rent	2,000	—	—	2,000	—	—	2,000	—	—	2,000	—	—
Sundry expenses	500	500	500	500	500	500	500	500	500	500	500	500
Drawings	400	400	0	400	400	400	400	400	400	400	400	400
Equipment	11,000	—	—	—	—	—	—	—	—	—	—	—
Summary												
Opening balance	0	(4,700)	2,400	(3,300)	(4,200)	(3,100)	(2,000)	(2,900)	(1,800)	(700)	(1,600)	(500)
Net flow	(4,700)	7,100	(5,700)	(900)	1,100	1,100	(900)	1,100	1,100	(900)	1,100	1,100
Closing balance	(4,700)	2,400	(3,300)	(4,200)	(3,100)	(2,000)	(2,900)	(1,800)	(700)	(1,600)	(500)	600

15.3 (a) (continued)

Profit and Loss Account for the year ending 30th June, 19–2

	£	£
Sales		96,000
Less: Cost of sales (75%)		72,000
Gross margin		24,000
Rent	8,000	
Sundry expenses	6,000	
Depreciation	2,000	
		16,000
Net profits		8,000

Balance Sheet as at 30th June, 19–2

	£	£	£
Fixed assets			
Equipment, at cost		11,800	
Less: Depreciation		2,000	
			9,800
Current assets			
Stock	6,800		
Debtors	8,000		
Bank	600		
		15,400	
Current liabilities			
Creditors		12,000	3,400
Capital employed			13,200

	£	£
Financed by:		
Capital:		
Opening balance	10,000	
Plus: Net profit	8,000	
	18,000	
Less: Drawings	4,000	
		13,200

(b)

Profit and Loss Account for the year ended 30th June, 19–2

	£	£
Sales		120,000
Cost of sales		90,000
Gross margin		30,000
Expenses		16,000
Net profit		14,000

Balance Sheet as at 30th June, 19–2

	£	£	£
Fixed assets			
Equipment, at cost		11,800	
Depreciation		2,000	
			9,800
Current assets			
Stock	6,800		
Debtors	10,000		
Bank	7,600		
		24,400	

	£	£
Current liabilities		
Creditors	15,000	9,400
Capital employed		19,200
Financed by:		
Capital		
Opening balance		10,000
Plus: Net profit		14,000
		24,000
Less: Drawings		4,800
		19,200

(c)
This is obviously a profitable venture, even if monthly sales are only £8,000. However, the cash budget at this level of sales reveals that an overdraft will be required for most of the 12 month period. The maximum overdraft is £4,700 in the first month, necessary to meet the payments for equipment and rent before cash in flows from trading begin.

If the bank is not prepared to meet this level of overdraft, then Blunt can pursue a number of alternative strategies to cover the deficit:

- inject more capital from the start
- try to defer payments for equipment and rent
- Generate cash inflow from sales in the first month by offering a cash discount

Obviously the level of sales will have a significant effect on profit and profitability. There is also a marked effect on liquidity, where although the maximum overdraft is still £4,700 in the first month, it is not required after October. This faster repayment would be much more attractive to the bank.

16.1 (a)
Operating statement for May

	Standard		Actual		Variance
	£	£	£	£	£
Sales		24,800		24,500	300(A)
Less: Direct materials	8,800		8,960		160(A)
Direct labour	10,080		9,900		180(F)
Factory overheads	4,032		4,850		818(A)
		22,912		23,710	
Profit		1,888		790	1,098(A)

(b) *Direct materials*

Price variance

$(SP - AP) \times AQ$

$= SP \times AQ - AP \times AQ$

$= £1.10 \times 6200 - £8,960$

$= £9,020 - £8,960$ $= £60(F)$

Usage variance   £160(A)

$(SQ - AQ) \times SP$

$= (8000 - 8200) \times £1.10$ $= £220(A)$

Direct labour
Rate variance

$(SR - AR) \times AH$

$= SR \times AH - AR \times AH$

$= £2.10 \times 4,600 - £9,900$

$= £9,660 - £9,900$ $= £240(A)$

Answers 323

16.1 (a) (continued)

Efficiency variance   £180(F)
$(SH - AH) \times SR$
$= 4,800 - 4,600 \times £2.10$ $= £420(F)$

Factory overheads
Expenditure variance
$= £4,032 - £4,850 = £818(A)$

(Note: This assumes that the overheads vary directly with hours worked.)

Sales variances

Volume   Not applicable
Price

$(SP - AP) \times AQ$
$= SP \times AQ - AP \times AQ$
$= £310 \times 80 - 24,500 = £300(A)$

16.2 (a) Operating statement for May

	Standard £	Standard £	Actual £	Actual £	Variance £
Sales		44,000		44,240	240(F)
Less: Direct materials	25,600		29,760		4,160(A)
Direct labour	3,648		3,456		192(F)
Factory overheads	4,800		4,620		180(F)
		34,048		37,036	
		9,952		6,404	3,548(A)

(b) Direct materials

Price variance
$(SP - AP) \times AQ$
$= SP \times AQ - AP \times AQ$
$= £10 \times 2,480 - £29,760$ $= £4,960(A)$

Usage Variance   £4,160(A)
$(SQ - AQ) \times SP$
$= 2,560 - 2,480 \times £10$ $= £800(F)$

Direct labour
Rate variance
$(SR - AR) \times AH$
$= SR \times AH - AR \times AH$
$= £1.90 \times 1,975 - £3,456$ $= £296.50(F)$

Efficiency variances   £192(F)
$(SH - AH) \times SR$
$= 1,920 - 1,975 \times £1.90$ $= £104.50(A)$

Factory overheads
Expenditure variance
$= £4,800 - £4,620$ $= £180(F)$

Sales variances
Volume   Not applicable
Price $= £240(F)$

16.3   Direct labour

Rate variance
$(SR - AR) \times AH$
$= SR \times AH - AR \times AH$
$= £2.20 \times 5,800 - £13,920$ $= £1,160(A)$

Efficiency variance
(SH − AH) × SR
Standard hours:
Super = 8 × 450   = 3,600
Deluxe = 12 × 450   = 2,340
                         5,940

= 5,940 − 5,800 × £2.20   = £308(F)
Net variance   = £852(A)

Variable overheads
Expenditure variance =
Actual hours × overhead rate
  5800 × £0.30   = £1,740
Less: Actual overhead   = £3,450
Expenditure variance   = £1,710(A)

Efficiency variance
 (SH − AH) × SR
= (5,940 − 5,800) × £0.30
= £42(F)

Fixed overheads
Budget = 8 × 420 + 12 × 250
       = 6,360 × £0.60
       = £3,816

Expenditure variance
= £3,816 − £6,940 = £3,124(A)

Volume variance
(Budgeted activity − Actual activity) × Standard rate
= (6,360 − 5,940) × £0.60
= £252(A)

Statement of Variances

Variance	Adverse £	Favourable £
Direct labour		
Rate	1,160	
Efficiency		308
Variable overheads		
Expenditure	1,710	
Efficiency		42
Fixed overheads		
Expenditure	3,124	
Volume	252	
	6,246	350
Net	5,896	

Assignment 1

1 *Sales performance over the last 5 years*

Turnover has increased by $\dfrac{28{,}645}{21{,}843} \times 100$

= 31% over the last 5 years.

This increase should be compared with the retail price index (rpi) or a more specific price index such as the one for alcohol to see if the increase is real or monetary. It would be useful to draw a graph showing sales and sales adjusted for inflation.

(a) As a tenant of the pub you would be restricted in the ways that you could improve turnover because of company (i.e. brewery) policy. Nevertheless, a tenant has a fair amount of operations leeway and can endeavour to keep a well-run house and give a cheerful and prompt service to the customers. Often revenue-earners such as food and bar snacks are left to the tenant's discretion.

(b) A wealth of accounting and statistical information might be available but it is important to determine which is relevant to the problem. Sources examined might include:
- previous profit and loss accounts, cash books and balance sheets for the Dog and Firkin
- comparable figures for other outlets supplied by the brewery
- licensed victuallars' data
- Government statistics, rpi trends in:
  - alcohol and food consumption away from the home
  - VAT and alcohol tax changes
  - rough data on local population changes in the area and the local unemployment rate

(c) Annual earnings:

	£
Drawings	3,710
+ wife	985

(d) Perks might include:
- free or cheap – accommodation
  – food and drink
- tips from customers
- profits from food

2 With the limited information it is difficult to make a decision but the factors for consideration are outlined in the flowchart below.

The key features are:
- Mr and Mrs King's objectives, e.g. do they want to be self-employed?

whether they think the Dog and Firkin can be made successful

- current ROCE $\dfrac{3,00}{60,000} = 5\%$

- whether they can raise the extra finance even if they wanted the place.
  This will involve persuading the bank manager, or someone else who can provide finance that the plans are well-founded.

(a) Given that the status is a free house, the owner would have much move flexibility than the tenant of a tied house. The following items might be considered:

Product – range
– choice of suppliers
– selling other breweries' ales, snacks and soft drinks

Place
– refurnishment, as fixtures are 10 years old
– diversification:
  leisure centre
  hotel or bed and breakfast
  beer garden
  children's facilities
  fruit and games machines
  restaurant

Pricing
– flexibility
– happy hours
  special offers to boost demand during quiet periods

Promotion
– advertising:
  local press
  leaflets
  tourist associations.
– special events, e.g. a lager evening
– company sponsors

Flowchart of DOG and FIRKIN decision process

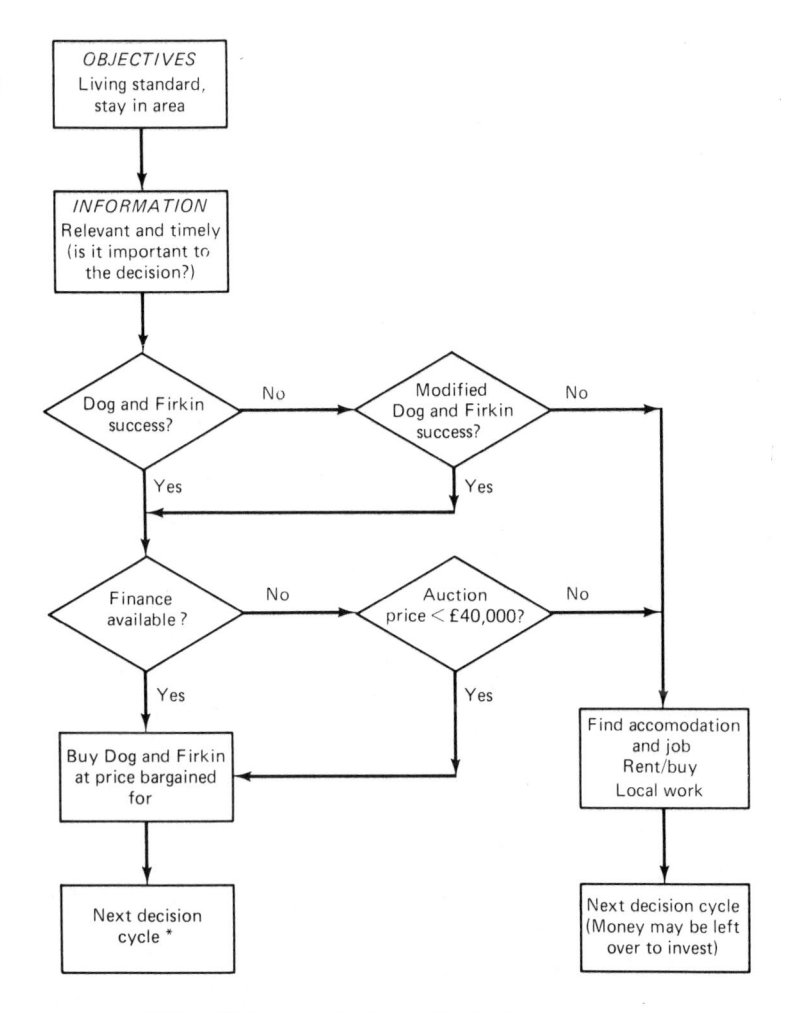

```
          OBJECTIVES
          Living standard,
          stay in area
                │
                ▼
          INFORMATION
          Relevant and timely
          (is it important to
          the decision?)
                │
                ▼
        ◇ Dog and Firkin ──No──▶ ◇ Modified ──No──────────┐
          success?                Dog and Firkin            │
                │                 success?                  │
               Yes                    │Yes                  │
                │◀───────────────────┘                      │
                ▼                                            │
        ◇ Finance ──No──▶ ◇ Auction ──No──────────────────▶│
          available?        price < £40,000?                │
                │                    │                      ▼
               Yes                  Yes           ┌─────────────────┐
                │                    │            │ Find accomodation│
                ▼                    │            │ and job          │
        ┌──────────────┐             │            │ Rent/buy         │
        │ Buy Dog and  │◀────────────┘            │ Local work       │
        │ Firkin at    │                          └─────────────────┘
        │ price        │                                   │
        │ bargained for│                                   ▼
        └──────────────┘                          ┌─────────────────┐
                │                                 │ Next decision   │
                ▼                                 │ cycle (Money may│
        ┌──────────────┐                          │ be left over to │
        │ Next decision│                          │ invest)         │
        │ cycle *      │                          └─────────────────┘
        └──────────────┘
```

*This will include planning for modification/improvements or longer-term projects
- Product — mix, choice of supplies
- Price — happyhours, specials
- Promotion — advertising, sponsors
- Place — hotel/restaurant/leisure centre

        — pub teams:
           darts
           pool
           soccer, etc.

(b) Economic trends can affect different products in different ways. Important points to note are:

Drink   — increasing consumption of wines and lager
         — relative decline of mild
         — popularity of real ale

These represent shifts in consumer tastes coupled with EEC policy towards taxation of wine and bear, which affects relative prices.

Food There is evidence to show that consumers are 'trading-down', i.e. switching from restaurant meals to bar-snacks, in an economic recession.

328 Accounting: A Practical Approach

3 The owner may first have to consider taking on partners, to raise the extra money. Almost certainly the owner should adopt limited liability to minimise losses if things go wrong.

4 This depends very much on the scale of the business. Initially the married couple may have planned to cope alone, with perhaps part-time bar staff to help out at busy periods. They may not realise the extra paper work involved and this might require a part-time accountant to look after the books. But long-term growth (see 2(a)) would add extra administrative responsibilities, not least the employment of full-time staff.

Assignment 2

It would be useful if students wrote to their local or favourite club for details of costs and revenues.

Cost-cutting exercises
- Major:
  - cut wages
  - reduce playing staff using part-timers as reserves
  - bring transfer fees under control
  - share stadium facilities with neighbouring clubs (often ruled out by fierce club loyalty, though rugby league and soccer can co-exist)
  - postpone ground improvements (not a sensible long-term option)
- Minor:
  - cancel pre-match meals
  - reduce overnight stays
  - travel by coach not train
  - no Christmas staff bonuses
  - reduce board-room hospitality

Sources of outside income
- *Share issues* All clubs are limited liability companies, yet until very recently the Football Association (F.A.) has frowned on investors seeking to make a profit out of professional soccer. It was an F.A. rule that 'the maximum dividend payable in respect of any year shall be 10% before deduction of tax'. No wonder the total share capital of Football League clubs was only £2.6m in 1981. Paid directors were not allowed until that year either; hence the lack of professionals and accountants at board level.

Recent public share issues have been very successful, however. Spurs, for example, wiped out most of their debts.

- *Supporters' clubs* – lottery, bingo, raffle and other fund-raising activities

- *BBC and ITV* television contract: an improved deal means more money for the clubs

- *Company sponsorship*
  - backing the team or individuals (e.g. Hitachi and Liverpool; Keegan, part of whose salary Scottish and Newcastle breweries pay)
  - includes such things as shirt advertising in return for personal appearances backing company products

- *Advertising* – ground
  - programme
  - shirt

- *Pools* – take from gambling is too low

- *On-ground concessions* – for shops, traders, etc.

'Product' improvements:
- to the game:
  amend the rules
  - no offsides?
  - shootouts?
  - sin-bins?
  - change in points structure, giving greater rewards for a win
  - change in penalising fouls

There are signs that some changes have resulted in brighter, more open football. Perhaps more experiments are needed.
play at different times
– on Sundays, evenings
– moratorium in December – February when it is too cold to watch
play fewer matches – form a 'super-league' of top clubs

- to the ground:
An obvious reform is to share facilities with a neighbouring club, particularly as most stadiums are commercially useful for only 50 or so hours a year.
omniturf
– ground can be used every day for practice etc.
– can be rented out for other events e.g. boxing matches, pop concerts
– is almost weather-proof and is good for television advertising
– gives the game a cleaner, up-market image
– but still traditional opposition to artificial pitches
all seater stadium – comfort encourages family attendance
executive boxes – often company sponsored for the season
better facilities all round – food, drink, toilets, bars, supermarkets?
entertainment complex – sports centre, squash courts beneath stand, etc.,

Assignment 3

1 From the sales value index (Table 17.4) it can be seen that January – June sales make up between 42% and 43% of the eventual annual amount. To date in 19–0, less than 40% of budget (220/560) has actually been achieved.

Target volume sales for 6 months = 316,720 (740,000 × 0.428) So sales are 316,720 – 290,000 = 26,720 short of the ½ year target. This represents a shortfall of about 8 percentage points.

Table 17.5 shows that labour costs are up by 20p per set on budget, which had allowed for a 15% increase on last year already. This must be because of an unforeseen wage settlement or a worsening of productivity. Either way, there is cause for concern. Other costs and material prices have risen but these were budgeted for.

Fixed costs are on course to be £400,000 over-budget, assuming that they are incurred at a steady rate throughout the year.

2 Assumption: actual level of sales in 19–0 will continue at the same rate (i.e. approximately 92% of budget), and so will fixed costs.

Average price of set		£30
Number of sets sold	£680,000	(92%)
	£m	
Total revenue	20.4	
Direct costs	5.644	
Contribution	14.756	
Fixed Costs	15.0	
Pre-tax profit/loss	(0.244)	

Hence the year-end estimate is a loss of £244,000.

Clearly the tax provision will be affected by this outcome and the directors will have to renew their recommendations for dividend payments.

3 'Rationalise' means, in this context, a cost-reduction exercise. For example, Hopkins suggests concentrating on successful products and phasing out loss-makers. This might result in plant (or line) closures and such capacity savings could lead to job lossess.

'Value-added' is the difference between sales and payments made to suppliers for raw materials, rent, rates and services etc. The value added, raised by the company's own efforts, is used to:
- pay wages and pensions
- pay dividends
- reinvest in the business

Prices should always be sufficient to cover all cost increases of materials and other services, but price rises may be difficult to implement in highly competitive markets.

4 Recommended courses of action

Again this calls for imaginative but practical thinking. Short-term solutions are needed to overcome the difficult liquidity position. Ways of getting quick money which could be considered are:
- getting stockists (debtors) to pay up more quickly by offering better discounts
- selling off stock at reduced prices under special offers
- factoring stock
- short-time working

Care should be taken that such contingency plans do not impair long-term profitability.

In the long term, careful consideration should be given to the corporate plan. Key decisions have to be made on objectives to decide in which direction the company should be going. This will involve investigating:

- product policy — rationalisation and/or diversification
- place — spreading sales abroad (see Table 17.6) for a balanced geographical portfolio
- price — strategy and tactics for a profitable business. Is the market really price elastic?
- promotion — cost-effective advertising and promotion

Such decisions will affect the nature and size of the operation and the materials, money and workforce required to support it.

5 Factors that should be considered:

- Careful advanced planning involving union representatives and the convenor if appropriate. The workers' representative should be fully versed in the reasons, numbers, names and redundancy pay, and any other factors.
- The timing of the message must be settled. How soon before the redundancy should it be announced?
- The boss, Mr Taylor, should talk to all the workers himself, ideally through a meeting where he could tell them the position and what was to be done, and answer questions. There should be an opportunity for Taylor or the personnel director (Knox-Johnson) to see every person concerned, individually.

In the communication the exact position of the organisation and any special reasons should be given. It should also be clear what action management is taking over the whole business, e.g. electronic games, new markets. Full details of the redundancy pay or terms should be given, as well as of any jobs that could be available elsewhere, training facilities, liaison with job centre etc.

6 (a) *Shareholders' viewpoint*

The return on owner's equity $\left(\dfrac{\text{profit after tax}}{\text{owner's equity}}\right)$ for 19–9 was 10% $\left(\dfrac{0.6}{6}\right)$ and is projected to be $\dfrac{0.8}{6.4} = 12.5\%$ this year (19–0). But the interim figures show a disquieting change and worse may still be to come. Even if fixed costs can be held in check (to £14.6m), pre-tax profits are estimated to be only £156,000 in 19–0. This would leave only £78,000 for distribution and, to maintain the same cover as in 19–9, the dividend payment would be only £39,000. Clearly the company looks vulnerable to future conditions and its money for new investment would be low. The profit before tax on sales (margin) has declined from 11% (19–7) to 6% (19–9) and, after an improvement in 19–8, the asset turnover ratio declined to 2.5 × that in 19–9. So the last 3 years' return on capital employed figures (calculated from appendix II) show a trend decline:

	19–7	19–8	19–9
ROCE %	24	20	15

In particular, labour and material increases and the larger than expected fixed costs, due in all likelihood to the increased borrowing charges for the bank overdraft, show cause for concern.

The liquidity position is potentially worrying also:

	19–9	19–0 estimate
Current assets to current liabilities	2.36:1	2.13:1
Acid test	1:1	0.9:1

The Balance Sheet shows that liquidity could be dependent on quick sales of stock and chasing up debtors. Current liabilities are largely creditors and there could be problems if suppliers wanted their money quickly. The projected increase in the bank overdraft (by 140%) and the unscheduled raising of £1¼m in long-term loans is also indicative of the company's inability to finance operations from internal funds.

The company's prospects depend on quick sales and the market potential for future profitable business. As a shareholder there is reason to doubt the whole toy sector, although it is probable that the Stock Exchange already reflects these problems in its share price, so the prospects may look good relative to the alternative of selling the shares.

Bank manager's viewpoint
The bank manager knows that the banks involvement with the company is £1.2m, £0.7m greater than the whole of last year. It is not known whether these overdrafts are secured and, if so, on what. (Default could mean that the bank has first claim on the company's buildings, for example.) Nor do we know what overdraft limit has been set or how the overdraft normally fluctuates in the year.

Given the 'profit' level and the liquidity situation, the overdraft seems very high and the bank may already be pressing for it to be reduced. It is almost impossible to pay back out of cash flow (assumed to be profits minus dividend plus depreciation) on current projections.

Thus, either the company may need to reduce its stocks, or reduce the general level of activity, or increase its long term borrowing/owner's equity. This will be difficult in the present climate, particularly as it has just borrowed £1m in loans.

The bank manager should clarify the limit on the overdraft and its security and ask for a planned reduction – seeing the company's plans for the coming period. Pressing for an immediate return would probably force closure, if not bankruptcy.

Assignment 4

1 Memorandum should observe the conventional layout and contain a clear statement of the amount the company can afford to repay and maintain the overdraft at £10,270.

The following accounts should be appended to the memorandum:-

Profit and Loss Accounts Six months ended 30th September, 1983

	£	£
Sales $\left(£1,468,470 \times \frac{1}{2} \times \frac{105}{100} \times \frac{105}{100}\right)$		809,494
Cost of sales (85%)		688,070
Gross profit (15%)		121,424
Salaries $\left(£150,530 \times \frac{1}{2} \times \frac{103}{100}\right)$	77,523	
General Expenses $\left(£25,450 \times \frac{1}{2} \times \frac{106}{100}\right)$	13,489	
Bank interest	15,200	
Depreciation $(£6,300 \times \frac{1}{2})$	3,150	
		109,362
Net profit		12,062

Balance Sheet as at 30th September, 1983

Fixed assets	£	£	£
Premises	185,000	—	185,000
Equipment	42,000	14,700	27,300
	227,000	14,700	212,300

Assignment 4 (continued)

Current assets

Stock $\left(140{,}760 \times \dfrac{105}{100}\right)$		147,798
Debtors $\left(58{,}500 \times \dfrac{105}{100}\right)$		61,425
		209,223

Current liabilities

Creditors $\left(64{,}800 \times \dfrac{105}{100}\right)$	68,040	
Loan	100,000	
Overdraft (balancing item)	1,781	
		169,821
Working capital		39,402
Capital employed		251,702
Share capital		200,000
General reserve		24,650
Profit and loss		27,052
		251,702

EITHER

Cash Flow Statement

	£	£
Sources of cash		
Net profit		12,062
Depreciation		3,150
Contribution from trading		15,212
Increase in creditors		
(68,040 − 64,800)		3,240
		18,452
Applications of cash		
Increase in stock		
(147,798 − 140,760)	7,038	
Increase in debtors		
(61,425 − 58,500)	2,925	
		9,963
Increase in cash		8,489

OR

Receipts and Payments Statement

	£	£
Receipts of cash		
Sales	809,494	
Debtors 31/3/83	58,500	
	867,994	
Debtors 30/9/83	61,425	
Receipts from customers		806,569
Payments		
Purchases (cost of sales + closing		
stock − opening stock)		
(688,070 + 147,798 − 140,760)	695,108	

	£	£
Creditors 31/3/83	64.800	
	759,908	
Creditors 30/9/83	68,040	
Payments to suppliers	691,868	
Salaries	77,523	
General expenses	13,489	
Interest	15,200	
		798,080
Increase in cash		8,489

The memorandum should therefore show that in maintaining the overdraft at £10,270, the company can afford to repay £8,489.

2 The letter should observe the normal conventions and cover the following points:

(a) There is an upturn in new car registrations in 1982. However, there is not enough evidence to predict confidently that this will necessarily continue into 1983.

(b) Even if overall demand is rising, it is possible for the company to perform below the general trend, e.g. they may be facing strong local competition or dealing in makes/models for which demand continues to be depressed.

(c) More reliable information is available from two sources:

- Society of Motor Manufacturers and Traders
- Motor Agents Association

3 The memorandum should show clearly how much the company can afford to repay on the basis of its present plans and the conditions about the overdraft imposed by the bank.

Supporting calculations should be in the following form:

	£
Increase in cash as per original budget	8,489
Reduction in interest (15,200 – 10,000)	5,200
	13,689
Reduction in overdraft	10,270
Increase in cash	3,419

Thus, on the basis of their present plans, the company could only afford to repay a maximum of £3,419, a shortage on the first instalment of £21,581.

4 Report should be given in appropriate form, with suitable heading, sub-headings and notation.

A full discussion of the major opinions open to Northborough is expected, ending up with conclusions and recommendations, e.g.

- reducing workforce
- reducing stockholding
- reducing prices/advertising
- closing smaller premises.
- reducing general expenses
- using spare workshop capacity for general servicing and repairs

Index

absorption costing 225
accounting concepts 35
accounting standards 35
applications of funds 117
AVCO 69

books of account 27
break-even chart 218
break-even point 216
budgetary control 251
budgeted final accounts 172

cash budgets 247
central processing unit 48
classifying costs 181
computerisation 52
constraints 3
contribution to sales ratio 217, 227
controllable costs 184
cost-effective information 7
cost of sales adjustment 152
current cost reserve 157
current ratio 136
current replacement cost 66

data storage 45
day book 29
depreciation adjustment 151
direct costs 182
direct materials budget 246
dividend cover 138
dividend yield 138
double-entry system 25

factory indirect costs 185
factory overheads 200
FIFO 67
fixed costs 182
floppy disk 49

gearing 139
gearing adjustment 154

gearing proportion 155

indirect costs 182
information systems 9
inter-firm comparisons 140
investment ratios 137

job costing 202
journals 29

labour time record 200
labour variances 260
levels of decision-making 17
LIFO 67
limiting factors 228, 244
liquidity ratios 135
loan capital 102

management information systems 55
manufacturing profits 186
marginal costing 225
margin of safety 216
materials requisition 199
materials variances 261
monetary working capital adjustment 153

net realisable value 67

obsolescence 73
organisational objectives 2
ordinary shares 101
overhead absorption rate 201
overhead budgets 245
overhead variances 262

partnership agreement 86
partners' capital accounts 87
partners' current accounts 87
peripheral units 49
planning budgets 243
preference shares 101
pricing 230

336 Index

process costing 206
production cost budget 244
profit ratios 133

qualitative data 5

reducing balance depreciation 77
reserves 102
residual value 75
return on equity 138

sales budget 245
semi-variable costs 184

share premium 103
sources of funds 117
SSAP 16 149
stock-taking 64
stock valuation 65, 229
straight-line depreciation 75
SYD 78

trial balance 31

variance report 265

working capital 115